Artificial Intelligence

Artificial Intelligence

An Introduction
for the
Inquisitive Reader

Robert H. Chen
Chelsea Chen

CRC Press
Taylor & Francis Group
Boca Raton London New York

CRC Press is an imprint of the
Taylor & Francis Group, an **informa** business

A CHAPMAN & HALL BOOK

First edition published 2022
by CRC Press
6000 Broken Sound Parkway NW, Suite 300, Boca Raton, FL 33487-2742

and by CRC Press
4 Park Square, Milton Park, Abingdon, Oxon, OX14 4RN

Library of Congress Cataloguing-in-Publication Data
Names: Chen, Robert H., 1947- author. | Chen, Chelsea, author.
Title: Artificial intelligence : an introduction for the inquisitive reader / authored by Robert H. Chen, Chelsea Chen.
Description: Boca Raton : CRC Press, 2022. | Includes bibliographical references and index.
Identifiers: LCCN 2021055530 (print) | LCCN 2021055531 (ebook) | ISBN 9781032103471 (hardback) | ISBN 9781032101842 (paperback) | ISBN 9781003214892 (ebook)
Subjects: LCSH: Artificial intelligence.
Classification: LCC Q335 .C4845 2022 (print) | LCC Q335 (ebook) | DDC 006.3--dc23/eng/20211116
LC record available at https://lccn.loc.gov/2021055530
LC ebook record available at https://lccn.loc.gov/2021055531

ISBN: 978-1-032-10347-1 (hbk)
ISBN: 978-1-032-10184-2 (pbk)
ISBN: 978-1-003-21489-2 (ebk)

DOI: 10.1201/9781003214892

Typeset in Minion
by MPS Limited, Dehradun

Contents

PART V Progression

PART VI Powers of Prediction

Preface

I N THIS BOOK, THE ADVENTURES IN THE QUEST FOR
artificial intelligence (AI) are exemplified by the entertaining
demonstrations of "man versus machine" competitions such as IBM
Deep Blue versus Garry Kasparov and Google AlphaGo versus Lee Sedol,
but the real significance of AI evolves from the human *ideas* behind the
machines' *algorithms* and what the machine may be capable of in the
future. Starting with mechanical calculation, the development of artificial
intelligence can be seen as a natural progression of technology abetted by
the generation of computer science. With the hardware, software, and
communications in hand, the quest for the long-dreamed of "expert
system" began in earnest with the pure logic-based "top-down" machine
where axioms go in and mathematical theorems come out, but because of
the inherent contradictions in pure logic and lack of data and computer
power, the *Logic Theorist* was replaced by Big Data and massively parallel
processing machines, in the so-called "bottom-up" approach.

Bottom-up AI mimics the structure and pattern recognition capability
of human brains with electrically activated artificial neurons forming
synaptic patterns of recognition and "thought" in an artificial *neural
network* formed in a parallel-processing computer. The synaptic patterns
are produced by Markov chain modeling of neuron activation with the
neurons weighted in accord with a training set in a process called
parameterization. The gradient descent of vector calculus minimizes the
difference between the machine patterns and the ground truth,
backpropagating the differences using the chain rule of calculus provides
the *machine learning*, and *hyperparameterization* fine-tunes the accuracy
and computational efficiency of the machine's "thinking" process.

The example of convolutional neural network used in computer vision
armed with Big Data and massively parallel processing has brought
machine vision into almost every facet of industry and society.

Predictive analytics AI is employed almost everywhere, especially
critically in business, science, politics, and the military. AI reinforcement

learning has produced machines that can best the top human video gamers without even *a priori* knowing the rules of the games being played, and in the real world of imperfect knowledge, AI systems have beaten the best in Texas Hold'em poker competition.

Because of the ambiguities and vagaries of speech, natural language processing using *generative recurrent neural networks* that can assess immediate speech in terms of what was spoken or inferred before are presently the most promising approaches.

The basic ideas behind the implementing algorithms and the processes enabling a machine to learn are described within the theme of the difference between human and artificial intelligence, with the touchstone question being the capability of machines to do mathematics.

That ability required by the reader, however, is only basic calculus, and explanations of the particular equations for artificial intelligence algorithms are provided with examples so that for those who have never learned, or have long forgotten their calculus, the ideas behind the algorithms can be easily understood, hopefully kindling an appreciation of the role of mathematics in artificial intelligence.

As for form, some methods of mathematical exposition, for example the boldface representations of vectors, and curly letter matrices are employed only when necessary for clarity, as their identities are evident from the context. Wording and spelling are in the American style but with British punctuation leaving quotes and parentheses inside sentences of which they are only a part, at the dreadful consequence of laying bare the period or comma.

Only the designs of the algorithms are presented, for those wishing to know the code, referrals are made to the relevant articles, and free code hosting platforms and excellent online programming tutorials offer great convenience and hands-on coding experience.

The authors would like to thank Callum Fraser of Taylor & Francis Publishing for professional guidance, to Mansi Kabra for expert handling of the manuscript, and the reviewers of the manuscript who provided excellent critical suggestions.

I

The Arrival of AI in the Human World

CHAPTER 1

Game-Playing Machines

H e was a man with two common first names, Arthur Samuel, born and raised in mid-America Emporia Kansas in a middle-class family, a graduate of the local College of Emporia, he appeared to be an ordinary young man brought up in a traditional American society. However, the genial but inherently cautious Arthur Samuel was soon to known as a man of great distinction in an unusual new realm. For from Emporia, his special talents allowed him to enter the citadel of engineering education MIT which provided him a sound electrical engineering basis, and thence to the fount of technical innovation AT&T Bell Labs where he worked on the telecommunications systems that transformed the whole world, and the radar technology critical to victory in World War II.

His contributions were significant, but he was not done, for after the War, closely tracking the locus of new technology, Samuel arrived at the University of Illinois to work on the giant ILLIAC scientific computer, and after being recruited by IBM, he was immersed in the design the world's first commercial mainframe computers that were soon to disrupt industry and education all over the world. But it was then that he came up with an audacious idea that would be the precursor of a transformative technology that would further disrupt industry and the lives of almost all the peoples of the world. His idea was inspired by a return to his everyman roots as the conjurer of a "thinking machine" playing a trivial game known and played by almost everyone in America.

DOI: 10.1201/9781003214892-2

THE IBM 701

Working in Poughkeepsie in 1949, Arthur Samuel noted that the storage and display matrices of the new IBM 701 computers, looked just like a checkerboard, and like almost everybody in America at the time, he played that common game of jumping about a board to capture an opponents' pieces and "kinging" your own pieces.

In his uncommon mind however, Samuel saw a clever way to create an image for IBM as the creator of a wondrous checkers-playing computer that could challenge and defeat humans at their own game, garnering publicity for the marvelous capabilities of IBM computers.

It was clearly a creative marketing scheme, but his company was not in the least supportive, for its venerable chairman Thomas Watson, Sr., like Samuel was conscious of IBM's image, but in the opposite sense of avoiding the spectre of a menacing "IBM thinking machine" going around beating up on humans all over the country.

The idea of the homey IBM *Selectric* typewriters and office machines souped-up like Frankenstein's monster to triumph over small-town residents at checkers was anathema to the friendly helpmate that was Watson Sr.'s marketing vision for IBM products.

Like Victor Frankenstein the earnest scientist, the dogged Samuel followed his checkered muse, jumping over the IBM powers by developing the 701 checkers machine on his own time. He encoded the rules of the game and programmed a *decision tree move generator*, evaluating moves by attaching numerical values to the move options that would most likely lead to a desired advantage. Included in the evaluations were nuggets of checkers wisdom familiar to any checkers player, for instance depleting the opponent's checkers by even challenges when ahead, simple gambits, and guile that today are called *heuristics*.

But this rote learning from rules, simple decision evaluators, and well-known heuristics would take the 701 checkers machine only to the level of its creator, which in Samuel's case, despite his technical brilliance, was below average, and so he consulted expert players for more advanced winning strategies and tactics.

Samuel found it difficult however to incorporate their checkers skill, being mostly based on knowledge of the proclivities and idiosyncrasies of opponents, and no little hard-to-codify "feel" and outright guessing.

Since this "top-down" encoding of rules, tree search results, heuristics, and learning from some expert players, although now "expert", the 701 could only as well as those players, it was clear to Samuel that the *701 expert system* needed to learn from playing *against* other expert players, and like a human player, 701 could accumulate playing skills "bottom-up" and from its own actual game experiences, gain knowledge on how to win by reinforcing its good move choices and degrading the bad moves.

Samuel now evaluated moves based upon their ultimate success or failure in training sessions based on the recorded matches of expert players, and the reward and punishment of good and bad moves in actual games against human players, and even in games played against itself. These were three learning schemes that would later be called respectively *supervised learning on training sets, reinforcement learning in game situations*, and *unsupervised learning by playing progressively improving versions of itself*, the basic methods of today's "machine learning", a term Samuel himself coined.

By means of machine learning, the IBM 701 checkers machine slowly improved, and in 1962 after 13 years of part-time development, Samuel's machine challenged and easily defeated the Connecticut state champion Robert W. Nealey.

After the match, the former champion said he had not had such competition from anyone since 1954, when he lost his last game, but in the rueful pride characteristic of accomplished human beings, he also circumspectly exhibited a clear approbation of the IBM 701's "intelligence".

Despite its successes, the checkers-playing IBM 701 had no such baneful pride, much less circumspection, but if pride instigates the will to succeed, thereby producing greater effort, a machine lacking such pride might make it inferior to humans in *determination*, but it has no equal in effort as it needs only electricity to practice tirelessly 24/7 against not only humans but other machines and itself.

And pride although motivating, if once broken can devolve to paranoia, as the great chess champion Garry Kasparov would later reveal in his acrimonious duel with IBM's *Deep Blue*.

Samuel's cool and collected IBM 701 in the ensuing years would have every reason to be proud, for it remained undefeated for 15 years until 1977 when it finally lost, not to a human, but to a rival checkers program developed at Duke University.

How prideful humans internalize defeat has been analyzed, but how a machine internalizes a defeat may never be known, for deep within the hidden layers of the artificial neural networks of today's AI machines, the germination and processing of a "thought" is largely unfathomable even to the learning algorithm's creator, and that unknown, contrary to the coldly logical computer ethos that usually makes it superior to an emotional human being, could conceivably leave room for machine attitude, willfulness, and even emotion.

The blessings of computers and artificial intelligence have been the machine's potential to increase production while freeing people from the drudgery of everyday work, allowing them to think about the work rather than just enduring the tedium of doing it, thus improving efficiency and leaving more time to pursue lofty goals and enjoy life. The bane of the machine is its potential to take over almost all human occupations, relegating humans' activities to the care and feeding of the machines.

GAME-PLAYING MACHINES

Possibly at odds with humanity's long term self-interest, organizations of humans for intellectual or commercial gain have initiated *Man vs. Machine* fair matches of supreme mental combat in the arenas of two of the primary indicia of human intelligence, IBM's *Grand Challenges* in Western chess and Google's *DeepMind* foray into the ancient Eastern game of *Go*.

Intelligence can be manifested in contests of strategic and tactical thinking within a game's metes and bounds, with superiority demonstrated by the rationality and creativity of moves that produce successful outcomes.

IBM DEEP BLUE

From Watson Senior to Watson Junior, IBM's attitude towards thinking machines reversed; for under Thomas Watson, Jr., the natural next step for IBM's electronic computers was to extend the machines' ken from simple checkers to sophisticated chess; engendering fear among the populace was not a concern to him, seeking admiration and subsequent income for IBM was the goal.

In 1996, the chess computer *Deep Thought* designed by Carnegie Mellon University graduate student F.H. Hsu, and further developed by his team at IBM, grand challenged Garry Kasparov, generally acknowledged as the greatest player in the history of the game, to a six-game championship challenge match.[1]

---

[1] Kasparov was the youngest world champion at 22, and the reigning champion for an unprecedented 225/228 months from 1986 to 2005. In 1999, Kasparov's FIDE Elo ranking of 2851 was the highest in history until Magnus Carlsen, a Grandmaster at 13 scored 2882 in 2014, the highest ranking to date.

Kasparov won the first match against Deep Thought 4-2, but the next year in New York City in May 1997, arrayed against Kasparov was the upgraded IBM massively-parallel RS/6000 SP Super Workstation *Deep Blue* chess-playing machine, replete with newly-developed accelerator chip sets.[2]

Deep Blue's specifically designed high-performance hardware and software could minimax tree-search 50 billion possible positions at a rate of 200 million moves per second. After *alpha-beta pruning* of the search tree, a tree-depth of six to eight moves was searched to select optimum moves.[3]

Kasparov (playing white) won the first game with an "anti-computer" strategy where deliberately suboptimal moves are made to confuse the rationally-wired computer; this seemed to work in the first game which he won with white advantage, but his confidence was shaken upon a devastating second game loss, after which he accused the Deep Blue team of illegal in-game human intervention. IBM denied this, saying that adjustments by humans were made only between the games, in accord with the rules. Deep Blue won the Match 3½-2½, the first time in history that a machine had defeated a Grandmaster in a Championship competition.

Afterwards, Deep Blue's game logs did reveal a random error in Game 1, and commentators speculated that Kasparov interpreted the subsequent fixes instead as Game 2 in-game changes by the Deep Blue team; in other words, Kasparov would not accept that he could be beaten by a machine.

The closeness of the match was not definitive of the superiority of machine over man, but Kasparov's paranoia throughout, and his abysmal resignation in Game 6 could at least establish that Deep Blue's cold logic could triumph over the warm frailty of human emotion and the pride of extremely self-aware human beings.

After its stunning victory, could Deep Blue the machine likewise be *self-aware* of its superiority? It will never be known because the fate of most innovative research devices is *dissection*; the RS/6000 SP was sent back to IBM's test floor and the shell returned, but two cards went to IBM headquarters in Armonk for visitor demonstrations, and the rest

---

[2] Thin 30 node, 120 MHz P2SC microprocessors at each node and 480 specifically-designed VLSI chess accelerator chip cards running C language software under the AIX operating system on a 32-bit microchannel bus.

[3] See Chapter 8 for a description of the basic technology and key points in the match. Minimax and alpha-beta pruning are discussed in that and later Chapters.

were inserted into the older version RS/6000 SP and dispersed to various workstations and parts shelves.

In the press conference after the match, Kasparov was cheered and heartily encouraged by an audience including many chess masters, expert commentators, the press, and the general public, but when IBM's Deep Blue team assembled on the stage, their notable technical achievement notwithstanding, they were met with thinly-veiled disdainful murmuring.

There is no sin in standing up for humankind against a machine, but Deep Blue's victory evoked unease, fear, even hostility, and the audience apparently sensed menace rather than hope. Perhaps Watson Senior was right after all.

After this challenge, the score was Machine 2, Humans 0, and after Nealey's prideful but acknowledged defeat came Kasparov's arrogance-fed emotional collapse, presaging psychological frailties that may or may not ever manifest themselves in a machine.

GOOGLE ALPHAGO

The West's explicit "kill the King" chess ethos was in full display in Manhattan with the machine defeating the human champion at his peak; would the masters of the East's implicit "surround and conquer" board game of *Go* meet the same fate?

In 2014, the new tech giant Google acquired Britain's *DeepMind* to challenge *Go* Masters from Europe, Japan, Korea, and China, paragons worshipped in East Asian societies as exalted members of the most sublime class of analytical geniuses.

The *19 × 19* board and possible 361 stone placements are simply played by capturing territory with your stones surrounding territory and your opponent's stones; the lower bound of 2×10^{170} possible positions is a prodigious number that is indeed greater than the sum of all the atoms in the Universe. Faced with such a daunting number of static decisions and the genius level creativity of *Go* Masters, computer scientists, many of them avid *Go* players, had always believed that a Masters-level *Go* playing computer was an absolute impossibility.[4]

---

[4] The number of atoms in the Universe, composing the galaxies, stars, planets, and interstellar gases (mostly hydrogen) is estimated at 10^{78} to 10^{82}, but in truth those atoms only make up about 4% of the total mass in the Universe, with the rest residing in the mysterious *dark matter* (16%), that cannot be seen and has not yet been identified but nevertheless holds galaxies together, and the mass-convertible *dark energy* driving the expansion of the Universe. See Chen, R.H. 2017, *Einstein's Relativity, the Special and General Theories with their Cosmology*, McGraw-Hill Education.

Nevertheless, early *Go* computers using simplified tree searches were developed that could play at an amateur level, but in 2015, for the first time, Google's *AlphaGo* won a sanctioned match without a handicap against a professional, the European champion Fan Hui, and then went on to defeat Japan's legendary top player Iyama Yuta, and the next year, in a highly-publicized match, AlphaGo defeated the then reigning world champion Korea's Lee Sedol 4-1, winning a US$1 million prize (which Google graciously donated to charity).

AlphaGo's sole game loss to Lee Sedol was attributed to a "delusion" resulting from incomprehension of Lee's "divine" move white 78; it was repaired in 2017, and the new improved *AlphaGo Master*, after a 60–0 win streak against humans and rival Go-playing computers, took on the new World's No. 1, the 18-year old prodigy Ke Jie in Wuzhen, China, believed to be the birthplace of *weiqi*, the Chinese name of the Japanese-named *Go*.

Ke Jie had been reluctant to accept AlphaGo Master's challenge, not as he said from fear of losing to a machine, but rather because he was afraid it would "copy my style" and indeed, AlphaGo Master had undergone supervised training on high-level *Go* match publications, and learned how to play from professionals, and its match against China's young genius very likely was a chance for another learning experience. AlphaGo Master easily won 3–0 and a US$1.5 million prize.[5]

Europe, Japan, Korea, and China's professional *Go* associations all awarded the highest 9-*dan* certification to AlphaGo, thus bestowing a *Go* Master's ultimate rank to a machine.

Ke Jie, after the match with AlphaGo Master, attributed his defeat to its "non-human playing style", adding a doleful prospection, "After humanity spent thousands of years improving our tactics, a machine tells us that we were completely wrong; we have only scratched the surface of the essence of *Go*".[6]

The implication was clear, the machine was more likely to discover the further mysteries in *Go* strategy than humans, and therefore in this realm

---

[5] See Chapter 28 for a technical description of AlphaGo and highlights of the Lee Sedol match.

[6] Ke Jie's quotes from Connor, N. 2016, *Google AlphaGo 'can't beat me' says China Go grandmaster*, The Telegraph and Silver, D. et al. 2017 *Mastering the game of Go without human knowledge*, Nature 550 (7676): 354.

of intelligence, Ke Jie recognized that the machine was already more proficient than the best *Go* Masters.[7]

Korea's Lee Sedol said, "After the first game, I was surprised I lost, but from the very beginning of the second game, I could never manage an upper hand for one single move. It was AlphaGo's total victory". In a kind but futile attempt at reassurance to the some 200 million humans all over the world who followed the match, he later added that "it was my defeat, not a defeat of mankind...."[8]

Although gracious, such words ring hollow then and now, for Lee Sedol, a child prodigy who gained professional rank at 12, won his first championship at 19, and was the No. 1 player in the world from 2002 to 2015, winning 18 world championships, was and is a national hero revered in Korea, and celebrated throughout the *Go*-playing world. He represented mankind nobly in a match with a machine, and he lost ....

Earnestly taking full blame for defeat at the hands of a machine, a shaken Lee Sedol retired in 2017 saying that no matter how hard he might try, "there is another entity that cannot be defeated". He however like Ke Jie wistfully added that "robots will never understand the beauty of the game as we humans do", displaying a little pique in losing, but unlike Kasparov, with an equanimity that only questioned AlphaGo's esoteric appreciation and not its playing skill.[9]

Lee Sedol and Ke Jie thereby revealed a cultural difference between an accepting East and a recalcitrant West represented by Kasparov that portends smoother acceptance of artificial intelligence in Northeast Asia than in Western Europe and America.

AlphaGo's artificial neural network was a *19 × 19 × 48* volume matrix input layer of artificial neurons and 13 filter-convolved hidden layers fully connected to a *softmax* rectifier. Using training sets based on published professional Go matches, AlphaGo's supervised learning employed a *Monte Carlo Tree Search* with alpha-beta pruning to reduce the number of possible move decisions to produce *playout* simulations that would reveal the optimum moves for various board patterns.

---

[7] A beautifully-done documentary film on the AlphaGo-Lee Sedol match is *AlphaGo Documentary* on YouTube, provided by Rajarshee Mitra.

[8] Lee Sedol quote from Byford, S. 2016, *Google's DeepMind beats Lee Se-dol again to go 2-0 up in historic Go series,*. The Verge.

[9] Lee Sedol quote from Le Roux, M. & Mollard, P. 2016, *Game over? New AI challenge to human smarts (Update)*, phys.org.

After this learning, different patterns of black and white stone positions could be recognized by a first *machine vision convolutional neural network* that revealed good and bad moves to form AlphaGo's *policy network* in a real match.

A second convolutional neural network evaluated the moves as to their contribution to the optimization of board position patterns. This *value network* could reveal the moves with the highest probabilities leading to acquiring the most territory.

But this, like Samuel's checkers program, only allowed AlphaGo to play as well as the best players in the training set, and did not provide a basis for *beating* those players. So AlphaGo began a rigorous regimen of self-training by playing games with reward and punishment for good and bad moves in *reinforcement learning* against *Go* Masters and different versions of itself, culminating in the unbeatable and constantly improving new version called *AlphaGo Master*.

The Anglo-American AlphaGo Master now could through relentless self-study determine optimum board position strategies as it iteratively increased the probabilities of ultimate victory against the best player in the world, itself. This classic instance of diligent self-strengthening leading to a game-playing virtue through comparison with oneself is quintessentially Confucian, entirely proper for a *Go* master in Northeast Asia.

AlphaGo Master when stripped of its supervised training module evolved into a pure-play thinking machine with zero *a priori* data input. *AlphaGoZero* thus could learn how to play any game just like a human player learns, from the bottom-up, learning the rules while playing and adjusting to the wide variety of opponent moves and strategies by observing the results of many, many moves and strategies, and then forming a policy and value network of moves therefrom that would lead to victory.

This policy of relentlessly maximizing the probability of final victory over and above winning particular instances of adroitly gaining territory in localized territorial *fights* indicates that for AlphaGoZero, it is not important *how* you win or *by how much* you win, or even *how you play* the game, the only goal is to win.

From the human perspective, Lee Sedol's "beauty" of the game is in the many instances of the clever manipulation of stones to disrupt, hem in, surround and capture your opponent's stones to win the martial arts-like fights for territory.

Rather like Premier League football, the "beautiful game" is attractive because of the superb skills of individual players in instances of cleverly outfoxing defenders with deft footwork and precision passing, actions that are beautiful to watch but seldom contribute to a final victory, something that often is the result of an *overall* positional policy, typically a stultifying defense that thwarts well-organized and crowd- pleasing shots on goal, but wins through break-away counter attacks.

So has AlphaGoZero taken the less beautiful but more efficient path to victory? Does AlphaGoZero perceive the game's objective victory/defeat reality more clearly because of its disregard for its aesthetic appeal? Can or do humans desire to emulate it? Do humans have the resolve to pursue AlphaGoZero's winning but wooden policy, and if so, is such a game worth playing?

It is of interest to note that some expert commentators have found AlphaGoZero to be perversely more *human* in its playing rather than what Ke Jie thought of AlphaGo Master's "less human style". That is, the result of the comprehensiveness of its optimizing algorithms was that AlphaGo Master developed a confidence that its moves were always the best, otherwise it would not have made them. AlphaGoZero might consider a human opponent's move clever, not bad, but nevertheless inferior to a response born of algorithmic rigor, data, and tireless self-study producing a superior match policy; that is, no matter what the opponent does, AlphaGoZero has a better counter, it has an ultimate confidence because after victories over all the *Go* Masters, AlphaGoZero cannot help but feel superior, and ultimately be quite aware of that superiority, a pride and arrogance that may produce a dangerous attitude toward humans.[10]

AlphaGoZero's reinforcement and unsupervised learning regimen could not just involve playing the same version of itself over and over again, because the algorithm would *overfit* the data and much like a pedestrian player, merely memorize responsive moves rather than creating new strategies and tactics. AlphaGoZero was invincible because different versions of itself were not only each in turn the best in the world, but the almost infinite loop of iterative improvement meant that AlphaGoZero would develop its skill such that it could never be defeated and become *infinitely* good at *Go*,

---

[10] For enlightening and thoughtful AlphaGoZero game review commentary, see Daniels, B., 2017 *Whatever you do is wrong*, YouTube.

whatever that means and portends, and unbeatable except by some other machine that somehow got ahead of AlphaGoZero's learning curve.[11]

IBM PROJECT DEBATER

So far, artificially intelligent machines have challenged champion checkers and genius chess and Go masters at their peak, and soundly beaten them all. But the victories were in highly *constrained domain* competitions.

How about the *open domain* of everyday life and that very human bane of arguing? There is no subject or opinion under the Sun that cannot be argued, and everyone and their spouses are experts, regardless of subject matter. Open domain environments require knowledge of almost any subject, rapid information-processing, creative construction of an argument, persuasive exposition of a position, quick understanding of the opposition's argument, and then analytical deconstruction and sharp rebuttal of the opponent's arguments, all buttressed by references and data, to finally persuade a skeptical audience, often by means of emotive elocution, humor, and a display of self-confidence.

The first debating Grand Challenge was held in San Francisco in 2019, the proposition was: "Should the government subsidize space exploration". IBM's *Project Debater* argued, supported by facts, that space exploration benefits humankind because it can help to advance scientific discoveries and inspires young people to think beyond themselves.

Noa Ovadia, the 2016 Israeli national debate champion, in opposition argued that there are better applications for government subsidies such as directly for scientific research here on Earth. Project Debater rebutted with historical facts that the potential technological benefits from space exploration outweigh most government subsidy spending that often leads nowhere. Noa countered by evoking the high cost of space exploration and the uncertainty of any useful results.

In their allotted seven minutes, both sides indeed presented succinct and emotive arguments among which it would be difficult to objectively determine the better. In accord with the pre-agreed to debating rules, a pre-debate poll *for* and *against* the proposition is held, the debater who

---

[11] AlphaGoZero is like the genius Einstein, who after recognizing his superiority, skipped classes and through thought experiments presented problems to himself which he solved by himself and thereby created the whole new fields of relativity physics and cosmology. The innately talented Michael Jordan also relentlessly practiced to improve to transcendent levels of basketball skill even when he had no equal.

produces the greater number of cross-over votes after the debate is the winner. Project Debater won by changing the minds of a greater number of the audience.

In a second debate, the proposition was, "We should increase the use of telemedicine". Project Debater once again won a greater number of cross-over votes. Faced with a previously unknown subject and proposition, and with no initial choice of side, in the far-reaching, diverse, dynamic environment of a professional debate, the machine had once again won.

The next year, Project Debater was improved and now named *Miss Debater* in respect of its synthesized female voice, and boldly took on the 31-year old world champion Debating Officer of the Cambridge Union Society, Harish Natarajan. The proposition was: "Should the government provide pre-school subsidies?" Miss Debater greeted her opponent respectfully but tinged with a veiled menace,[12]

> *I have heard that you hold the world record in debate competition wins against humans, but I suspect that you have never debated a machine before. Welcome to the future!*

Harish hesitated, but courteously nodded in response and the great debate began.

Miss Debater's reflexively gleaming façade's three blue orbs tantalizingly rotated as she searched her database of over ten billion sentences from 300 hundred million newspaper, scientific journals, and other articles, and then meticulously but quickly formed an argument.

Harish was also combing his memory, but instead of computer memory fetches, and microprocessors churning logic for arguments, he was busily scrawling notes on a notepad outlining arguments for his position.

Miss Debater produced research data and media quotes to show that subsidizing preschools is not just a matter of finance, but a moral and political duty to protect some of society's most vulnerable children; again, a seemingly evocative argument rising above practical matters, albeit unfortunately sounding a little like a left-wing politician's speech.

---

[12] Reference for further details, see IBM research director Arvind Krishna's online blog.

Sensing and taking advantage of a general disdain for politicians among the public, Natarajan countered that too often subsidies function as politically-motivated giveaways to the middle class, and that even with subsidies there will be many who still cannot afford pre-school for their children; a realistic but rather cynical rebuke in response to what apparently sounded to the audience like a politician's bleeding heart jabber from Miss Debater.

Although Miss Debater occasionally flashed un-machine-like humor during the debate, she was likely incapable of cynicism, and perhaps because of the rather harsh political climate of conservative self-help at the time, Harish the human won over more of the audience to his side.[13]

After the debate, a commentator noted that "While Miss Debater was clearly better than Harish at citing meaningful facts, Harish had better rhetoric and better counters, and brought up tough rebuttals that Miss Debater did a poor job addressing".[14]

After the debate, Natarajan, a man from the East but brought up in the West's debating tradition, proposed an amalgam of East and West for the future development of artificial intelligence,[15]

> *After the first minute of getting used to the shock of it not being a human being, or the surprise of what that actually meant, it became much like a human being ... what the machine is better at than any human could ever be is finding relevant evidence, studies, examples, cases, and get that context. Another thing I think is very impressive was not only [Miss Debater's] ability to present evidence, but also its ability to explain why it matters in the context of the debate. Combining Project Debater's skills with those of a human would be incredibly powerful!*

Is Man still in control and the Machine as helpmate the best combination? Miss Debater's demonstrated fact-finding prowess, logical argument formation, debating ability, and persuasiveness, for better or worse, sooner or later may very well obsolesce the entire class of lawyers in our society ... and perhaps more distressingly, dispose of human and humane teachers and professors as well.

---

[13] For a description of the debate, refer to Fortune, 2019.02.12 and many other online accounts.
[14] Inevitablehuman.com, 2012.02.12.
[15] Quote from *Project Debater*, top500.org.

TORONTO/DEEPMIND VIDEO GAMER

Apart from the rather serious contests of mental acuity, it seems that since video games were created on computers, it is logical to think that silicon-based machines (although having no thumbs) could also learn to play them, and play them well enough to defeat carbon-based human gamers in what is a decidedly fast-paced reflexive contest of manipulative skill, planning, and intelligence.

In action video games, the so-called "Non-Playing Characters" (NPCs) in video games exhibit what appears to be intelligence in surprise attacking, hiding, counter-attacking, and so on, while the agent player is engaged in the so-called optimal *pathfinding* from one point to another taking into consideration terrain, obstacles, enemies, adverse situations, and costs of certain actions, for instance types of weapons to procure and ammunition supply in war and "survival instinct" games.

The artificial intelligence *finite state* player matched against physical barriers and apparently intelligent NPCs that was seen as the breakthrough was the Toronto/DeepMind Technologies' convolutional neural network reinforcement learning AI Video Gamer, which with no *a priori* knowledge of even the rules of the game, from scratch defeated expert video game-playing humans in the highly competitive environment of the classic Atari games, *Beam Rider, Breakout, Enduro, Pong, Q*bert, Seaquest,* and *Space Invaders.*

The University of Toronto's Volodymyr Mnih and colleagues' goal was to create a single artificial neural network agent that is able to learn to play a variety of games. The network was not provided with any game-specific information or hand-engineered visual features, and was not privy to the internal state of the Atari 2600 emulator that was used in the competition.

The Toronto/DeepMind Video Gamer learned from nothing but raw pixel video input, the reward and terminal signals, and it generated a set of possible actions using purely experiential replay memory. There were no adjustments of the architecture, learning algorithm, or hyperparameters for different games, the Toronto Video Gamer performed just like a human player across all seven games, clearly demonstrating a robust general game-playing capability.

The Toronto Video Gamer defeated expert human players in three out of seven of the games (with ties), with superior benchmark performance. Although conceptually similar to checkers, video games rely more on rapid reflexive responses rather than the relatively deeper strategies of chess and *Go*, but computers are best at effective quick survey and response, as demonstrated in basic word processing.

IBM WATSONQA

In 2011, IBM Watson Grand Challenged two all-time champions in the popular "given the Answer, pose the Question" television game show *Jeopardy*. The hardware had to be formidable because in order to ensure a fair match with humans depending only on their immediate memory, *WatsonQA* could not have any access to external information. The self-contained, forced air-cooled, ten refrigerator-sized Power 750 Servers that stored 200 million pages of information for 3000-core processor massively-parallel processing was backstage in a sound-proof holding room that muffled the sound of fans cooling the overheating processors.

Because *Jeopardy* is a contest of information knowledge and retrieval, and not the ability to accurately understand the moderator's speech, WatsonQA was simultaneously given the Answers in text that it would parse and parallel process tree-search threads based on keyword matching, factoids, grammar, verbal relationships, and risk management of responses (there is a penalty for incorrect responses and contestants can wager winnings in the later stages of competition). WatsonQA could quickly jump from branch to branch of the tree depending on how the combination of words was playing out to definiteness at the tree leaf node.

Natural language open-domain information is almost always imprecise, subject to context and often ambiguous, so the recognition within the millisecond range that champion contestants can press the buzzer to pre-empt competitors obviously required sophisticated natural language processing and search and logic processing speed.

WatsonQA used Wordnet, Wikipedia, and myriad other information sources, and was trained against a hundred previous Jeopardy winners to search and weight information as to its probable contribution to correct responses, and positively bias correct and negatively bias incorrect threads.

WatsonQA roundly defeated legendary Jeopardy champions Brad Rutter and Ken Jennings, and won a million-dollar Grand Challenge prize and $77,147 in game winnings, and could have continued to win every contest it entered, but for obvious reasons was banned from further Jeopardy competition. After the defeat, a chastened Jennings displayed an equanimity that Kasparov sorely lacked and Lee Sedol only ac-knowledged with a caveat,[16]

> *Just as factory jobs were eliminated in the 20th Century by new assembly-line robots, Brad and I were the first knowledge-industry workers put out of work by the new generation of "thinking" machines. "Quiz show contestant" may be the first job made re-dundant by Watson, but I'm sure it won't be the last.*

CARNEGIE-MELLON TEXAS HOLD'EM PLAYER LIBRATUS

So far the machine has bested humans in contests of logic, speed, and memory, but those are what humans already regard as the computer's strength; can a machine beat man in the quintessentially human game of bravado, cunning, baiting, deceit, bluff, intimidation, and subterfuge that is *Texas Hold'em* poker? A high-stakes poker game victory would de-monstrate that a machine can be vulgar as well as refined.

In 2017, a perfectly poker-faced computer from Carnegie-Mellon University soundly defeated four top-ten professional players each in 120,000 hands of heads-up (two-player), no-limit (can bet total of chips owned) Texas Hold'em, with Professor Tuomas Sandholm and graduate student Noam Brown's *Libratus* ahead by $1,700,000 in simulated chips at the end of the 20-day competition.

Libratus employed game theory mathematical models of strategic interactions between rational decision-makers, something seemingly at odds with the dare-devil machismo of poker, but in truth directed at the calm assessment of the winning bet probabilities necessary for victory.

Indeed, behind the façade of bravado lies a cold-faced logic that parlays the luck of the draw with the skill of the bet using Nash equi-librium game theory and Monte Carlo simulations of probability distributions.[17]

Heads-up, no-limit Texas Hold'em has been a benchmark challenge for *imperfect information* situations where an agent does not have all the information (as one does in the board games by just looking at the board) but must still make critical decisions in order to be successful.

---

[16] Quoted from Ford, J 2011, *Paging Dr. Watson ...*, singularityhub.com.

[17] Game theory, Monte Carlo simulation, and the Nash equilibrium as well as the other technical issues of this Chapter will be described in later chapters.

In Texas Hold'em, a player does not know what cards the opponent is holding, nor the order of cards not dealt, and so poker is like most real-life situations where decisions must be made with limited information. Imperfect information game theory is employed in more serious undertakings than poker, for instance in the stock market, business, geopolitics, and warfare.

The stakes are much higher, but given past human folly in those endeavors, in light of the demonstrated capabilities of *Libratus* and its progeny, perhaps we should leave more momentous decisions to machines rather than humans.

After his victory, Professor Sandholm was asked by a reporter what game might be beyond a computer's capability, to which he replied that "AI had already surpassed the best human and achieved superhuman performance".

That was one-on-one poker. In 2019 Noam Brown's new multiplayer pokerbot *Pluribus*, in a six-player 12-day session of 10,000 hands of no-limit Texas Hold'em defeated 15 top professional players playing a hand every 20 seconds, more than two times faster than the best professional poker players.

Final score in games: Machine 21, Humans 1, with the one victory by a human the result of a number change of position decided by a human audience, likely covertly betraying a subjective prejudice for the human against the machine, as overtly displayed by the audience at the Deep Blue-Kasparov chess match. Indeed, Harish Natarajan said after the debate that "I felt I had an advantage because I was not a machine, I was a human". That emotional advantage may well persist in the eyes of many observers, but the machine's functional advantages would become clearer as its domain broadened.

CHAPTER 2

Working Machines

U p to this point, artificial intelligence has been used for playing games, if the idea is just to prove that machines can think, the machine has already surpassed humans in restricted domain endeavors. With that capability, aside from trivial quiz show games like *Jeopardy*, for instance WatsonQA could just as well provide more useful functions, for example given its supreme ability to know the question from the answer (is that diagnosis?), assisting physicians in the treatment and alleviation of suffering or robot physicians even taking over a patient's entire medical treatment, while at the same time creating new business opportunities for the machine's proprietors.

In the Jeopardy-like medical diagnosis game *Doctor's Dilemma*, there was once an answer:

> *The syndrome characterized by joint pain, abdominal pain, palpable purpura, and a nephritic sediment*

The question is (of course) "What is *Hanoch-Schonlein Purpura?*" The same game format used in Jeopardy can be used by WatsonQA in serious and indubitably non-trivial medical diagnostics that requires knowing the question when you have the diagnosis.

IBM PHYSICIAN'S ASSISTANT

In addition to the on-board memory of the Jeopardy machine, an *IBM Watson Health* doctor or physician's assistant machine could be connected

DOI: 10.1201/9781003214892-3

to the Internet and thereby immediately access many different medical information sources and the latest developments in research. Then quickly analyzing, diagnosing, and advising treatment, all with a competence that a local general practitioner would be hard pressed to match.

IBM Watson Health has programs for example in oncology, genomic interpretation, and diabetes management. It employs *Nuance*'s speech recognition software specifically designed for medical terminology to act as a patient interface, so in response to a query, medical information from the cloud can be searched in seconds, and questions and answers are processed in the cloud, allowing access to voluminous medical information and expert diagnosis for anyone with a verified connection.

For instance, a physician might say to Watson Health, "My patient has had digestive issues and has lost interest in bowling, her favorite pastime." IBM's *Blue Gene* supercomputer then searches the *Diagnostic and Statistical Manual of Mental Disorders* (DSM) for "lost interest" and classifies that as a symptom of depression, and then scans journals looking for the logical AND of "depression" and "digestive problems" and finds an article on *celiac* disease, an autoimmune disorder. If there are other articles supporting this diagnosis and no clearly contradictory evidence found, the physician can order lab tests to confirm or dispel the celiac diagnosis. If confirmed, a gluten-free diet would be advised, and the patient hopefully will soon be happily back at the bowling alley.

To refine the automated diagnoses, Watson Health could assign weights to articles, for example based on the number of positive citations, and consider for example epidemiological factors that increase the probability of a given diagnosis in a given region.

Eighty percent of healthcare data is unstructured, and just like *Jeopardy's* WatsonQA, Watson Health can read and understand unstructured data by natural language processing to identify, classify, and encode clinical information from virtually any source, and just as in every other field today, Big Data can substantially improve medical predictive analytics with voluminous data.

An artificial neural network trained on massive amounts of medical data is used by Watson Health to classify diagnoses, with reinforcement learning improving its diagnostic accuracy. Again, a human cannot endure 24/7 training and tireless study, and indeed many controlled experiments have shown that Watson Health's machine learning can be equal to if not superior to diagnoses by human physicians.

Once up and running, Watson Health can perform problem identification and automatically produce a summary of care from a patient's medical record, then after classification of patients with clinical similarity, dynamic patient cohorts can be created for path selection for a given group of patients, with the optimum care paths becoming an integral part of healthcare Big Data available to all practitioners.

For medical research, Watson Health can find information in the medical literature to support new hypotheses and create new diagnostic tools; for example, quickly scanning and reading a complete set of medical literature such as the journal *Medline*, and from there identify documents that are semantically related to the research topic in question.[1]

Notwithstanding, many practicing physicians oppose the use of artificial intelligence for diagnosis or other medical matters, often citing a machine's lack of empathy for the patient (as well as sympathy for the one-upped doctor), and the likely increased liability risk of malpractice stemming from machine misdiagnosis.

Furthermore, having a machine take over medical diagnosis is against a human physician's professional self-interest, and the storied arrogance of some physicians may prevent their acceptance of machine diagnosis, no matter how great the benefits.

Perhaps the debater Harish Natarajan's suggestion of man/machine collaboration would encourage a machine doing the hard work of diagnosis with the human physician deciding on treatment and handling the emotional care of the patient, with augmented machine malpractice insurance, and premiums paid from the higher profits derived from the lower costs of research- and diagnosis-performing robots compared with human physicians.

This is in accord with the first sentence of the Hippocratic oath below, but should the physician's unease and/or pecuniary concerns at the thought of a robot physician taking over patient diagnosis outweigh the duty set forth in the second sentence below?[2]

I will remember that there is art to medicine as well as science, and that warmth, sympathy, and understanding may outweigh the surgeon's knife or the chemist's drug.

---

[1] Ref. IBM Watson Health online.
[2] This 1964 revised version of the Hippocratic Oath is used by most medical schools.

I will not be ashamed to say "I know not", nor will I fail to call in my colleagues when the skills of another are needed for a patient's recovery.

When the "colleagues" are physician's assistant machines or very capable *Doctor Robots*, are human physicians violating their Hippocratic oath when they are not receptive to artificial intelligence to help care for a patient?

NYU CANCER DIAGNOSTIC

An artificial intelligence automatic recognition and diagnosis of lung cancer from images of diseased and normal tumors was developed by the NYU School of Medicine with tumor image data downloaded from the *Cancer Genome Atlas*, which was prepared by expert pathologists' detailed microscopic examinations of tumors and their diagnoses. This data constituted a training set of 800,000 images from 1200 cases of diseased and healthy lungs for machine learning. The *Google Inception v3* computer vision convolutional neural network (CNN) learned diagnosis from the image data recognition, and after two weeks of training, the CNN could correctly diagnose tumors at 97% accuracy, better than the three expert pathologists who served as a control group.

Taking a step further, NYU's CNN was asked to extract more than just the cancer diagnosis from the training set images. Expert oncologists cannot discern genetic mutations solely from images of tumors, but rather must read the tumor's DNA sequencing and compare it with the normal DNA of the patient to detect genetic mutations, a tedious and error-prone process.

The NYU automatic cancer tumor diagnostic tool was able to automatically predict the mutational status of a key lung cancer-driving gene with greater than 80% accuracy, and it was found that more training set data could further increase that accuracy rate to far surpass the best human detections of genetic mutations.[3]

CORONAVIRUS ATTACKERS

There was great hope that artificial intelligence could help to overcome the transformative coronavirus pandemic of late 2019 that decimated societies and economies worldwide. Many turned to artificial intelligence in the hope that AI could find ways to predict the outbreaks and attack the virus.

---

[3] World Intellectual Property Organization (WIPO) Technology Trends 2019, *Artificial Intelligence*.

Since this was a novel virus, there was insufficient data to model the coronavirus pandemic spread. Thus for example, a *Kalman filter*, as used in predicting the position of a self-driving automobile on a journey using trip data, measures the current motion state vectors and estimates their uncertainties, then updates and weights the data as more information from multiple sources is collated. The Kalman filter would require similar data to predict the locations of virus spread.[4]

This data was gleaned for covid-19 spread prediction by among others a Canadian company called BlueDot that continuously collected online disease-related news, official reports, social media mentions, and air traffic data, and then cross-referenced the data with the National Institutes of Health and Global Microbial databases. A natural language processing (NLP) algorithm correlated the data through the interpretation of a *focal word* (for instance "fever") that influences the interpretation of other words, thereby helping to identify covid-19's distribution. This allowed BlueDot to predict 127,000 cases for March 30, 2020, and outbreaks in China, Italy, Iran, and the United States that were spot-on., however the new mutation variants appearing have been more difficult to model.[5]

There are more than 200 viruses known to infect human beings, each with different infection mechanisms, behavior, and response to treatments and vaccines. When the *severe acute respiratory syndrome coronavirus -2* virus enters the body, mostly through the mouth or nose, it infiltrates healthy cells by binding to the cell receptors on the surface of human cell by means of the protein spikes studded on the *coronavirus* surface. Infiltrated by the virus, that cell then replicates its RNA, as well as the structural proteins needed to assemble new viral particles, which are then released into the body causing an infection.

Since there is no known cure for the new *covid-19* virus, it was thus necessary to find a vaccine to control the pandemic. Universities and research institutions all over the world pursued at least eight different types, including inactivated viruses and DNA and RNA vaccines.

The approach was to find protein antibodies that can recognize parts of the virus that it can bind to, and thus stimulate an immune response. There are, however, tens of thousands of possible virus targets. DeepMind's

---

[4] The Kalman filter is similar in operation to a *Hidden Markov Model* used in speech recognition, see Chapter 30.

[5] See Chapter 31 for Natural Language Processing (NLP).

AlphaFold neural network was used to predict the three-dimensional shape of the coronavirus based on its genetic sequence; then machine learning was employed to predict which parts of the virus can be recognized as targets based on training set data of known pathogens.

It was found, reasonably enough, that the spike proteins arrayed on the surface of the virus were the best targets for rendering the virus incapable of binding to the human cells. The targeting proteins, conventionally *inactivated viruses*, are then integrated into vaccine candidates and tested for immune response.

Instead of inactivated viruses, however, DNA and RNA genomes can mimic a part of the virus' genetic sequence to prompt the cells to produce the antigen that triggers an immune response.

Because of its 3D structure, mimicking viral proteins requires the complex chemical sequencing technique called *protein folding*, as developed by DeepMind and Moderna, among many others, and artificial intelligence was used to design and synthesize the genetic components of DNA-based vaccines that to date have been largely successful.[6]

SELF-DRIVING CARS

Practically every major automobile manufacturer, ride-hailing service, and information industry tech giant is in the process of developing self-driving cars. In an attempt at classification standardization of a burgeoning new industry, the Society of Automotive Engineers (SAE) has established five levels of progression for the automated driving automobile industry:

1. Shared Control Driver Assistance, for example, adaptive cruise control, automated parking and lane-keeping assistance;

2. Automated-Driving but Monitored Intervention, for example unforeseen encounters such as roadblocks where the driver must take over control;

3. Self-Driving and Vehicle Warning for Intervention, for example the autonomous car will not automatically respond but warn the passenger;

---

[6] For more on the coronavirus and the protein-folding process, see Chapter 31 Speech Recognition, which algorithms curiously can be used in protein-folding.

4. Complete Self-Driving in Specific Environments, for example on designated roads where the passenger need not intervene; and

5. Complete Self-Driving in any Environment where the passenger relinquishes all control to the autonomous car, which may not have a steering wheel, but likely has an emergency brake.

Early autonomous cars undergoing road testing can be easily identified by the stark light detection and ranging (LIDAR) tower on the car roof sweeping out low-powered laser beams to map the vehicle's surroundings without blinding passersby.

The laser beam is reflected by objects and photoelectric cells pick up the return beams and convert the light intensity to electric current, and from the time span of the returned light signals, the distance of scanned objects is measured, and in accord with the change in wavelength upon reflection, the relative motion of scanned objects and the car can be computed using the Doppler effect.[7]

Fusing information from LIDAR, radar, sonar, odometry, GPS, inertial measurement units (IMUs), computer vision, and navigation systems, Bayesian *simultaneous localization and mapping* (SLAM) software constructs a *point cloud* map of the surroundings while keeping track of the car's position within that environment. Following the SLAM output, actuators and servos on the car control the direction, speed, and braking of the car for autonomous driving. Object recognition is by computer vision pattern recognition employing deep artificial neural networks that can learn from training sets of actual driver experience.

Of course the more training data, the more apposite is the response of the autonomous car; that is, the autonomous car learns to drive like a human drives, gaining skill by driving more. If the driving data of a full fleet of autonomous vehicles are loaded into a computer and serves as training sets for all the autonomous cars in the fleet, the shared driving experience gained will far surpass what any one human can accumulate over a lifetime of driving.

Studies have shown that over 90% of automobile accidents are the result of human error, so if all the cars on the road were autonomous, the wealth of driving experience and proper responses to traffic, obstacles,

---

[7] The Doppler effect is the change in wavelength (frequency) of a wave source moving away (increasingly lower pitch for sound and redshift to longer wavelengths in light spectrum) or towards an observer (higher pitch sound and blueshift to shorter wavelengths).

and pedestrians would significantly increase overall traffic safety. At the very least, the driverless car will do away with drunken and reckless driving, and road rage.

A major obstacle to the more general use of self-driving cars has been the initial psychological disinclination of turning control over to a machine in a potentially dangerous environment, but research has shown that after the pronounced misgiving upon getting into the car and starting up, in only about ten-minutes after nothing untoward has happened, even control-freak drivers are quickly at ease letting the car do the driving.

Furthermore, there is technology to dispel misgivings, for example, soft blue panel lighting or mood music as the car is safely moving along, with lights turning to yellow and faster music only when something is remiss, and red lights and blaring beeps calling for driver intervention when needed.

ASSEMBLY LINE QUALITY CONTROL

In the complex mass manufacture of liquid crystal displays (LCDs), in spite of almost completely automated production, final inspections of LCD panels were done visually and if a defect in a panel is found, it can cause an entire production run to be downgraded or just discarded. Moreover, the cause of a defect and when and how it was generated is often difficult to ascertain, such that the term for a defect whose cause is unknown has been ruefully called *mura*, a generic Japanese term for "irregular" or "non-uniform" and a word used by car manufacturers as "wasted".

China Star, a subsidiary of TCL, the world's third largest producer of television sets, engaged IBM Watson to develop an *Artificial Intelligence LCD Panel Inspection System* that obviates human visual inspection of defects using computer vision convolutional neural networks to automatically detect, identify, and classify defects from pattern recognition comparison with a database of defect images and their causes.

The almost completely automated LCD fabrication assembly line has robots at virtually every station, and in addition to a final inspection scan, mounting CMOS sensors on the robots' heads can scan the panels at critical fabrication stations for defects, and if found, the production line can be stopped at that stage and the process adjusted as needed to prevent the defect, and then continued, saving time and avoiding a completely unproductive production run.

The trained AI inspection system can also store new defect data in the database in real time, and thus improve its defect detection skills as it works on the assembly line, and so increase yield.[8]

COMPUTER PROGRAMMERS

There are many online program-drafting competitions organized by programmers themselves that have attracted developers of code-writing machines to generate human-readable source code given a programming objective in an input-output test.

Automatic programming generation employing *recurrent neural networks* (RNNs), wherein some hidden layers change in response to activation from succeeding layers, can model sequential programming steps to formulate a working program that satisfies the output test objective.

Researchers at Microsoft and Cambridge have developed a *Learning Inductive Program Synthesis* (LIPS) machine called *DeepCoder* that determines the attributes of programming language for a specific task utilizing text recognition to generate a programming dataset of the character-by-character sequences used in the C++ and Python high-level computer languages. LIPS learns the probability distributions of attributes for the given programming task employing an artificial neural network, and then guided by the machine-learnt input-output mapping derived from the task objectives, searches existing computer programs for program steps consistent with the input-output test objectives.[9]

In 2020, the Elon Musk founded *OpenAI* and announced its *Generative Pre-trained Transformer version 3* (GPT-3) that could not only write computer programs, but through enormous database training from crawling the Internet and billions of parameters. its algorithms, through reinforcement and unsupervised learning, could compose prose and poetry, and indeed write any text up to 50,000 words.

The dependable, tireless, non-complaining robot programmers are particularly suited to the Red Bull®-driven all-night sessions of intensive programming, and the unerring placement all the semicolons and parentheses in C++, and it will need only electricity for sustenance, with no infrastructure requirements of free Coke®, La Croix®, nuts, pizza, fried won tons, and ping-pong tables.

---

[8] Regarding LCD fabrication, ref. the author's book Chen, R.H. (2011), *Liquid Crystal Displays, Fundamental Physics and Technology*.

[9] Balog, M. *et al.* 2017, *DeepCoder: Learning to Write Programs*, ICLR paper.

The ideas for new program applications at present are the province of human ingenuity, but it looks like that as GPT-3 and its progeny gain programming skill, they will develop entirely new programming techniques and find new uses and entirely new areas for computer programming.[10]

DIGITAL ASSISTANTS

The stand-alone digital assistant can handle personal and business communications, providing information in synthetic speech in response to human speech commands. Its mobile derivative, a service robot can be a helpmate and companion.

Everyone is familiar with the speech commands understood and responded to by today's personal computers, smartphones, digital assistants, and service robots, which actually do a fairly good job. From America's *Defense Advanced Research Projects Agency* (DARPA) sponsored continuous speech recognition development and natural language front-end recognizers, to the clumsy adventures of IBM's pioneering but flawed *Newton* and Apple's early malapropistic *Siri*, great strides have been made in *natural language processing* (NLP), and *intention-driven interfaces* such as Nuance, Apple's Intelligent Siri, Wolfram Alpha, IBM Watson, Google Assistant, Now, Nest, Microsoft Cortana, and Amazon Echo and Alexa, all of which are probing the "known unknowns" of ambiguity and inference in speech.

These robots are already among us, either helping or bewildering us; will they eventually replace all of the service class for business, government, home, and although they can appropriately respond to human voice commands, will they ever really "understand" human needs and be able to deliver information like learned humans?

EXOPLANET ASTRONOMER

The search for extraterrestrial life is one of humankind's most compelling pursuits. Presently over four thousand planets orbiting relatively near stars have been discovered, more than half of which were made by the Earth-trailing heliocentric orbiting *Kepler Space Telescope* (KST) launched in 2009.

---

[10] All these algorithms will be discussed in detail in the following chapters.

KST looks for the tiny periodic changes in stellar brightness caused by exoplanets moving in front of stars. However, in 2012 and then in 2013, two of Kepler's four stabilizing directional reaction wheels failed, and the space telescope could not hold a stable pointing position, resulting in less precise and very noisy observational data.

However as long as KST was still looking, there should be exoplanets passing through its field of view at the same rate as before, so Anne Dattilo at the University of Texas designed *AstroNet-K2*, a deep neural network that after training on known exoplanets, could systematically remove the instability and noise from KST's signals, and not only reveal new exoplanets, but also find exoplanets in the old observational data *that even experienced exoplanet astronomers had missed.*

Furthermore, from December 2016 to March 2017, as Mars passed through the crippled KST's field of view, its direct and scattered light obfuscated any exoplanet signatures, but AstroNet-K2 heroically discovered two exoplanets through all the instability, noise, and the reflective glare of the Red Planet.

One detected exoplanet was a super Earth-sized, volatile-enveloped "puffy" planet whipping around a Sun-like star with a 13-day period and a surface temperature of 750°C, a little too hot for humans, but fast-paced, heat-loving beings would love the quickly-passing seasons of super-tropical weather.

The second exoplanet was also super Earth-sized, but with an even shorter 3-day period that would truly make "the hours pass like minutes", and a surface temperature of 1400°C, hot enough to melt aluminum let alone humans. One wonders what the beings on these exoplanets would look like ....[11]

The first Earth-sized exoplanet was discovered in 2015 also by the impaired Kepler Space Telescope. Prosaically named *Kepler-45b* is orbiting in the habitable *Goldilocks* zone around *Kepler 45* a star similar in size to our Sun with an orbital period of 385 days, almost exactly the same as an Earth year. But because Kepler-45b's star is older than our Sun by about 1.5 billion years and considerably brighter, Kepler-45b is slightly warmer than our Earth, but assuming a suitable atmosphere and pressure, it is amenable to an H_2O triple-point, and therefore has human being-like habitation potential. However, at about two times the

---

[11] Datillo, A. *et al.*, 2019, *Identifying Exoplanets With Deep Learning II: Two New Super-Earths Uncovered by a Neural Network in K2 Data*, arxiv.org/abs/1903.10507.

size of Earth, it has stronger gravity, so any *Earth 2.0* animals would not need much fur, and its humanoids would be tanned, stocky, and very muscular.

If these super-strong "Kepler 45b-ings" are intelligent enough to develop themselves or their robots to travel the 1402 light years distance to Earth, at close to the speed of light, it would take them at least 1400 years to reach and colonize Earth (and in the absence of spacetime wormhole travel, according to Einstein's theory of special relativity, they would grow even more massive but age much more slowly on the journey because of *time dilation*, the latter relativistic effect allowing them to discount some of their accumulated travel years).[12]

In light of this dire possibility, in 2017, astronomers at MIT and the Carnegie Institute for Science released two decades of data, and the software and an online tutorial to analyze that data, and called on amateur astronomers to help with observations of the more than 1600 stars within 325 light years from Earth in the hope that "fresh eyes" would quickly find new nearby exoplanets, not only for the scientific adventure, but also to gain time to prepare for eventual alien landings on Earth.[13]

The Kepler Space Telescope could have helped, but its reaction wheels finally ran out of fuel and it was officially retired on October 30, 2018. Fortunately, a new space telescope, the *Transiting Exoplanet Survey Satellite* (TESS) had been launched on Elon Musk's Space X Falcon 9 rocket on April 18, 2018, and is continuing the epochal search for extraterrestrial life, no doubt primed to find nearby exoplanets with the help of artificial intelligence machines.

The few hundred years travel time makes it incumbent upon us Earthlings to train TESS to quickly find the nearby exoplanets, and communicate with them if possible. Advanced extraterrestrial beings would no doubt first communicate and send advance scouts before landing *if* they meant no harm, otherwise we should prepare our defenses to alien attack.

Well before such an invasion takes place, for our very survival, Earthlings must develop artificial intelligence to supplement our meager native intelligence, and send our robots to get to them first. In this sense,

---

[12] For a description of the time dilation and mass increase of extraterrestrial travel at close to the speed of light, see the author's book, Chen, R.H. 2017, *Einstein's Relativity, the Special and General Theories with their Cosmology*, McGraw-Hill Education.

[13] Call for crowd-sourced astronomers, see *Astronomy*, June 2017, p. 13.

we will need AlphaGoZero's supreme intelligence not just to amaze us, but more importantly to save us.

AstroNet-K2 could automate much of the work of exoplanet hunters, working tirelessly at any time and place under any conditions, and without the biases that humans might have, particularly in the urgency to find Earth-like planets peopled with human-like beings in this most glamorous, and possibly most *critical*, field of astronomy.

CHAPTER 3

Intelligence

A re AI machines really and truly intelligent? "Intelligence" has been variously and controversially defined, perhaps the most general being,[1]

The ability to acquire and apply knowledge and skills

All the game-playing and working machines described easily satisfy the elements of this definition, so coming to the rescue, cognitive psychologists have added,[2]

The ability to perceive or infer information, and to retain it as knowledge to be applied towards adaptive behaviors within an environment or context

The machines can still easily pass this test of intelligence, so in an apparent attempt to *ad hoc* distinguish human intelligence from animal intelligence, these definitions have been buttressed with,[3]

understanding, reasoning, critical thinking, planning, emotional knowledge, creativity, consciousness, and self-awareness

"Understanding", "reasoning', "critical thinking", and "planning" clearly are in danger of circling definition. What is meant by "emotional knowledge" is anybody's guess, but if it means the perception of emotion

---

[1] Kumar, M 2018, ResearchGate.
[2] Dezhic, E 2018, *What is Intelligence?*, towardsdatascience.
[3] *Intelligence*, Wikipedia.

DOI: 10.1201/9781003214892-4

in others, then modern computer vision's facial recognition of mood clearly fills the bill.

As for creativity, AlphaGo's "shoulder hit" move 37 in the Game 2 has been lauded by an expert commentator as a truly creative original move beyond human teaching.[4]

Lee Sedol before the match had confidently predicted "total victory", but he was astounded by AlphaGo's move 37, calling it a "spark of genius", the hallmark of human creativity.

In Game 4, AlphaGo's performance declined after Lee Sedol's "divine wedge move" 78, perhaps an indication of a machine's emotional knowledge of a formidable challenge, and possibly a kind of self-awareness that it had no appropriate response. Indeed, game-playing computers commensurate with a "probability of loss" index, can assess the likelihood of ultimate defeat and display a forlorn "resign" output.

Given time to recover after the loss, AlphaGo went on to win Game 5 with many of what Lee Sedol later described as "weird moves", which could be seen as acknowledging the opponent's new moves, reasoning about them, critical thinking of its responses in Game 4, and subsequent planning for Game 5, all evincing an acute adaptive intelligence.

After the epochal match with AlphaGo, a chastened, but now more formidable Lee Sedol went on to win all of his subsequent matches against human *Go* Masters, stating that conversely to what Ke Jie had feared, Lee Sedol "learned from AlphaGo", and that "it has changed the way Go would be played in the future". That is, the machine had something new to teach the supremely expert human in accord with the board game adage,

Sometimes you give them a lesson, sometimes they give you a lesson.

That leaves the *consciousness* and *self-awareness* elements of the augmented definition of intelligence to be addressed. Consciousness could be no more than a brain's particular neuron activation pattern, which occurs naturally in animals and humans and artificially in computer neural networks.

Oxford mathematical physicist Roger Penrose has suggested that the realization of a particular recognition is an instant of intelligent consciousness. For example, when viewing Escher's famous *Angels and*

---

[4] For analysis of moves 37 and 78, see Chapter 28.

Demons, typically first the demons, and then in a sudden flash of perception, the angels are also discerned, and further observation reveals that the fractal is never-ending, extending forever to infinity. In observing the drawing, each new step of recognition constitutes a new awareness and thus a newly conscious intelligence.[5]

In optical illusions, humans can never know when one may recognize the illusion; however, the decisional probability of the illusions should be equal in machine pattern recognition, which means that if an illusion is palpable, the machine will know at once that there are two possibilities, each at 0.5, while a human must wait for conscious awareness of the possibilities, and some humans will never be able to discern the different illusions. In this sense, the computer vision machine's perception of the possibilities is superior.

This shows that an artificial neural network's pattern recognition capability can be equal or superior to human pattern recognition, and as such represents an awareness and consciousness similar to a human's that can satisfy those elements of the cognitive psychologist's definition of intelligence.

Continuing with the definition, *self-awareness* is something that a *non-playing character* (NPC in a video game appears to possess, apparently knowing what he/she/it is capable of *vis à vis* the agent-player and the game environment, so the computer program and the hardware and software that drives the NPC apparently also has some modicum of self-awareness. However, is that merely an awareness designed by the human programmer? That is, is it the human who created the machine actually providing the intelligence that the machine is apparently displaying?

A human, once conscious and aware of a concept, for example the existence of two opposing states in an optical illusion, can sort out the situation by reasoning about the concepts in the abstract. Many can agree that mathematics is something that requires that abstract reasoning, and in almost every society there is an often uneasy respect for the very apparent intelligence of those who are *good at mathematics*, which may be just the ability to abstractly and logically reason in its purest form. A definition of *mathematics* is:[6]

---

[5] Figure 3.1, Escher image from researchgate.net under *Creative Commons*, Attribution 4.0 International (CC by 4.0) without any modification; image also used by Penrose, R. 1989, *The Emperor's New Mind: Concerning Computers, Minds, and the Laws of Physics*, Oxford.

[6] The definition of mathematics and doing mathematics are the author's amalgams gleaned from various reputable sources over time, with references now long forgotten.

A discipline that logically investigates inductively and deductively the relationships among concepts in a very compact formthat gets to the heart of the matter

If there is a touchstone of intelligence, perhaps it is this ability to do mathematics, as many have believed, the purest manifestation of abstract human thought. *Doing mathematics* can be defined as

the discovery of relational aspects of disparate functions that can lead to some reasonable conclusion.

Instead of a human-invented *discipline*, Plato for one saw mathematics as an æthereal logic residing in the Heavens but controlling the Earth, flittingly visited by mankind through an incipient awareness of mathematical forms; as Penrose explains it, mathematical concepts and mathematical truths inhabit an actual world of their own that is timeless and without physical location distinct from the physical world, but in terms of which the physical world must be understood and our minds do have some direct access to this Platonic realm through an "awareness" of mathematical forms, and our ability to reason about them.

Galileo believed that the Universe is a grand book written in the language of mathematics, and Penrose thought that *only* humans can access the Platonic world and Galilean Universe of mathematics as it is a highly specialized and peculiarly human activity. Indeed as Penrose added, some might say that it is an activity confined to certain peculiar humans.

The artificial intelligence pioneers Allen Newell and Herbert Simon in a computer program written by John Shaw in 1955 at the RAND Corporation confronted the classic *mind-body problem* of whether a machine composed of inanimate matter can have the thinking capability of an animate mind.

Their *Logic Theorist* was the first computer program specifically designed to simulate the thinking process in problem-solving by the human mind, and chose the abstruse discipline of proving mathematical theorems as the testing ground. It proved 38 of the first 52 elementary theorems in Alfred North Whitehead and Bertrand Russell's epochal tome on the logical basis of mathematics, *Principia Mathematica*. Proving theorems is certainly doing mathematics, but the *Principia* theorems selected were very basic.[7]

---

[7] For more on the *Logic Theorist*, see Chapter 9.

Not so basic was Paul Dirac's electron equation which by the appearance of ± in front, elegantly foretold the existence of the anti-matter positron, and Albert Einstein's gravitational field equation wherein the Riemann tensor revealed the manifold structure of the Universe. That makes mathematics at least the handmaiden of physical reality, and if the machine is to surpass human abilities, it will have to demonstrate that mathematical capability.[8]

In 2018 AlphaGoZero's inference engine AlphaZero, with no human input or training, learned how to play board games simply by playing, and although designed by humans, improved to be the very best player in each of those games simply by autonomously playing against itself.

So if AlphaZero can by itself do the abstract, creative manipulation, and strategic thinking required in matching wits in the structured logic of chess and *Go*, in fact reasonably performing just the relational aspects (stone positions) of disparate functions (chess piece moves) leading to a desired conclusion, then it is doing mathematical thinking and is thereby intelligent in and of itself.

IBM Watson, of course also created by humans, has found relational aspects of disparate functions far beyond what its human designers could find to defeat very accomplished humans in debating and *Jeopardy*; its intelligence in that regard clearly surpassing that of its creators.

Following these examples, an "AlphaMathZero" or "IBM MathQA" with some supervised training from the best mathematicians doing classical math problems, and then by doing millions of problems, improving along the way by reinforcement and unsupervised learning, in principle could become superlative robot mathematicians.

Today's computers of course can numerically solve complex non-linear differential equations and has proven such abstruse mathematical conjectures as the classic four-color map theorem.[9]

However, the former is done by the finite-differences number-crunching formulated by humans, and the latter by try-all-possibilities brute force, and as such are not really "thinking" but merely following an iterative process to its end. It seems that it is really the machine's

---

[8] Refer to the author, Chen, R.H. 2017, *Einstein's Relativity, the Special and General Theories with their Cosmology*, McGraw-Hill Education.

[9] The four-color theorem: Given any separation of a plane into contiguous regions in a map, no more than four colors are required to color the regions of the map so that no two adjacent regions have the same color.

designers who are paving the way, and the machine is merely mechanically following in the path.

The proprietary software application program *Socrates* can read math problems and produce step-by-step solutions and explanations, but is based on categorizing known solutions for use in mathematics education, just finding an appropriate solution to a given problem by search, and not actually solving the problem itself.

The human visual cortex has 140 million neurons, and Google's deep convolutional neural network (DCNN) only has a few million artificial neurons, but ever more massive and efficient DCNNs are under development, and it is conceivable that a very deep CNN, through reinforcement learning and a large variety of algorithms could scale up to human brain capacity.

Researchers at *Facebook* have used a neural network to map input sequences to output sequences as in speech recognition, and applied that to sequences of mathematical symbols in equations to map integrals and ordinary differential equations problems to solutions. The mathematical expression is represented by a tree with operators as nodes and operands as leaves could produce results that were more accurate than the equations-solving programs of *Mathematica, Matlab*, and *Maple*.

Plato and Penrose believed that only a human could access the Heavenly world of mathematical forms, and indeed we have not yet found any non-human who could mathematics. Lee Sedol and Ke Jie also believed that only humans could appreciate the "beauty" of *Go*, however they both lost to AlphaGo the machine, showing that the "beauty" of *Go* does not absolutely imply success in practice

It seems that the simple *Turing Test* of the ability to reason about mathematical forms could determine whether an AI machine can join those peculiar humans in their peculiar activity: The AI machine could be presented with some mathematical puzzles to see if it can solve them as well as or better in a competition with humans.

Ostensibly a simple and effective test, it is nonetheless plagued by the fact that the relatively simple mathematical puzzles can be solved by tree-search, and solutions from logical ANDs would seem to be no more than a copying and collating test rather than proof of reasoning about mathematical forms. Nonetheless, much of mathematics actually is done by analogy with other mathematics problems, but in assessing the AI machine's mathematical ability, the separation of analogizing, reasoning, and creativity may well be as difficult as any math puzzle itself.

Perhaps a step down from doing mathematics, another test of intelligence may be based on the psychologist's view of intelligence as ability at "general cognitive problem-solving" where "cognitive" includes all the above listed attributes of intelligence, and the key word here is "general".

That indeed has been the machine's bugbear; its lack of *general purpose* ability that derives from a broad intelligence that can address and adapt to different conditions and situations. The criticism of machines and robots is that although they do some things very well, even better than humans, but each machine can only do its own thing.

However, AlphaGoZero's appendage "zero" came from the idea that "less is more", meaning that *less complexity produces greater generalization*, and in accord with Apple's design philosophy, *simplicity is the ultimate sophistication*, a *zero* human input, randomly initialized deep policy and value network could produce a "thinking machine" that can perform ever higher-quality "policy iteration".

Indeed, AlphaZero did quickly learn not only *Go*, but also checkers, chess, *xiangqi*, and *shogi*, and beat human champions in each of those board games after only a few hours of reinforcement and unsupervised learning.[10]

This naturally brings up the notion that in principle such a thinking machine embodying the artificial neural networks, tree-search and game theory algorithms could engage in any activity without any prior knowledge of the specifics of the activity and excel in that activity; isn't that kind of take-on-all-challenges the essence of *general* adaptive intelligence?

So going beyond the mind games, AlphaZero was assigned the task of creating unique pharmaceutical drug molecules based on the principles of organic chemistry. However, AlphaZero's creativity led to drugs that were theoretically possible and decidedly innovative, but impossible or impracticable to combine and maintain, meaning that the machine went too far, something that humans often are too guilty of as well. Of course, with some further intensive reinforcement learning from rewards and penalties for success and failure, AlphaZero should be able to come up with some useful new drugs, among them therapeutic cures and immunological vaccines for covid-19.

---

[10] For details of the algorithm Silver, D 2018, *DeepMind AlphaGoZero mastering games without human knowledge*, online. AlphaGZero's learning curve for each game is shown in this video.

The research problem then is to develop a general purpose robot comfortable in a variety of environments and possessing a number of different skills.

All the genius-level *Go* Masters and great chess Grandmasters were prodigies, for example Korea's Lee Sedol was only 26 when he became a world champion, and the heir apparent new world champion China's Ke Jie was only 18 at the time of his match with AlphaGo Master. The American Bobby Fisher won the World Chess Championship at 28, after startling performances from age 13, and of course there is Russia's great Garry Kasparov, and the current World Champion Norway's Magnus Carlsen gained Grandmaster level at only 13. Of course, well-known child prodigies abound throughout the histories of mathematics, as well as music and art. So the touchstone of genius-level intelligence is likely something innately present in the organization of neurons in the human brain at birth, an innate and specific intelligence.

The brain material of geniuses and the so-called idiot-savants have been dissected and analyzed to show synaptic neural networks densely concentrated in particular areas of the brain that process different extraordinary capabilities, *just like densely hard-wired microprocessor ASICs.*[11]

Analysis of Einstein's brain revealed atypical inter-hemispherical connections and an enlarged *lateral sulcus* allied to analytical/mathematical function. Observations of portraits of René Descartes and his pronounced frontal lobe bulge associated with spatial and analytic perception has been proposed as the source of his formulation of the graphic-analytic Cartesian coordinate system.[12]

Furthermore, neuroscientists have observed that individuals with high IQs and knowledge of a lot of facts have the enhanced ability to quickly recognize patterns to classify those facts; in effect the neuron hard-wiring and rapid synaptic neural connecting upon external stimulation are the source of their innate intelligence and later-acquired intellectualism.

Indeed, it has been found that during the process of deep thinking, the neural activation of the *dorsalateral prefrontal cortex* allied with self-awareness and self-consciousness is actually lower, and the *medial prefrontal cortex* allied with stimulus-independent internal idea generation

---

[11] The author has never forgotten the Indian savant in Taipei who within seconds could respond to my question of what day of the week was August 13, 2029, and any other date asked by the people gathered around him.

[12] Einstein himself however deprecated his own mathematical ability, but that was in comparison with his genius-level pure mathematician colleagues such as Hermann Minkowski.

is higher, thereby allowing an uninhibited "free-flow" of thought rapidly through synaptic patterns, essentially closing off the external environment to allow the unobstructed transmission of neural signals.[13]

Many have no doubt experienced that when deep in thought, for example doing a math problem, computer program coding, analyzing a situation, writing an essay, business report, or legal brief, painting, or playing a difficult piece of music, one becomes oblivious to surroundings, and ideas surge from within; that is, from the *medial* at the expense of the *dorsalateral* prefrontal cortex.

This can explain why superior thinkers are often lost in a world of their own, and may not be aware of their environment and the consequences of their acts and words on others, thereby being perceived as lacking social grace. Lost in thought, they perversely display annoyance when that environment intrudes on their thinking.

Humans are stuck with the neurons and patterns that they have at birth, but can refine the synaptic flow from education, experience, and practice with effort. The AI machine however through training sets and intense iterative reinforcement and unsupervised learning can dynamically generate the synaptic neural connection network necessary for specific tasks, and refine the cognitive flows through the network.

A general-purpose AI machine then can be hard-wired as a top-down expert system for specific tasks, with more circuitry for the more difficult tasks. That hardware then can be driven by a very deep neural networks and an ensemble of clever algorithms to deep learn from the bottom up through reinforcement and unsupervised learning. Adding a central control unit, actuating sensors, feedback loops, and servo-mechanical constructs constitute an extremely capable "robot for all seasons".

This single AI robot in principle will be able play chess and *Go* better than Kasparov and Ke Jie, compose and play music like Mozart, paint like Picasso, write like Tolstoy, do physics like Newton and chemistry like Lavoisier; and hopefully mathematics like Gauss and cosmology like Einstein.

---

[13] For details of human brain structure, see Berlin, H 2015. *The neuroscience of genius, creativity, and improvisation*, YouTube.

CHAPTER 4

The AI Singularity

M erely using available data to machine learn is called "Weak AI", using that data and being able to recognize and make inferences from it is called "Strong AI". If Strong AI can equal or surpass human intelligence, it will mark the arrival of the *AI Singularity*, and challenge the of humankind's dominance of this Earth.

Alan Turing devised the first test of the AI singularity, a human and a robot respondents are placed behind a curtain, and a human questioner in front of the curtain asks many questions; the questioner is then asked which respondent is human and which is robotic, if the questioner is correct in half or less of his answers, it means that he cannot distinguish the robot's answers from the human's answers, and humankind has first-encountered the AI singularity.[1]

This rather simplistic test was meant to be performed on the rudimentary computers of Turing's day, in a better test of equality of intelligence, conducted in the late Seventies, the Carnegie Mellon University computer program called *BACON* (in honor of Sir Francis) was given data about the motion of planets around the Sun, and lo and behold, it came up with Kepler's Third Law that the square of the orbital period of a planet is directly proportional to the cube of the semi-major axis of its elliptical orbit.

Stanford physicist Zhang Shoucheng in a *Google Talk* described the following scientific test: given data regarding naturally-occurring material interactions, could the robot provide an explanation for all the

---

[1] Alan Turing's life was portrayed in the 2014 movie *The Imitation Game*.

DOI: 10.1201/9781003214892-5

observed phenomena? And again lo and behold, the AI machine came up with Mendeleyev's Periodic Table of the Elements![2]

The AI machine thus can see patterns in physical data and infer relationships, implying that it can do the scientific discovery of physics and chemistry, but can it "deductively find the relationships among *concepts* in a very compact form that gets to the heart of the matter"; that is do mathematics?

Further, critics of the "proofs" of the AI Singularity point out that the machine had perfect data, but to come up with their theories, Kepler and Mendeleyev had to parse mountains of sometimes mistaken observations, erroneous conclusions, crack-pot and half-baked interpretations, and from masses of inchoate and amorphous data select the relevant from the irrelevant and contradictory, all in the face of doctrinal religious and wrong-headed science opposition, to finally produce their theories.

The machine could demonstrate intelligence equivalent to the best minds in science given perfect data, but if it could devise a theory from imperfect data that explained phenomena for which mankind has not yet found a theory, then the AI singularity has definitely entered mankind's intellectual house, and for the greater good.

But beyond the logic of natural phenomena, Kepler embodied a spirit of inquiry and the drive to understand essential to a good scientist that, unlike a machine, ponders the mysteries of Nature, faith or both in the "natural light of reason". Does a machine have an uninstructed *spirit* of inquiry to use that reason to discover the intelligible plan, and the courage of conviction to pursue it in the face of doctrinal opposition, and even if it does, to what end?

No less a philosopher than Nietzsche proclaimed this ascendency of mankind's intellect derived from the human spirit,[3]

> *He stands proudly on the pyramid of the world-process; and while he lays the final stone of his knowledge, he seems to cry aloud to listening Nature: "We are at the top, we are at the top; we are the completion of Nature!"*

Humans pursue the Truth in the spirit of enriching and bettering society, why should an AI robot do the same for the betterment of an insensate

---

[2] Zhang, S 2018, *Quantum Computing, AI, and Blockchain; the Future of IT*, Talks at Google. YouTube, June 6. Tragically Professor Zhang committed suicide later in 2018.

[3] Nietzsche, F 1957, *The Use and Abuse of History*, Bobbs-Merrill.

robotkind? Would robots have any motivation to improve its environment? Air and water pollution are of no concern, but extreme weather, earthquakes and floods are, and with better sensing producing more data, analysis, and pattern recognition capability, robots will likely be more attuned to, for example, the dangers of climate change.

Will human scientific endeavor cease as inadequate and irrelevant after the AI Singularity and be replaced by the considerations of robot science? Do robots have any, like Nietzsche, philosophical motivations?

Will the AI robot of its own volition measure the skies, probe the Universe, produce great works of literature and art, seek the sublime ideals of philosophy and intellectualism, including the contemplation of human (and robot) consciousness and awareness as the better part of mankind has done? Will an intellectual robot continue to follow the productive course set by humans and produce new robots to allow old robots to enjoy more leisure time and pursue higher interests?

Will the uninstructed AI machine resolve the problems of disease, environmental degradation, species extinction, war, climate change, and inhumanity by itself? Why should robots redress what mankind has stupidly done? After subjugating mankind, will the singular AI robot display its own mechanomorphic stupidity in launching devastating internecine robot wars, just as humans have so cruelly done?

If the history of mankind's realization of superiority and its manifestation in the cruel, abusive, and exploitive treatment of Nature's animals is any guide, perhaps the best that can be hoped is that we humans won't be slaughtered by the AI robots; fortunately they have no need to consume us for nourishment, but they may find other uses for our bodies, such as fat for fuel and lubrication, bones for landfill, skin for basketball and footballs, or gut for their robot tennis rackets.

What AI robots do with us will depend on their *attitude* towards us, and that attitude will be a function of their intelligence and how it is used, and poses the question: Does intelligence beget attitude, and if so what attitude?

Human attitude emanates from the 100 billion neurons, 100 billion glial cells, and 100 trillion connections among neurons of the human brain, and although artificial intelligence research has helped to understand how a *thought* is developed in the hidden layers of artificial neural networks, because of the billions of backpropagation passes through the network, when the thought was conceived cannot be fully known, and something as complex as an *attitude* makes the problem all the more difficult.

Furthermore, there is a serious problem, if the search for a theory of intelligence is being carried out by that very intelligence, can one probe and understand something by means of that very something? According to Kurt Gödel's *Second Incompleteness Theorem*, the full validity of any system cannot be demonstrated within that system itself; that is, human intelligence cannot be established and defined by humans using their own intelligence to study human intelligence. The completeness of a theory cannot be established unless there is something outside the frame of reference against which it can be tested, so it appears that the only legitimate testers of human intelligence are superhuman robots or aliens from another planet.

Anatomically modern humans' intelligence has developed over only 200,000 years from hunter-gatherer existence to an understanding of those hunted and gathered life forms as they evolved in accord with Darwin's *Origin of Species and Theory of Natural Selection*, and human intelligence has ostensibly improved through natural selection, but this is merely human intelligence studying its evolution at its earlier stages and not modern intelligence *per se*.

After the AI Singularity, perhaps superior autonomous AI machines will teach humans to be even more intelligent to participate in the robot world, or perhaps their attitude towards us humans will devolve to just a minor problem of how to dispose of us in the most efficient manner.

A defense against this rather distressing end is to control artificial intelligence development within the rules of Asimov's *Three Laws of Robotics*:

1. A robot may not injure a human being or, through inaction, allow a human being to come to harm.

2. A robot must obey orders given it by human beings except where such orders would conflict with the First Law.

3. A robot must protect its own existence as long as such protection does not conflict with the First or Second Law

However, the first law has already been violated by autonomous military drones finding and killing terrorist leaders, an explosives-carrying police robot's pursuit and detonation killing of an active mass shooter, and of course, fictionally, the *Terminator*.[4]

Perhaps a more philosophical approach will help to assuage our fears, if the human mind is taken as Fontenelle's *historical collective* mind; that is, a good cultivated mind containing all the minds of preceding centuries. If it continues to iteratively develop, humankind intelligence will never degenerate, and perhaps be able to compete with robot intelligence.[5]

However, our current investigation and construction of artificial intelligence is going off on a locus away from human intelligence to robot intelligence, and robots presently are just products of that human intelligence, so humans ostensibly should remain the *primus inter pares*, at least until a super smart robot is developed or intelligent beings from other worlds show us their surpassing intelligence.

The *Search for Extra-Terrestrial Intelligence* (SETI) has employed giant radio telescopes and multichannel scanners to analyze spectra from beings operating other-worldly transmitters. In this sense, "intelligent creatures can be defined merely as those with the means and inclination to engage in interstellar communication via electromagnetic waves", and if they succeed in contacting us humans, they presumably have a superior intelligence since they have contacted us and not us they. Perhaps they will tell us what "intelligence" apart from humans really is, and thereby have a basis for the AI Singularity.[6]

---

[4] Afghan war veteran Micah Johnson killed five police officers and injured nine civilians in Dallas, Texas on July 7, 2016, a police bomb disposal robot *Andros MarkV-AI* killed Johnson with a bomb.

[5] Bernard Le Bouvier de Fontenelle (1688), quoted in Nisbit, R 1969, *Social Change and History*, Oxford and Fukuyama, F 1992. *The End of History and the Last Man*, Avon.

[6] The author participated in a SETI program at Stanford under a program directed by Harvard's visiting Professor Paul Horowitz, and often wondered what we would do if we really detected an intelligent transmission from outer space. The electromagnetic wave definition of intelligence is from Ferris, T 1988, *Coming of Age in the Milky Way*, Doubleday.

II

The Artificial Intelligence Infrastructure

CHAPTER 5

Hardware

M any Western science historians have marked the beginning of the Scientific Revolution at 1543 with the publication of Copernicus' *De Revolutionibus*, an indeed revolutionary idea of the Earth revolving around the Sun; a rational heliocentric replacing the self-absorbed homocentric regard of man's natural surroundings.

Johannes Kepler's *Astronomia nova* published in 1609 presented a new ephemeris based on planetary orbits later derived analytically in Newton's *Principia Mathematica* and expounded upon in Leibniz' *Specimen Dynamicum*, and LaPlace's *Traité de Méchanique Celeste*.

The new scientific method of observation, hypothesis, and confirmation, armed the natural philosophers of the day with new medicine, chemistry, mathematics physics, endowing their adherents with powers of healing and feats of astronomy and engineering, that having a predictive capability, attracted the patronage of many of the paranoid European rulers of the time. But the Age of Reason would not only amuse and strengthen the monarchs' rule, it would enlighten the whole world through science.

The predictive power of science was founded on the calculus of Newton and Leibniz in the late 17th Century, a new mathematics that was to be employed first for the greater understanding of Nature and then for new constructs and weapons that would not only advance the power of nations, but also produce industries that would change human society forever.

The calculus of Newton and Leibniz can describe the rate of change of a body having position x with time t, a first derivative velocity v, and the rate of change of velocity with time that is a second derivative of position, an acceleration a, thence from Newton's second law $F = ma$, a force F applied to a body with mass m will accelerate that body,

$$F = ma = m\frac{dv}{dt} = m\frac{d^2x}{dt^2}$$

Humankind thus could know precisely what force could produce a desired motion, and conversely what acceleration could result in what force, and design machines to those ends.

Furthermore, that force F times velocity v, when integrated over time t gives the amount of work W done by that force over distance s, and from that it could be known how much of that net work will generate how much kinetic energy, and conversely how much kinetic energy is required for the machines to do that work,

$$W = \int_{t_1}^{t_2} F \cdot v dt = \int_{t_1}^{t_2} F \cdot \frac{ds}{dt} dt = \int_{s_1}^{s_2} F \cdot ds$$

Net Work = Kinetic Energy

The "d" in the equations denotes a very small change, the fundamental idea of *limits* in calculus where for example in going from A to B by continually halving the distance results in getting *infinitely* close to B but never arriving, with the distance becoming infinitesimally small. From this, changes in distance, time, velocity, force, work, energy, and so on all can be made infinitesimally small, allowing representations of dynamic systems and their changes to the finest detail.

For artificial intelligence, the calculus has been employed to minimize the error between the belief of an artificial neural network and the ground-truth, allowing the network to learn, while the chain rule of calculus joining past changes (first derivatives) pushes the network to improve its understanding. A system employing the calculus thus can learn and ultimately predict, and so can be said to be "intelligent" in its ability to predict through learning.

The Industrial Revolution of the late 18th Century in England was founded in large part on Robert Boyle's steam engines as the drivers of the Newtonian machines that gradually replaced human, bovine, and equine labor. Faraday's experiments and Maxwell's mathematics found that a turning magnetic field could generate an electric current in a stator and conversely, an electric current in the stator could produce a magnetic field to turn a rotor, resulting in the idea that electricity generators and driving motors could provide the energy and impetus for the machines to do the work of manufacturing and transporting people; this idea would quickly transform the life and society of the day, and ultimately drive machines that could "think"; that is, the computers and algorithms operating on Big Data,.

Burning coal to boil water to produce steam to turn electromagnets to generate electricity in 1882 was scaled up by Edison and Tesla whose great steam-powered turbines began to produce electricity not only to run machines in factories, but also to light up those factories for work into the dark of night. Electricity as well lit the homes in London and New York for the reading, study, and leisure that would develop an urban culture that would generate a new industrial society.

In 1908, Henry Ford's assembly-line mass manufacture of petroleum-powered internal combustion engines for automobile transport thrust the world towards the crude oil-cracking industries of gasoline and plastics that would dominate the 20th Century.

The assembly line, however, relegated the erstwhile master craftsman to the mind-numbing routine of servicing the machines that now did the crafting. This led not only to labor unrest and subsequent social revolution, but advanced into the horrifying thought that the machine could be intelligent as well, and take over "thinking" from humans.

On the other hand, the saving grace was that although man serviced the machine at work, the machine would serve man at home: the refrigerator, washing machine, and vacuum cleaner saved time and labor, the radio provided information and entertainment, and the phonograph provided music for enjoyment. Later on, the computer would help humans do their work and marvelous electronic devices provide hitherto unimaginable communications and information; and artificial intelligence ultimately might do almost all the "thinking" for humans.

The portents of the European industrial revolution were duly noted in far-off Japan. After the 19th Century Meiji Restoration, the traditional social hierarchical order of *warrior, farmer, artisan, merchant* was turned on its head by the previously unthinkable, a titled samurai, honor-bound to the rigid frugality of his spiritual class, began taking up the mundane and at times venal affairs of civil administration and the materialism of commerce.

Iwasaki Yatoro, the great grandson of a revered samurai, in 1870 founded Japan's first *keiretsu*, Mitsubishi Heavy Industry and Shipbuilding. The builder of the agile Zero fighter planes and giant *Yamato* class battleships was understandably disbanded by the Americans after World War II, but upon the Korean War, to counter the rise of communism by demonstrating the virtues of capitalism, Mitsubishi was re-organized and re-branded to become an electric appliance manufacturer.

The hearts of those appliances would beat from electricity, but their brains would soon depend on a new electronics based on the physics of quantum mechanical uncertainty. That is, because electrons could not concurrently have an absolutely determinable energy and position, they could probabilistically tunnel through an ostensibly insurmountable potential barrier in a semiconductor material, permitting current flow and amplification under the control of an electronic gate.

From this mostly Germanic physics, first America's Bell Labs invented the transistor in 1947, and then Texas Instruments and Fairchild Semiconductor in 1958 independently created an integrated circuit of transistors, propelling TI and Fairchild's successor Intel to semiconductor device dominance in the late 20th Century, and RCA and General Electric to the forefront of consumer electronics production using those semiconductors, albeit to be quickly over-taken by the design and miniaturization wizards at Japan's Sony and Toshiba.

In nearby South Korea, after the devastation of the Korean War, with American aid and under the autocratic leadership of President Park Jung-hee, the cozy relationship of the central government, the banks, and the family-run *chaebols* fostered the dominating emergence of the Big Four of Samsung, LG, Hyundai, and Daewoo in steel, shipbuilding, consumer electronics, and finally semiconductor fabrication.

At the same time, on the small island of Taiwan, taking full advantage of counter-communism American aid, the Republic of China began textile, plastics, and passive electronic components manufacturing for export, and the much-maligned but inexpensive and useful "Made in Taiwan" products flooded the US market, the fledgling precursors of a major electronics supply chain specializing in the mass production of semiconductors chips by TSMC, personal computers by Acer, and liquid crystal displays by Chimei, all the while bringing down prices so that people all over the world could utilize and enjoy the new electronics.

Japan's exquisite product design, together with South Korea and Taiwan's efficient mass production, brought high-tech products to the masses, the globalization lifting the *tiger economies* of East Asia, but driving the pioneering RCA, Westinghouse, General Electric, and Telefunken to consumer product desuetude.

America quickly made a comeback with Texas Instruments' handy pocket calculator, the unprecedented computational power of IBM's mainframe computers, and Apple and IBM's personal computers, all of which together with the Asian tigers' low-cost, high-efficiency production would change work and society all over the world.

The 20th Century thus saw the high-technology consumer electronics globalization paradigm at its best: European science, American invention, Japanese design, Korean and Taiwanese production. And all the while, Asia's sleeping giant, the Peoples' Republic of China, mired in a regressive cultural revolution, was left out in the cold.

Later in the Century, American research universities and the innovative spirit of Route 128 in the east and Silicon Valley in the west attracted engineers and entrepreneurs from all over America, and then the world, particularly India, China, Russia, and the Middle East. The new information technology companies Yahoo, Google, Facebook, and Amazon quickly rose to Internet commercial dominance, and the personal computer and smartphone communications began to generate the Big Data that empowered the rise of modern artificial intelligence in America, and finally awoke the sleeping dragon China with the new AI-intensive tech companies Alibaba, Baidu, and Tencent leading the way.

The seminal changes in industry and society of the late 20th Century were propelled by the computer; the middle of this Century will be dominated by the implementation of artificial neural networks driven by clever new algorithms parsing the ever-growing Big Data derived from the ever-shrinking but more powerful computers in the smart phone.

THE COMPUTER

As artificial neural networks are totally dependent on the constructs and calculations performed by computers, artificial intelligence depends on the computer just as human intelligence depends on the human brain.

Computer processing can be said to have started centuries ago, first with the idea of logarithms for analog mechanical computation, then binary numbers and Boolean logic for semiconductor logic, and finally integrated circuit switching electronics for fast and massive computing.

It is an obvious and proven fact that the brain is more sensitive to proportion when there is a large difference factor, so logarithmic difference of orders of magnitude (10x) is more easily perceived than say the unit differences of a centimeter scale, so it seems natural that the fundamental operations of a brain-mimicking computer would be based on logarithmic scales that have the further advantages of being able to conveniently perform multiplication and division and increase the range of computation.

The modern-use idea of logarithms was formulated in the early 17th Century by Scotland's John Napier as an aid for doing mathematical calculations. The logarithm of a number is the exponent to which another number, called the base, must be raised to produce that original number, thus practically allowing all numbers to be represented by exponents (for example, the log of 10 to the base 10 is just 1.0 ($log_{10}(10) = 1$) and so very large numbers can be represented more compactly as exponents to the base 10 (for example, $1000000 = 10^6$, (just count the number of zeros); furthermore, multiplication and division can be performed by adding and subtracting logarithms, leading to very convenient analog computation first by mechanical calculators, then the engineer's slide rule, and eventually digital computation by computers.

Two luminaries of the 17th Century Scientific Revolution, the French mathematician Blaise Pascal and the German Gottfried Wilhelm Leibniz designed hand-cranked cogwheel adding machines that could also logarithmically multiply and divide, the mechanical principles of which would drive calculators for the next 300 years.

These calculating machines would later be controlled by the principles of Joseph Marie Jacquard's automatic weaving loom that used a deck of punch-hole cards read by movable rods to interweave different color threads for cloth manufacture. Different sequences of cards could produce different designs, the Jacquard loom thus constituting as early as 1804 the first programmable weaving robot, who would soon be promoted to scientific and engineering work.

In 1822, England's Charles Babbage designed a calculating machine with numbers etched on interacting cogs and wheels that by cranking could step-by-step iterate the small differences in derivatives with respect to an independent variable to produce solutions of differential equations for engineering tables. In 1834, he expanded the scope of his *Difference Engine* with a locomotive-sized, steam-powered mechanical calculator having a "store" that could hold one hundred 40-digit numbers etched on those cogs and wheels, and a "mill" that could fetch the numbers and perform calculations such as iterations (do-loops), conditionals (if-then), and transfers (go-to), requiring many, many complex mechanical interactions.

This was the beginning of computers that could do calculus, be programmed, and handle large amounts of data, the life-blood of artificial intelligence machines.

It was Babbage's assistant, the lovely daughter of the great poet Lord Byron, who, using Jacquard's punch cards devised the first ordered sequences of the above logical operations for the calculations of Babbage's *Analytical Engine*. The self-taught mathematician Ada, Countess of Lovelace in 1843 thus was history's first computer programmer.[1]

The Countess' punch-card programs designed to control Babbage's Analytical Engine could solve different differential equation problems just as the woven cloth designs produced by Jacquard's loom could be changed simply by changing the order of the punch-cards in the stack, so as the Countess wrote in her operational instructions,[2]

We may say most aptly that the Analytical Engine weaves algebraical patterns just as the Jacquard loom weaves flowers and leaves

Alas, Babbage's analytical engine was never built because of lack of funding, mankind thus had to wait more than one hundred years for Vannevar Bush's analog *Differential Analyzer* that still required cogwheels which shaft rotations recorded small difference iterations for solving differential equations that were still set up laboriously by hand using screwdrivers and wrenches.

Bush's cranked mechanical shaft rotations were gratefully replaced by Lee De Forest's vacuum-tube triode amplifiers and George Philbrick's electric voltages in 1938, thereby increasing computation speed and greatly reducing set-up time. The results were displayed on an oscilloscope, signaling the arrival of the graphical representation of electronic scientific and engineering calculations.

Bush's Differential Analyzer was employed in the War effort, but it required ten different logical states to represent the decimals 0 to 9 and depended on the often unstable and noisy analog voltages of vacuum tubes to perform its operations.

---

[1] Babbage's Differential Analyzer was built, in 1991 when the London Science Museum constructed a working Babbage machine using materials and techniques available at Babbage's time as proof of concept. The Countess was self-taught because as a woman she was not allowed to enter university to study mathematics; it was obviously the university's great loss.

[2] Lovelace quote from *BBC Science Focus Magazine* (13 October 2020).

The conceptual breakthrough to today's digital computers was recorded in his 1847 book, *The Mathematical Analysis of Logic*, wherein George Boole revisited Leibniz' study of ancient China's *I Ching* divination that all under Heaven are dualities, for instance dark and light, male and female, up and down, left and right, good and evil, and so on. Following Napier, Boole formulated a base 2 logarithmic system, and with only those two states, laid the foundations for the binary logic of digital computing to replace decimal calculation with the eponymous *Boolean Algebra*.

In contrast to base 10 decimal numbers where each position to the left of the decimal point increases by a power of *10*, each place to the left in a base 2 binary system represents an increasing power of *2*, with "1" signifying the very religious Leibniz' active "God" existence and "0" signifying an inactive "Void" in *I Ching* mysticism, so read from right to left, for example 8 is represented by the binary sequence 1000, where read from right to left, only the fourth place is "on", so $2^3 = 8$.

The basic binary logical operations of AND, OR, and NOT in combination can express all arithmetic operations, and the NOR, NAND, XOR operations can make operations simpler. Arrays of these logic gates can add, subtract, multiply, divide, compare, classify, and perform all the basic mathematical and logical operations.

Logic gates receive high or low coded pulses through the logic gate cascades to produce high and low voltages allowing current to flow or not flow according to the truth tables of Boolean algebra to produce desired logical outcomes for programming computer computations.

The implementation breakthrough came from Vannevar Bush's graduate student Claude Shannon. He noted that since the binary representation of any number can be strings of binary bits, the two-state on/off logic of electronic switches could easily represent all the numbers, for example the number 8 (binary 1000) can be easily set by binary switches as (right to left), *off, off, off, on* and combinations of bits could form bytes of information, so that combinations of switches as gates could control logical operations represented by truth tables of either True (on, open, high) or False (off, closed, low) that led to a desired logical cascade that represented the results of the computation.

Mathematical calculations thus could be very efficiently performed solely by simple electronic switches, as Shannon outlined in his 1938 MIT master's thesis entitled *A Symbolic Analysis of Relay and Switching Circuits*, proving that it is after all possible for a graduate student thesis to have some value.

Analog signals, such as voice and music, are digitized by sequentially sampling a small interval of the voltage signal, giving each a decimal value which is translated to binary form by an analog-to-digital-converter (ADC), and decoded back to analog voltages by a DAC for playback which, because of the number assignments of each sound, is not subject to noise or distortion; that is why the music on digital CDs sounds better than that of analog tapes.

The theoretical breakthrough for computing hardware was set forth in Alan Turing's 1936 Cambridge University research paper, *On Computable Numbers*, which defined the binary logical operations that could be sequentially recorded and stored on a theoretically infinitely-long paper tape to constitute what he called a *universal machine* that could in principle compute any solvable problem, and therefore in principle also could actually "think" electronically and thus was the first instance of a machine-generated artificial intelligence.

As proof of this intelligence, the deciphering of the Nazi secret code *Enigma* during World War II by Turing and the "Backroom Boys" at British Intelligence's Bletchley Park and their 2,000 vacuum-tube *Colossus*. Intercepted German messages, encoded and punched into paper tape which was fed to a photoelectric reader that iteratively scanned at a then astonishing rate of 5,000 characters per second, it was then compared with the Enigma codes captured by the Polish resistance to find a match. Even though the Germans scrambled messages by systematically rotating alphanumeric rotors and changing the plug settings and keys of the encoding machine three times a day (the German receiver would know the settings), the "Backroom Boys" broke the code, and as one of the Boys said.[3]

I won't say what Turing did made us win the war, but I daresay we might have lost it without him.

A *Turing Machine* running Boolean algebra on electronic circuits was constructed in 1942 at Iowa State College by John Atanasoff. The prototype's vacuum-tube logic and capacitor memory would later be cited as the prior art that in 1974 invalidated the ENIAC computer patent, and so laid legal claim to be the world's first digital electronic computer.[4]

---

[3] Quote by British mathematician I.J. Good who worked under Turing at Bletchley Park.

[4] The term "digital" is sometimes used to describe just a logarithmic design, either base 10 decimal, or base 2 binary, and sometimes just for base 2 binary.

Jacquard's 1804 weaving loom and Countess Ada's punch-cards would reappear in 1890 in a tabulator that read the holes in the punch-cards by trailing them under metal brushes and over a bath of electrically conductive mercury so that when the brushes penetrated a hole, a circuit between the brushes and the mercury was closed producing a signal to add to a counter. Used for tabulating census data for the United States Census Bureau, the effort took only one-third the time of the last census to count, sort, and statistically analyze a population that had increased by 13 million to almost 63 million citizens.

The inventor, Herman Hollerith, would later start a machine tabulating business that many years later would grow under Thomas Watson Sr. to become the giant IBM that produced mainframe computers using the eponymous *Hollerith* punch cards to enter data and programming instructions for batch-mode computer processing.

Despite being a consummate profit–maximizing businessman, Watson Sr. was not immune to government calls to assist in the War effort and, as he put it, "making a virtue of necessity", he publicly vowed that IBM would never make more than a 1% profit from its government work. Watson Sr. then donated punch-card tabulators for the Army's ballistic table calculations, and critically, when the physicist Hans Bethe's equations for nuclear fission bomb designs could not be solved at Los Alamos, IBM provided the computing machines for the top-secret Manhattan Project development of the Atomic Bomb.

With the ever-increasing sophistication of computing machines, IBM agreed to a joint venture with Harvard University's Howard Aiken who had conceived a design for a scientific computer that is fully automatic, capable of handling positive and negative number and carrying out calculations in a natural mathematic sequence, and it could utilize a variety of mathematical functions, such as the sine and cosines of trigonometry.

The Harvard Mark I was a decimal-coded, 50-foot long monster with 3,304 relays, 500 miles of wire, and 750,000 electromechanical switches which clattered like "a roomful of old ladies knitting away with steel needles" while it crunched numbers up to 23 digits long, added three 8-digit numbers in a second, subtracted in 3/10 of a second and multiplied in 3 seconds. Using the progression of reading data from continuous paper tape punch holes instead of separate punch-cards, it could perform calculations in a single day that formerly took months.

Its first job was to calculate ballistic trajectories for the Navy, and what with the swaying of ship-borne guns on an unstable sea, an extremely difficult problem to begin with was made almost intractable by the sea winds buffeting the shells.

When shipped to the Navy for operations, Watson Sr. the inveterate salesman saw an opportunity to enhance IBM's image with a sleek, gleaming steel and glass casing for the Mark I, contrary to Aiken's plan for an open frame exposing the workings for easier monitoring and adjustments.

In the introduction of the new machine to the press in 1944, Aiken barely mentioned IBM, and the announced "Harvard" surname for the Mark I further rankled Watson as diminishing IBM's role in the development of the machine and depriving the company of much sought-after publicity. The *Harvard Mark I*, born in acrimony, nonetheless performed admirably for the Navy, but personal animosity followed both of the midwives to their graves.

Meanwhile in the land war, artillery pieces firing on the North African shore against Rommel's *Afrikakorps* were recoiling into the soft sand throwing off their aim. New firing tables were urgently needed. The War Department's Ballistic Research Laboratory at the Aberdeen Proving Grounds found revising the calculations beyond their differential analyzers' capabilities, so a branch was set up at the University of Pennsylvania, and the Army awarded the Moore School of Electrical Engineering $400,000 to do the new firing tables calculations.

The director of the effort, John Mauchly, had visited John Atanasoff at Iowa State to see his prototype computer, and in the fog of invention conception, he and Presper Eckert designed an 80-feet long, 30-ton *Electronic Numerical Integrator and Computer* (ENIAC), employing, like Atanasoff, capacitors for memory and vacuum tubes for logic that could add a thousand times faster than the Harvard Mark I.

However, when work was finally completed, ENIAC's unveiling found a country no longer at war, obviating the immediate need for soft-terrain artillery firing tables, but it nonetheless could compute new, more accurate firing tables in 20 seconds, less than the time for the shell to reach target.

A big-time test soon took the place of the firing tables, the development of the Hydrogen Bomb for the incipient Cold War required many, many calculations of controlled fusion reactions, and since ENIAC's vacuum tubes could switch a thousand times faster than the electromechanical switches of the Harvard Mark I, it was called upon to serve its country in a cold rather than a hot war.

The H-Bomb designs of Edward Teller and the Monte Carlo calculations of Stanislaw Ulam were spot-on, Elugelab island in the Enewetak Atoll was obliterated, and ENIAC was sanctified in the miasma of vaporized coral reefs in 1952. ENIAC although obsolete well before The Super detonated, it was the first mainframe "general-purpose" computer (artillery shell firing tables to nuclear fusion bombs), but not the first, and surely not the last technology, that was created to destroy, but ultimately served the good of humankind.

The mainframe computer was now seen as benign but with a cool reverence-inducing capability operating with unnerving detachment, as described by a reporter witnessing IBM's *Selective Sequence Electronic Calculator* (SSEC) calculating a high-precision lunar ephemeris at IBM Headquarters in New York City in 1948:[5]

There is the quiet clicking of printers, the steady shuffling of punched cards, the occasional rotation of a drum with memory tape, and a continual dance of little red lights as number-indicating tubes flick on and off in far less time that the twinkling of an eye. All else is hushed, and even the operators speak quietly in this streamlined sanctuary.

The SSEC was one of a succession of acronymic computers, ILLIAC, IAS, MANIAC, ENIAC, EDVAC, EDSAC, UNIVAC, and BINAC, each contributing to the long march of automatic computing technology and each experiencing a heyday, but all quickly lapsing to desuetude after being outperformed by new designs and better technology. In this sense, Watson Sr. need not have lamented IBM's lost publicity for the Mark I whose crude electromechanical switches became a symbol of backwardness in light of the ENIAC's fast vacuum tube switches.

Although a seminal advance, ENIAC's shortcoming was that it was a base 10 decimal architecture, requiring 17,468 vacuum tubes that handled 100,000 pulses per second such that there were more than 1.7 billion chances of a tube failure every second. So ENIAC of necessity ran at low

---

[5] Scientists used the SSEC free of charge in fluid flow, nuclear physics, and optics calculations, and the lunar ephemeris tables it calculated were used to plot Apollo's course to the Moon in 1969. Quote from *Revolution in Science, Time-Life Books* (1989).

voltages with great fans for air-cooling, reducing failures to one or two per week, but large-scale computing generally requires sequential operations, so that the already tedious searches for the burnt-out vacuum tubes that were arrayed in thousands of plug-in modules, once found dismayingly meant re-starting the interrupted calculations from scratch.

Furthermore, ENIAC's "general-purpose" appellative was misleading, for its internal storage could only hold the numbers it needed for the calculations at hand. This meant that particular operations had to be connected within the circuitry by hand-plugging and unplugging hundreds of wires for each different computing task, a tedious, tiresome, and error-prone procedure that often took days to complete.

ENIAC's successor, the *Electronic Discrete Variable Computer* (EDVAC) operated in (discrete) binary logic rather than decimal, reducing the number of vacuum tubes, and adopted the *von Neumann architecture* used at the Institute for Advanced Studies (IAS) computer that stored programs in an expanded electronic memory with automatic fetching replacing ENIAC's primitive hand-plugging.

In 1945, the amiable, bon vivant master of all technical disciplines, John von Neumann, in his famous *First Draft on the Report of the EDVAC* had divided computer operations into a *processor* that comprises a central arithmetic logic unit (ALU) and state registers, a *central control unit* with an instruction register and program counter, *memory* that stores instructions and data, external mass storage units, and input and output registers, altogether defining a serial architecture for the modern central processing unit memory-fetch digital computer that is still in use today in most computers. However, in today's artificial intelligence computers, the *von Neuman architecture*'s serial processing would be replaced by the much faster massively-parallel processing architecture required for the operation of the matrices of Big Data required for artificial intelligence computation.[6]

One of these von Neumann machines was Cambridge University's *Electronic Delay Storage Automatic Calculator* (EDSAC) that was ironically completed two years before the EDVAC in 1949 because of turmoil at the Moore School over Mauchly and Eckert's belief that von Neumann was overly credited for *their* development of EDVAC.

With thoughts of striking it rich to assuage hurt feelings, Mauchly and Eckert left the University of Pennsylvania because of its policy that

---

[6] For parallel processing, see Chapter 22.

employees should not benefit financially from research performed at the University. They formed their own company to produce a truly general-purpose *Universal Automatic Computer* (UNIVAC) using magnetic tape for high-speed programming and data input.

The design was sound, but lacking business acumen, their financially distressed company was sold to Remington Rand in 1950. Mauchly and Eckert each made only about $300,000 from the sale and patent royalties.

Under the professional management of Remington Rand, UNIVAC was a commercial success as the first large-scale truly general-purpose computer. A total of 46 machines were sold to government and industry, one of which predicted the winner of the 1952 American presidential election, a feat that created an aura of machine intelligence that could awe the public, in contrast to the esoteric ENIAC Monte Carlo simulations that were by law veiled in the secrecy surrounding the development of the Hydrogen Bomb.

UNIVAC's lead in commercial mainframe computer sales clearly irked Watson Sr. He ordered IBM to accelerate the development of IBM's entry into the general-purpose computer market, just the IBM 701 that Arthur Samuel was adapting to play checkers. The 701 would later replace the SSEC in IBM's New York showroom in 1952.

For computer memory, Fred Williams at Manchester University developed a cathode ray tube, which beam painted binary dots and dashes on a phosphor screen that was read by a scanning electron beam that stored a distinctive current on a collector plate to represent data in memory that could be *randomly accessed*. This *RAM* display allowed a machine to on-command fetch programs and data, and Watson Sr.'s IBM 701 immediately used the *Williams Tube* to gain an edge on Remington Rand's UNIVAC.

For large amounts of data, An Wang's *pulse-transfer controlling device* is generally cited as the prototype of the *magnetic core memory*, whereby networks of ferrite cores stored binary bits specified by the circulation direction of magnetization produced by coaxial currents of opposite circular direction that provided the massive disk data storage for the later IBM 704 and 705 computers.

A then commercially disinterested Harvard University allowed Wang to obtain personal patent rights, which he used to establish the eponymous Wang Labs in 1951 that pioneered the earliest desktop calculators, word processors, and scientific and business minicomputers.

Progress was being made on all fronts and the computer age was looming clear upon the horizon, but the dawn was held back by the bulky, hot-running, failure-prone triode vacuum tubes. Although good enough for radios where a millionth second short-circuit would have no noticeable effect, they would cause crash-worthy errors in the non-stop operations of electronic computing.

Originally researched for AT&T telecommunications and modeled after the familiar "cat's whisker" crystal radio sets, the germanium spring-loaded point-contact transistor invented in 1947 by John Bardeen and Walter Brattain at Bell Labs could coolly take over the vacuum tube's work both as a stable amplifier and switch at a fraction of the size while emitting far less heat, the bane of all electronic devices. It was successfully utilized in radios and calculators, shrinking their sizes and increasing their useful lives by orders of magnitude.

However, the spring-loaded contact was fragile and difficult to mass produce, so the irascible head of the Bell Labs transistor team, William Shockley, driven by his dismay at being one-upped by underlings Bardeen and Brattain, in the same year developed a more robust germanium flat-interface *junction* transistor.

But although only 8×10^{-4} ounce was used per transistor, germanium was practically available only from coal fly-ash and as a by-product of zinc, silver, lead, and copper ore refining, it cost more per pound than gold. The $8 price of a germanium junction transistor compared to the $0.75 price of a vacuum tube, and pennies for hordes of resistors, inductors, switches, and capacitors, inhibited its wide-spread use.

Although germanium has a higher electron/hole mobility, its chemical cousin silicon has a larger operational band gap, is more stable at higher temperatures, and is abundant as the grains of sand on the beach. But pure crystalline silicon was difficult to produce and the minority-carrier dopants injection necessary for semiconductor function was difficult because the surface of silicon became rough and brittle from differential temperature materials' expansion.

The breakthrough came from the impossible-to-pronounce Czochralski crystal-growth puller process that produced 99% pure crystalline silicon ingots just right for semiconductors. When Bell Labs tried doping the pure silicon in a hydrogen gas atmosphere, it accidentally ignited, and because of silicon's high chemical affinity for oxygen, a smooth SiO_2 (glass) coated the silicon. SiO_2 is a natural insulator through which holes could be etched by hydrogen fluoride to inject the dopants smoothly into the silicon to provide semi-conduction.

Gordon Teal at Texas Instruments in 1953 engineered the Bell Labs process for industrial production and gradually lowered the cost of silicon junction transistors to $2.50, opening the door for their wider use, starting with TI's popular rugged little transistor radios and pocket calculators.[7]

The price of transistors, however, was still far above that of vacuum tubes, and for large-scale electronics requiring many vacuum tubes, the high per unit costs inhibited transistor use, but the cost-overrun insouciance of the US military and the National Aeronautics and Space Administration fortuitously came to the rescue.

Avionics, weapons, electronic warfare, and computers for space exploration with all their inherent risks called for electronic components that were robust, reliable, cool-running, long-lasting, low maintenance, small and light; just what the silicon junction transistor was all about. With guaranteed government sales, the economies of scale soon lowered the unit costs and propelled the transistor industry take-off, literally from war into space and then to the consumer marketplace, where the benefits of the junction transistor were soon clear to all in the sleek miniaturization of beautiful new consumer electronics products, and finally to computers.

The transistorized products and their ever-increasing features, however, required ever-more complex circuitry with much greater numbers of transistors and passive components, and the ever-increasing power of the acronymic computers could be unleashed only by thousands of transistors taking the place of vacuum tubes.

The transistors were batch-processed by photoengrave etching on large wafers of silicon and then cut apart to produce the individual transistors, only to be soldered to other components on circuit boards inside the devices. Although expertly wired and soldered by the nimble fingers of legions of young women, the sheer number of wires in the ever-smaller devices was fast becoming intractable, particularly for the hundreds of thousands of wiring connections for the tens of thousands of transistors required for the ever more powerful and versatile mainframe computers.[8]

---

[7] For the basic physics of semiconductors and their development, see the author's book, Chen, R.H. 2011, *Liquid Crystal Displays, Fundamental Physics and Technology*, Wiley. For a detailed technical description of the commercial development of transistors, see Burgess, M., *Early semiconductor history of Texas Instruments*.

[8] Men who are proud of their soldering skill could not hold a candle to those young women who deftly soldered thousands of components every day.

The great potential of the digital computer was being literally strangled by the tangle of wiring connecting the transistors; a "tyranny of numbers" suppressing the freedom of the great new machines.

Coming to liberate the computers was not a revolutionary leader, but chefs of the Italian culinary arts. To avoid the tangled webs of wiring *spaghetti* connecting the transistors meatballs, one could simply make *lasagna* instead.[9]

The active silicon semiconductor transistor meatballs and the connecting-wire spaghetti could be integrated into meat layer components and a layer of metal wiring pasta separated by layers of silicon dioxide cheese.

The active transistors and passive resistors and capacitors were all fabricated from single semiconductor "mesas" on a desert substrate, a *monolith* of all the different components into a single body.[10]

Thus in 1958, with a nod to showmanship, Jack Kilby turned on his monolithic phase-shift oscillator that converted a DC into an AC signal and easily impressed his Texas Instruments bosses as they watched the straight-line voltage dramatically change to a sine wave on the in-line oscilloscope display.

Funding was immediate, but in the rush to file a patent application, Kilby used a "flying wire" drawing with all the gangly wiring connections exposed, and his prototype did not properly claim any integrated wiring connections.

In the same year, those flying wires were evaporated and embedded as a *metal layer* that seeped through tiny holes pre-etched in the SiO_2 insulating layer to form printed circuit conduction channels for the planar semiconductor layers. Robert Noyce at Fairchild Semiconductor thus

---

[9] Spaghetti and lasagna images are from en.wikimedia.org and used under Creative Commons.

[10] The idea of an *integrated circuit* was first proposed by the British radar expert G.W.A. Dummer in 1952, combining wired-together transistors, resistors, and capacitors in a single semiconductor block, but he never fabricated a working device.

could demonstrate a two-state *flip-flop integrated circuit* ideal for computers that not only obviated the tedious soldering of thousands of wires, but with the micron distances between components and electrical signals traveling at about half the speed of light, the flip-flop switch heralded the age of the superfast integrated circuit.[11]

Quickly, computer memory capacity increased by orders of magnitude with TI's *dynamic and static random access memory* (DRAM and SRAM) and Fairchild and later Intel's *central processing units* (CPUs) that respectively would become the silos and workhorses of the new personal computers that were looming on the horizon.

The digital computer was at last free from its wiring bondage, millions of transistors and components now could be integrated and inserted on motherboards as complete electronic entities. The sizes of the switches and amplifiers progressively shrank from the relatively massive, hot glass-walled triode vacuum tubes to the cool point-contact transistor, to the junction transistor, and finally to the completely integrated transistor circuits.

The tyranny of numbers was overcome by a *monolithic integration*, and the legions of skilled young women solderers spawned by the new technology of transistors were set free by the newer technology of automated semiconductor planar-process fabrication in an oft-repeated tale of machines replacing humans.

Invented in 1963, the soon to be dominant low-noise, cool-running, zero-volt static power (needs voltage only when alternating between *0* to *1*), thin-gate *Complementary Metal-Oxide Semiconductor* (CMOS) that "complemented" *n*-type (NMOS) and *p-type* (PMOS) transistors could be formed under dense design rules on a wafer bringing down sizes and prices in abeyance to Moore's Law.[12]

The CMOS would soon become the workhorse semiconductor for almost all the integrated circuits employed in personal computers, and in

---

[11] A *flip-flop* is a circuit that can store two independent states that can be stored in memory. Kilby received the Nobel Prize for Physics in 2000 for the integrated circuit, but Noyce had died in 1990, and thus was ineligible for an award. Kilby graciously acknowledged Noyce's contributions in his acceptance speech.

[12] In *n*- type (negative) semiconductors, the majority atomic charge carriers are the negatively-charged electrons and in *p*-type (positive) semiconductors the majority carriers are positively-charged holes. Since the number of defects per wafer is generally constant, larger wafers and more transistors per unit area of wafer (small logic density design rules) means more defect-free transistors per chip, bringing down the price of each chip, and together with greater efficiency and higher production yields, roughly every two years doubling the number of transistors on a chip and halving the price (Moore's Law).

the thin-film version used in liquid crystal displays that made possible the notebook computer, flat-panel monitors, wall-hanging television sets. CMOS sensors also replaced the more expensive Charge-Coupled Devices (CCDs) in optical sensors and digital cameras, and indeed the LCD made possible the mobile phone, which not only made possible continuous telephone contact, but also instant information, music, and ride-hailing, all the while amassing Big Data for the training sets of artificial intelligence.

In the late 1960s, after soundly defeating Remington Rand and fending off local rivals Control Data Corporation (CDC), Digital Equipment Corporation (DEC), and Amdahl, then Japan's NEC and Fujitsu, IBM's System/360 integrated circuit computers extended its mainframe hegemony to all corners of the world.

Off the silicon shores of Northern California, however, a sea change soon would not only downsize computers, but also IBM itself.

The world's first microprocessor, the 2250 transistors 4-bit Intel 4004 was made for the Japanese calculator maker Busicom in 1971. A later version in 1972, the 8008 microprocessor arranged 8-bit bytes into 256 unique arrays of ones and zeros that could handle the ten numerical digits, all the letters of the alphabet, punctuation marks, and other symbols, and after conversion to NMOS, the faster 8080 microprocessor, together with its competitor Zilog's Z80, was the heart of home-build computer kits such as Altair for teenage boys to tinker with.

Among those older boys, Steve Wozniak built the first general-purpose, compact, stand-alone home computer in 1976, and Steve Jobs promoted the derivative Apple II so aggressively as to force a reluctant IBM to join the personal computer parade with its PC, an open system effectively mandated by fear of Antitrust investigation, and so run by CPUs from Intel, memory from TI, and an operating system from start-up Microsoft.

The open system allowed cloning by Compaq and price reduction by new manufacturers such as, Acer in Taiwan, who sold PCs all over the world under their own brands but mostly as OEMs for almost all the other brands, including IBM, Dell, HP, Toshiba, and Sony.[13]

While the capabilities of even super-thin notebook computers have already far surpassed the bulky early acronymic mainframes, much

---

[13] "OEM" stands for "Original Equipment Manufacturer", which for obvious reasons means two different things in the West (the branded product) and in the East (the contracted actual manufacturer).

greater computer speed and power are required for the massively-parallel calculations of the multi-parameter, interdependent, non-linear differential equations of physical and chemical quantum mechanics, astrophysics, fluid dynamics, weather prediction, physical and engineering simulations, and indeed the Big Data of artificial intelligence.

More recently, supercomputers have been used in, molecular and genetic modeling, cryptanalysis, cosmological calculations of the beginning of the Universe, and now crucially in biological system simulations of viruses and climate change models; they can and likely soon will be used in overarching artificial intelligence.

For example, solving the equations of stellar evolution for a star from birth to death would take an astrophysicist 3,000 years, while a supercomputer can do it in seconds. Closer to home, simulations of nuclear weapons explosions could allow nuclear-armed belligerents to just exchange simulation print-outs and computer graphics to determine whose bomb was more destructive, bringing warfare from the battlefield to the laboratory, if only world leaders knew something about science.[14]

In the 1970s, Control Data Corporation and Cray Research began the race for the title of world's fastest computers. Initially virtually alone in the field, CDC and Cray met competition first from Japan's NEC and Fujitsu, then later from China's Sunway and Tianhe, the latter two recently taking turns with America's IBM Summit and Sierra in the race for global supercomputer supremacy.

Summit regained the crown from Sunway in 2018 with an HPL benchmark 122.3petaflops, but China's supercomputers claimed 227 of the top 500 in the 2018 supercomputer rankings, that also included supercomputers from Japan, France, and Germany. While performing useful scientific and engineering simulations, the supercomputers have also become symbols of national technological prowess.

The massively-parallel processor cores running the supercomputers were primarily from IBM, Intel, Sunway, Fujitsu, ARM, and Nvidia, and the design architectures were from the individual supercomputer entities which included many universities, research institutions, and semi-public concerns.[15]

---

[14] The author has programmed Cray supercomputers, and suggested the print-out exchange in lieu of hydrogen bomb Armageddon to the government, receiving no response.

[15] HPL (High Performance Linpack) measures how fast a computer can solve a dense $n \times n$ system of linear equations, $Ax = b$. A *petaflop* = 10^{15} floating point operations per second. Although hard to grasp, such fantastical speeds are a result of the very short atomic distances in semiconductors, about 10^{-10} meter so the electrons and holes don't have far to travel to do their work.

These fantastical speeds and capabilities, combined with Big Data and deep artificial neural networks cannot help but evoke disturbing images of a supercomputer controlling a vast army of general-purpose robots running rampant over human civilization, or at least in the very near future, automating all manufacturing, services, and monitoring humans at home and at work, together with controlling almost all the vehicles on the roads and tracks of first America, China, Europe and then the whole world.

CHAPTER 6

Software

T he punch-hole cards of Jacquard's loom instructed the a machine to weave cloth, the Countess of Lovelace's punch-hole cards instructed Babbage's Analytical Engine how to calculate, and Boole's binary algebra instructed a computer how to compute. The machines could comprehend these *instruction sets* which then could be seen as written in a *machine language*.

In a binary computer, encoded strings of zeros and ones constituted the instruction where, for example, in an 8-bit instruction, the first four bits may tell the computer what to do and the last four bits tell it where the data to use can be found.

There are more than 200 fundamental computer operations so encoding and keeping track of all the instruction sets in machine language was a nightmare, made worse by the fact that different machines would have different designs and structures, and even if they were similar, there were no rules for program step sequences and register addresses, so a program written for one machine, even in machine language, was not transferable to another machine.

The computational logic problem had been solved by Turing and von Neumann, but the practical implementation of programming in machine language was difficult and error-prone, the programs could not be used on different machines, and were almost impossible to understand even by the programmers themselves after the fact.

This provided the impetus for *software generalization*, and Grace Hopper, an assistant on the UNIVAC project, was assigned by John Mauchly to

DOI: 10.1201/9781003214892-8

make their new machine, the *Binary Automatic Computer* (BINAC), capable of accepting algebraic equations *as written* by the user.

Hopper realized at once that "one could use some kind of higher code other than the machine code" to program a computer, a code that was more easily understood by humans that could be translated *by the computer* into machine language for the computer to translate and read.

Since many processes and mathematical computations are repeated during an operation, Hopper and co-workers devised short command mnemonics such as LOAD, STORE, and PRINT, associating them with the relevant machine language instruction sets and combinations thereof, so that simple commands could be used to call up the performance of a desired process.

These *subroutines* also included mathematical computations, for example taking a square root (SQRT) that, once assembled in machine language, could be stored in a subroutine library, and when *compiled* with other operations, could be called up by the programmer using the short mnemonic commands to perform the calculation. A sequence of such commands assembled using this *assembly language* was easier than machine language for someone to write and others to understand.[1]

These subroutines once compiled in the computer could then be used by anybody to write programs in assembly language, with the machine doing the work of translating from assembly language to machine language by simply accessing the called-upon machine language instruction sets. Hopper in 1952 called the language translation *compiling*, and the translator was called a *compiler*, terms that are still in use today.

During her work for the Navy on the successor to the Harvard Mark I, the Mark II mysteriously crashed, and upon investigation, Hopper found that a moth had wandered into the maze of circuitry and died in shock blocking an electric relay switch that caused the malfunction. And so the term "debugging the computer" became the term for any computer malfunction.

Although much easier to master and use than machine language, assembly language still required designating address registers and knowing all the short instruction mnemonics which may vary from machine to machine; it also still required an intimate knowledge of each

---

[1] For example, to ADD X and Y in assembly language involves fetching the values of X and Y from their registers, thereby requiring knowing their addresses, commanding the ALU to add them together, and sending the result to another register address in memory.

machine's design and workings. The next step thus was to formulate a *higher-level language* that was easier to write and understand, and again have the computer translate that language into assembly language and then into machine language, using compilers.

Software development pioneer John Backus at IBM in 1957 created FORTRAN (*Formula Translation*) that could be compiled for use on the new IBM 704, going from high-level to assembly, and finally to machine language. FORTRAN employed relatively natural language statements that convolved several assembly and machine language instructions into single statements that could command a computer to perform mainly scientific and engineering calculations.

When a computer is turned on, built-in programs instruct the CPU to find the operating system which then takes control of the system hardware, a few functional programs are permanently stored in the ROM and the CPU executes the instructions in machine language after being translated from a high-level language computer program through an assembly language using a compiler; a RAM typically holds information and programs during processing.

Primarily for business and commercial use, the *Common Business Oriented Language* (COBOL) could more efficiently file, sort, merge, add, subtract, and calculate percentages over large sets of data, and conveniently generate reports, all using syntactical English. COBOL is still used by businesses and often is a legacy language stored in many companies' mainframe archives for reference.

As an example of the syntactical nature and universality of COBOL, when Grace Hopper was stranded at a computer center in Japan, and having difficulty in communicating her wish to go back to her hotel to the non-English speaking Japanese programmers, she resorted to COBOL, pointing to herself and saying "MOVE", and then pointing outside the center, said "GOTO Osaka Hotel".[2]

Primarily in Europe, the *Algorithmic Language* (ALGOL) was designed to be more in tune with fundamental computer science syntactical principles ostensibly to do mathematical computation more elegantly than FORTRAN, but in truth was Europe's putative counter to America's FORTRAN hegemony. Not surprisingly, ALGOL became the *lingua franca* for European-developed software for a time, but for lack of

---

[2] "Hotel" in Japanese is just "hoteru", copied directly from English. *Computer Languages* 1989, *Time-Life Books*.

built-in utilities such as a standardized input/output regime, FORTRAN still held sway in America where most new software was written.

All these languages were based on the *imperative* programming approach that at any time the program has an implicit state defining the values of all the variables and current point of control, and as the program executes by means of the von Neumann architecture, the programmer can know each and every step and state through which the computer passes by examining the program's *dump* files.

The primarily mathematical logic and operational functions of imperative programming were expanded to *objects* in an *object-oriented* programming approach that simulated systems by grouping data and instructions into direct and explicit representations of modular objects having a set of instructions and relevant discrete portions of data each representing one facet of a given system run.

For examples, a banking program would define objects such as savings, checking, and certificate of deposit accounts, and concepts such as balance, interest, bank charges, and so on, while an electrical engineering program would define objects such as resistors, capacitors, and transistors, and concepts such as resistance, capacitance, and gate voltage, and then following operation instructions, classifying and comparing the objects. Object-oriented languages would later be employed by artificial intelligence programs written in *C++, Java, Python, and JavaScript*.

High-level language computer programming progressed from the mainly FORTRAN batch-mode computer punch-card to remote dumb terminal time-sharing, and then to minicomputers like the paper-tape instructed PDP series, to the Intel microprocessor-run BASIC Altair microprocessor, to personal computers that can access any language over the Internet, and finally to online host-computer coding platforms such as *GitHub* where the more direct control C++ language and the higher-level Python and Java are dominant in the production of new programs with source code published and freely distributed. This *open source software* (OSS) was a critical resource for the development of artificial intelligence.

CHAPTER 7

Computer Communications

T he first electronic communication over distance was the three-state (off, dot, dash) *trinary* system of Samuel Morse representing letters of the alphabet which combinations thereof could form words and a message. The signals were sent over dedicated transmission lines, but although successful, it could only send messages sequentially one at a time and was so limited in its use as a long-range communications system. To carry more messages, Emile Baudot thought of changing the time between states for different messages, allowing the messages to be differentiated by their *frequency* and sent simultaneously over the same line.

This concept of *multiplexing*, was employed for machine communications over dedicated lines, in the two-state (on, off) binary-coded telegraph using a teletypewriter and a five-bit *Baudot* code to instantly transmit messages, or record messages on paper tape for delayed transmission or storage.

Alexander Graham Bell in 1876, constructed a diaphragm in contact with a bag of loose carbon particles and ran a dc current through it, so when a sound vibrates the diaphragm, it will impact the carbon particles changing their density in the bag thereby modulating the current, thus producing an electric current that represents the sound. Thus a "voice" current can be transmitted to a destination receiver in a wire which is wrapped around an electromagnet in contact with a diaphragm, the

DOI: 10.1201/9781003214892-9

diaphragm will then vibrate in accord with the voice current thus reforming the speech at the destination.

Multiplexing allowed simultaneous transmission of telephone calls over a single line. Today the multiplexing by different frequencies is called *frequency-division multiple access* (FDMA), division by coding messages is called *code-division multiple access* (CDMA) (which is used by the GPS Global Positioning System, using allocated time-slots is *time-division multiple access* (TDMA), and using synchronized switches at each end of the transmission line to divide messages is called *synchronous-division multiple access* (SDMA). In addition to all that, there are many variations and combinations of the different multiplexing schemes as used for example in Europe the tandem TDMA/FDMA *Global System for Mobile* (GSM) and in China a duplex synchronous time/code-division system called TD-SCDMA.

For Internet communication, *space-division multiple access* (SDMA) is used on the early wired *Ethernet* and the IEEE802 family of standard protocols was used for wireless routing for local area networks (LANs), WiFi, and accessing the Internet. Improved speed was provided by the capability of electromagnetic waves to be polarized as in *polarized-division multiple access* (PDMA) which was used for cordless telephones, digital radio, ADSL and LTE. For Internet transmission over fibre optic cables, *wave-division multiple access* (WDMA) is used.[1]

For 4G and 5G mobile device communications, including mobile phones, autonomous cars, robots, and many other communication systems, *orthogonal frequency-division multiple access* (OFDMA) is used, however multiple access causes *inter-carrier interference* (ICI, cross-talk) because frequency deviations of the sub-carriers will affect the polarization orthogonality, so each sub-carrier must be individually *shaped* to prevent sub-carrier frequency overlapping. Needless to say, all kinds of multiplexing were essential for handling the explosive growth of electronic communications.[2]

Voice electronic communications are efficiently transmitted by dividing them into *packets* that can be simultaneously sent over the least

---

[1] ADSL (asymmetric digital subscriber lines) where "asymmetric" means the bit rate (number of bits used per second to represent audio or video communication) at the receiver end is faster than at the sender end; long term evolution (LTE) refers to the advances in communications after 2G GSM such as 3G up to 4G.

[2] Regarding optical polarization, refer to the author's book Chen, R.H. 2011, *Liquid Crystal Displays, Fundamental Physics and Technology*.

busy lines and then reassembled at the destination to re-form the message in a process called *packet-switching*.

Early personal computer communication was carried by telephone lines through modulation of a carrier wave at the transmitter to the receiver *modem* at a rate of transmission called the *baud rate* (in honor of Baudot). Anyone of a few years will remember the consternation of dealing with unstable modem communications.

Directly-wired inter-computer communications were much faster and more reliable than the telephone line transmissions, but in the beginning directly-wired computers could only communicate through their host network server, and since each host network server communication operating system may not be compatible, not all computers could communicate with each other.

Oversight, regulation, and standards-setting were clearly necessary for personal computer inter-communications. Rules for compatible communicating were set by the *Internet Engineering Task Force* (IETF), a loose non-profit organization through which anyone can contribute expertise to form *protocols* such as the *Internet Protocol* (IP), *Hypertext Transfer Protocol* (HTTP), and *Simple Mail Transfer Protocol* (SMTP), which dictated the form, transmission rate, and error-checking methods for inter-computer communication. Each host server communication operating systems thereafter was obligated to follow the protocols in order to communicate with each other, thereby *de facto* mandating transmission standardization for inter-computer communication.[3]

Among the earlier protocols for form was the *American Standard Code for Information Interchange* (ASCII), the coding system of 128 strings of seven ones and zeros, each sequence representing an Arabic numeral, a letter of the English alphabet, punctuation marks, symbols, and actions such as keyboard ENTER, became the universal standard for all computers in 1963.

In the beginning of the computer age, the computers were all *centralized* mainframe batch-processing and on-site time-share dumb

---

[3] The term "protocol" is taken from diplomacy where diplomats and high officials are very sensitive to relative rank, so that there are rules for gatherings regarding titles, addressing formalities, priorities such as who goes first, seating, and so on. The analogy is that every communication has a rank and certain rules to be observed for smooth interaction. The story is that after being name Secretary of State the press asked him, "Do you prefer being called 'Mr. Secretary' or 'Dr. Secretary'", Henry Kissinger replied "I do not stand on protocol, if you just call me 'Excellency' it will be okay". Isaacson, W., 2005, *Kissinger, a Biography*, Simon & Schuster,

terminals that required the user to trek to the computer center to use the computer. "Computer time" was a fare-based proposition charging for use, and although it may have improved program efficiency, it may also have dissuaded some to not use the main computer at all because of the "computer charges".

Earlier, in 1961, John McCarthy, a co-founder of the MIT Artificial Intelligence Laboratory, suggested remote time-sharing on the IBM 709, and the proposal subsequently led to the Department of Defense Advanced Research Project Agency's ARPANET in 1969 linking defense-work research laboratories in Utah and California, this was the first fully-functional packet-switched network whose progeny would be critical for the communication among the developers of artificial intelligence.

With the advent of distributed computing power came the idea of distributed computers themselves. The demand was met primarily by the Digital Equipment Corporation's (DEC) series of newly-coined *mini-computers* in a series they called *Programmed Data Processors* (PDP-n), and by other companies such as Hewlett-Packard, Honeywell, and General Electric. The minicomputers did not have a mainframe's processing power, but they were smaller and cheaper, and could be programmed for specific tasks for the projects of the individual entities, as well as linking to a mainframe.

At the time, however, each company's minicomputer came with its own specific design and operating systems, so programs for it had to be written from scratch in assembly language for each minicomputer, and if a company or department upgraded or changed to a different vendor's minicomputer, all the old programs and routines were useless and had to be re-written for use on the new minicomputer.

At Bell Labs, researcher Ken Thompson's *Solar System Simulation* program was loaded on a PDP-7 with good graphics, but that mini-computer to his chagrin lacked basic *utility* routines such as copy and print, so he and colleague Dennis Ritchie wrote the utilities in assembly language and added file management and text-editing. They then loaded these routines into one of Bell Labs' newly-purchased PDP-11s that was faster with more memory than the PDP-7.

Although impressed by Thompson's *Space Travel* graphics, other re-searchers at Bell Labs were more interested in the utility routines, and so in response to many requests, Thompson and Ritchie wrote up an *op-erating system* manual for the PDP-11s, calling the system *UNIX* which was upgraded for time-share management in 1972, and further expanded to hold 100 modules for recording instrument readings, sorting, linking, and analyzing data that could be sequenced to run a user's specific research program. All the programs and utilities could be stored in a single PDP-11 and thus were available for a researcher's specific needs as a stand-alone computer.[4]

Most of the scientists and engineers at Bell Labs, however, did not know how to write computer programs in assembly language, let alone machine language, so Thompson and Ritchie wrote a higher-level language for programming the UNIX operating system that they called "C" (as the successor to the limited *Basic Combined Programming Language* called "*B*" then in use). Born in 1973, C is the progenitor of the C++ language now widely used for coding artificial intelligence algorithms.[5]

With a nominal-fee license for UNIX to industry and universities using PDP computers, the publication of C in 1974 on DEC's $50,000 PDP-11 loaded with UNIX soon became the *de facto* standard distributed minicomputer for science and engineering use. The PDP-11 minicomputer could not only serve as a stand-alone, multipurpose computer, it could manage data and program files, control laboratory equipment, text-edit and data-format reports using a central *kernel*, and through a *shell*, time-share and program-share over multiple local and remote networks.

Berkeley in 1977 established a free and open "host-computer coding platform" based on UNIX called the "Berkeley Software Distribution" (BSD), the harbinger of today's platforms such as *GitHub* and *Red Hat* that are now critical for the development of artificial intelligence.

In 1978, DEC's faster and more powerful VAX 11/780 with 4.3 gigabytes of memory took over as the mainstream distributed computer for industry, universities and research institutions.

Since any computer with a UNIX OS and a C compiler could employ the UNIX system, so that by 1983 more than 80% of university computer science departments had adopted the free UNIX inter-computer communications system.

However in the same year, the Department of Justice's antitrust consent agreement with AT&T was lifted and UNIX suddenly became a

---

[4] Ken Thompson, a Turing Award winner, was also a pioneer in computer chess, and the outside member of Deep Blue developer Hsu Feng-Hsiung's doctoral committee at Carnegie-Mellon.

[5] Critics of the arcane and hard to spot punctuation symbol commands and parentheses ubiquity of C++ can blame the B language for the curly bracket delimiters, but perhaps can be mollified by knowledge that it was designed to be concise and has roots as an assembly language for the first general-use operating system to be used by scientists and engineers who have an eye for detail.

commercial product in high demand, and because the source code was only licensed *as is*, after much travelling through the commercial computer world, almost every stop produced many different versions of UNIX, each with its own idiosyncrasies, the erstwhile standard communications formats were Balkanized decreasing UNIX's reach. The the high-price commercialization of UNIX led to Richard Stallman's free GNU ("GNU is not UNIX") to be described in the next chapter.

Way back in 1971, Ray Tomlinson sent the first *email* using the @ symbol for the address, and in 1973, the *local area network* (LAN) for computer connections within institutions and companies began using high-capacity Ethernet coaxial cables for sharing data and information.

At Stanford in 1980, Computer Science grad student Leonard Bosack wanted to computer-communicate with his girlfriend Sandy Lerner, also a Computer Science Department graduate, who was managing the Stanford Business School Computer Lab. They legendarily trudged through the underground cross-campus maintenance tunnels stringing cable to connect their computers, and so came up with the idea of *routers* and *servers* to make LAN connections for the different departmental computers at Stanford, the basis for starting a company in 1984 called *Cisco* to provide hardware and software for networking computers.[6]

To further expand *wide area networks* (WANs), client computers could access the packet-switching servers in accord with the 1983 *Transmission Control Protocol/Internet Protocol* (TCP/IP) that today governs how messages are broken up into packets, sorted, transmitted to IP addresses (currently *IPv6*) and transmitted using the *Domain Name System* (DNS), to be reassembled at the destination.

In the next few years in quick succession, Tim Berners Lee at CERN launched the *World Wide Web* in 1989 that identified websites by *Uniform Resource Locaters* (URLs) that were linked using *Hypertext Markup Language* (HTML) so that all the nascent web browsers could access websites all over the Internet.

Marc Andreessen at the University of Illinois developed *Mosaic*, the first general purpose web browser for public use in 1993 and co-founded

---

[6] The author was at Stanford on the second floor of Durand Hall programming a PDP-11 connected to a national Cray supercomputer while Len Bosack was downstairs in the Computer Science Department serving as a support engineer; my roommate was a student in the Graduate School of Business using the Computer Lab minis; we talked about computer connections but were not sufficiently prescient to join in the nascent LAN/WAN development that would have made us both rich beyond imagination.

Netscape in 1995; Brian Pinkerton at the University of Washington in 1994 invented the *WebCrawler* (*Spiderbot*) for universal Internet searching, and in the same year, Jerry Yang and David Filo at Stanford unveiled the first tree-structure hierarchical Web directory *Yahoo*.

Everyone knows the story of graduate students Sergey Brin and Larry Page's further development of the web crawler also at Stanford, and the 1998 search engine that turned the company's name "Google" into a verb for online search. The revolution in data acquisition and the very volume of data that has been progressively accumulated, such as Google *ImageNet's* more than 14 million labeled images serving as AI training sets for computer vision, would have a profound influence on the progress of the bottom-up learning of artificial neural networks.

All the data and information swirling about the exponentially-increasing number of computers required the faster and more reliable transmission of broader bandwidths. Of course the early transmission over telephone lines of 9600 Baud (bits per second) was inadequate, and now satellite communications, 1000 Mbps fibre optic networks, terrestrial wireless microwave transmission with its 2–4 GHz frequencies today are the main carriers of 4G and 5G telephony and Internet data and information.

CHAPTER 8

Open Source Software

W idespread, fast, and convenient computer communication would be of little help in developing new ideas and innovative software if their source code and techniques were proprietary and kept confidential. The free and open publication and use of *open source software* (OSS) for software development and even crowd sourcing for new ideas particularly using the free access of host-computer coding platforms are critical to the development of artificial intelligence.

The open source software ethos was born at the MIT *Tech Model Railroad Club* where a successful design of some complex railroad operation was completed by someone who just "hacked away" at the circuits until the model train behaved as planned. The good circuits of course were incorporated into the grand model and thereby accessible to all the members of the club.

From the old realm of railroads, the Club's interests naturally turned to the new world of computers. The free-spirited young men informally promulgated a completely unrestricted flow of ideas while they developed the first rudimentary computer games running on a PDP-1 minicomputer.

The hacker spirit quickly crossed the country to Palo Alto's *Homebrew Computer Club*, and the magazine *Popular Electronics* spread the Hacker Gospel to all points in-between where boys with a mathematical/electronics bent could try their hand at the new tech, so that not only Apple, but also Microsoft and many other pioneering companies, were eventually spawned in the juvenile but heady atmosphere of computer

DOI: 10.1201/9781003214892-10

hardware and software development spurred on by the free and open exchange of ideas and programs.

The most popular home-build hardware was based on the Altair 8800 home computer kit running on an Intel 8080 CPU that was featured on the January 1975 cover of *Popular Electronics*, and the software initially used the DOS assembly language operating system, later changing over to the more popular CP/M.

But it was one of the hacker acolytes, Bill Gates, who crossed the Rubicon with his lambasting of the Homebrew boys for copying and distributing his $500 BASIC programing system without paying him for it.

While the inventor of the personal computer Steve Wozniak remained true to the hacker ethos in freely distributing his computer designs to his confreres at Homebrew and indeed to anyone interested. But after Wozniak hacked AT&T's very expensive long-distance calling by electronically mimicking AT&T's 2600 Hz switching tones for free long-distance calls, he demonstrated his "Blue Box" to his 17-year-old friend Steve Jobs, who early-on displayed his marketing acumen by going around to university dormitories where students made many calls home and to friends, selling more than 100 Blue Boxes for $170 each, earning substantial pocket change for himself and Woz.[1]

Jobs credits their blue box for the invention of the Apple computer,[2]

> *If we wouldn't have made blue boxes, there would have been no Apple. Because we would have not had not only [sic] confidence that we could build something and make it work ... but we also had the sense of magic that we could influence the world*

But the Blue Box clearly infringed AT&T's technology and trade secrets and Woz and Jobs were fortunate to evade the police and an FBI investigation. Both Jobs and Gates however later turned to the law as helpmate in their excoriation of copyists, conveniently forgetting the fact that many of Apple computers' later features were copied, being invented by others at Stanford Research Institute (today SRI), Xerox Palo Alto Research Center (PARC), and the Berkeley Software Distribution (BSD), and many of Microsoft Windows' features were simply copied from Apple's Macintosh.

---

[1] Lapsley, P. 2013, "The definitive story of Steve Wozniak, Steve Jobs and phone phreaking", *The Atlantic*, February 21.

[2] Haden, J. Aug. 1, 2019, *Inc.*

Jobs' desideratum however was to establish an enduring company that would create innovative new products and supply demands (some of which even consumers themselves were unaware), and thus provide new utility that would benefit society if properly used (for example, the mobile phone makes ride-hailing possible), but Apple seemed to be forever in court charging copyright and patent infringement of very simple technology (for example the curved iPhone edges and proportions) in an effort to drive out competitors.

The less innovative but more opportunistic Gates was simply riding on IBM and the PC clones' near monopoly to make exorbitant rent-seeking profits from his operating system and applications software licenses. The never-ending new *Windows* versions reflect Gates' concentration on a commercial strategy that exploited consumers' desire to have (not necessarily useful) new features and the latest tech-fashion products.[3]

After amassing his fortune from his personal computer operating system monopoly, Gates' late-blooming philanthropy for well-selected worthy causes, although laudable, appeared to some as conscience-stricken amends for past commercial transgressions, perhaps being purchases of wishful tickets to an undeserved Heaven.

Microsoft ostensibly has been re-engineered as a more open and socially responsible company with the publication and licensing of its holy operating system source code and a promise to be more cooperative under direction of the new CEO Satya Nadella. But can the ultimate commercial predator really change its spots?

Fortunately for the development of artificial intelligence, software has been blessed by the rebirth of the hacker spirit in the *Open Source Initiative* (OSI), a non-profit organization promoting free use and openly

---

[3] "Rent-seeking" has been defined as "increasing one's share of existing wealth without creating new wealth". Gates had piggybacked on IBM's personal computer and disproportionately increased his share of the wealth based on the debatable extension of copyright laws to source code and object code. In economic analysis terms, with virtually no capital expenditure (only workstations), low labor, and practically zero reproduction costs, Microsoft collects exorbitant license fees and copyright infringement awards out of proportion to its minimal creation of new wealth, resulting in economic waste; that is, licensing fees, court awards, and attorneys' fees could be better spent, say in research and development or for charitable causes. The secrecy of Microsoft's source code also inhibited research as evidenced by the fact that practically all new software research is based on the publicly licensed GNU and Linux operating systems; Microsoft finally came around after Gates had left and opened up its source code for public use. Apple with its innovative iPod, iPad, iPhone products has created wealth, and more deservedly profits from it, but overly so by exploiting low pay-level countries' assembly workers and extreme overpricing of its products.

distributed source code for participation in new software development through host-computer coding platforms.

Corporate open source however was incongruously hatched at AT&T, a fierce protector of its intellectual property rights. The reason is that before the 1960s, AT&T was designated as an officially sanctioned monopoly of America's telephone system under a Consent Decree by the Department of Justice to ensure compatible public utility services, and indeed for generations the stodgy black dial phone was the only telephone model available, while all the phones, switchboards, relay stations, and land lines were produced by AT&T's manufacturing subsidiary Western Electric. To prevent the further expansion of AT&T's monopoly, the Justice Department prohibited AT&T from any activities outside of telephone communications, and particularly in the burgeoning new field of computers.

And so in the 1970s the source code for Ken Thompson's UNIX operating system and its derivatives for inter-computer communication developed at Bell Labs was freely distributed to universities under a *General Public License* (GPL), and for a nominal $20,000 for commercial use. UNIX quickly became the *de facto* standard science and engineering communication link serving universities, research institutions, technology companies, and government agencies.

However, after the government-mandated dissolution of AT&T in 1983 into regional "Baby Bells", and the grievous dissolution of the great Bell Labs, at last free from the antitrust Consent Decree, AT&T quickly reverted to its commercial roots, deeming UNIX proprietary and its use subject to substantial licensing fees up to $250,000. Its source code was strictly confidential and protected by copyright, the distribution of copies were in object code only, and although not human-readable, also protected by copyright.[4]

---

[4] The freeing of telecommunications from monopoly no doubt accelerated the development of many new telephone products through freer competition, but the concomitant disbanding of the legendary Bell Labs, the cradle of much of today's high technology, is no doubt an irreparable loss to science and technology innovation and development. The copyrighting of source code as literary expression is by itself debatable for the compiled product of source code, object code's sequences of binary 0's and 1's, to be copyrightable "expression" is pushing the limits of definition, rendering such protection clearly a product of established commercial interests rather than legal theory and logic. Furthermore, a work protected by copyright by law should be published for society to appreciate and licensed to copy if desired, proprietary software source code has long been an egregious exception as being neither published nor licensable (only the object code is licensed and for use only), a situation at once rigorously exploited by corporations such as Microsoft and Apple, and also roundly denounced by open source advocates, mainly academics.

And so, although birthing the concept of a General Public License, AT&T turned around and terminated the idea of commercial open source software by establishing the onerous royalty-bearing licensing regime subsequently employed by, among others, Microsoft, and the legal basis for infringement suits that would be aggressively pursued by, in particular, Apple.[5]

The AT&T UNIX now closed system rankled the young members of the fast-developing academic discipline of computer science, and BSD created many competitive alternatives, but in particular the acknowledged computer science genius Richard Stallman took it upon himself to develop a competing inter-computer operating system he called "GNU", a recursive acronym, "GNU's Not UNIX", the source code of which was public, free, and freely distributable, and included a developmental toolkit to encourage participation in further development of the open operating system and its implementation and applications.

Mounted on the open range wildebeest GNU trampling through the halls of computer science departments and the homes of hackers worldwide, the wild-eyed Stallman offered open source software for all to freely use and distribute, all the while excoriating Apple and Microsoft's denials of public access to source code as veritable "crimes against humanity" that would stifle the growth of the new computer software discipline and its related industries.

Apple and Microsoft, nonplussed, in effect replaced AT&T and IBM's monopolies with their own, and were busily restraining the trade for personal computer operating systems and applications software with onerous licensing programs (Microsoft) and vigorous enforcement of patents and software copyright (Apple).

It is of utmost irony that one of the first permissive host-computer coding platforms, BSD, was sued by AT&T for copyright infringement of UNIX in 1992 (delaying BSD's further development for two years) exemplifying the copyright enforcement zeal of Microsoft and Apple, while Microsoft later cynically used BSD-produced code in Windows 2000 and Apple's macOS and IOS operating systems were largely based on *FreeBSD*. It seems that in the commercialization world of computer software one can have one's cake and eat it too.[6]

---

[5] Ref. Weber. S. 2004, "The success of open source", Harvard. The author while at Acer Computers negotiated many agreements with Microsoft and Apple and experienced first-hand their aggressive use of intellectual property rights.

[6] The lawsuit was brought by AT&T's Unix System Laboratory (USL) and justifiably settled in BSD's favor.

In his fight against secret and proprietary software, Stallman's crusade found a kindred spirit during a speech in far-away Finland. Inspired by his talk, the University of Helsinki grad student Linus Torvalds, using the GNU toolkit, developed the eponymous *Linux* as an open source competing operating system for personal computers. He published the source code online in 1991 under a GPL, attracting many young hackers to not only use it as a substitute for Microsoft's OS, but also inviting them to improve it and develop new utilities and application programs based on it in an early instance of crowdsourcing.

Linux liberated the development of computer operating systems and application software from the tyranny of Microsoft's secret source code, providing new tech start-ups an operating system platform on which to develop their own new software. Apple has remained a bastion of closed-system, overpriced proprietary hardware and software that despite its products' planned obsolescence and marketing subterfuges, by means of his now *de rigueur* new product stage performances, each new product became the darling of the high-tech *fashionista*.[7]

Notwithstanding, while the world mourned the death of the tech icon in 2011, when asked for his reaction, ever-true to his open source creed, Stallman was reported to have said, "I'm not happy that he died, but I am glad that he is gone".[8]

It has come to pass that the conflict between the harsh commercial despotism of Apple's Steve Jobs and Microsoft's Bill Gates against the dreamy idealism of Richard Stallman and Linus Torvalds would find common ground in a compromise between crass rent-seeking and idealistic free and open software in the development of artificial intelligence.

It can be understood that the notoriety that motivates a boy to freely show off his coding skills may not suffice for the man who has to feed a family. The creativity and hard work in his field no doubt deserve proportionate remuneration, but on the other hand, the free and open exchange of information and ideas in that field are necessary to its development, and now critically so for the far-reaching science and technology of artificial intelligence.

So the tech idealists at the University of California, in conformance with the Berkeley quintessence, together with kindred spirits at the

---

[7] Aside from its designed-in incompatibility with other brands, for example, the iPod's non-replaceable battery and iPhone6's deliberate slow-down and accelerated battery run-down to goose sales of later (more expensive) models, are instances of Apple's commercial subterfuges.

[8] Quote from Stallman's personal blog.

citadel of enlightened engineering MIT, devised a GPL derivative, the *Permissive Software License* (PSL), and established the *BSD* and *MIT License* regimes that advocated the open source development of new software, but with a nod to entrepreneurship, permitted the exploitation of newly-developed commercial software that did not require publication of the source code.

So a potentially lucrative software product could be protected as intellectual property, rewarding its creator with exclusive rights, but the software genesis of that product was open source, free for anyone to use. In this way, commercialization could encourage new ideas, but the tools necessary for manifesting the idea would be free. For example, the languages *C++, Java, Python*, and canned numerical analysis and linear algebra programs such as available on *Wolfram, Matlab* and *Octave*, plus numerous free tools, toolkits, and applications programs together with online programming tutorials and host-computer source code platforms such as *RedHat* and *Github* are all available to help guide and realize the new product. This type of a developmental regime was instrumental in the creation of new artificial intelligence algorithms.[9]

For example, in the fight against the corona virus and its variants, the Harvard Medical School protein folding algorithm source code was publicly available on GitHub; Baidu's *Linearfold* mRNA protein folding algorithm, the Washington University (St. Louis) *Folding@Home* open source personal computers link that ran at *exaflop* (10^{18} ops) capacity for crowd-sourced protein folding development, and IBM, Google, Amazon, and Microsoft have all made their computer power available to research vaccines against the corona virus. The Intel-Argonne National Laboratory cooperative *Aurora* supercomputer project also will take part in protein folding calculations to find anti-viral drugs for treatment and vaccines.

The proposal of the waiving of patent rights for vaccine development and manufacture is also an indicator of the trend towards open source. It is gratifying that the world is progressing to open source in the face of an overwhelming global pandemic; let us hope that open source remains the basis for the development of artificial intelligence after the pandemic withers away.

---

[9] GitHub was acquired by Microsoft in 2018, the speech recognition company Nuance in 2021. IBM acquired RedHat in 2019 to operate out of its Hybrid Cloud Division, but Microsoft has brought RedHat Enterprise Linux into its global cloud Azure; it remains to be seen how independent GitHub and RedHat will be going forward.

III

From Top to Bottom

CHAPTER 9

Top-Down Artificial Intelligence

I n 1956, at the inaugural *Dartmouth Summer Research Project on Artificial Intelligence*, the AI pioneers John McCarthy and Marvin Minsky set out their goal of a pure *top-down* artificial intelligence machine in a grant proposal,[1]

> *The study is to proceed on the basis of the conjecture that every aspect of learning or any other feature of intelligence can in principle be so precisely described that a machine can be made to simulate it*

Their conjecture was philosophically based on the *monism* of Descartes' *mind-body problem*; that is, an abstract thought and the physical brain are not separable, and thus a thought could be produced by a physical machine.[2]

Two attendees at the conference, Allen Newell and Herbert Simon, picked a task that they believed would be an ultimate proof of the conjecture: a machine that could prove mathematical theorems.[3]

From the rules of symbolic logic as set forth in 1913 by Alfred North Whitehead and Bertrand Russell in their epochal three-volume tome *Principia Mathematica*, a set of symbols is used to represent *tautologies*

---

[1] *Proceedings of the Dartmouth Summer Research Project on Artificial Intelligence* 1956.

[2] *Monoism* thus implies that upon the material destruction of the brain, any consciousness or ideas are also destroyed, and death means the end of any type of "being" contrary to many religious beliefs. *Dualism* in the mind-body problem means that mind and matter are distinct, and therefore some kind of conscious "being" may exist after death, perhaps the "soul" or "reincarnation" of many religions.

[3] Herbert Simon won the Nobel Prize in Economics in 1978 for his work in organizational behavior.

DOI: 10.1201/9781003214892-12

such as "All unmarried men are bachelors", *inferences* such as "if *A* implies *B*, and *B* implies *C*, then *A* implies *C*", and the mathematical concepts of *uniqueness* ($\exists!$) and *completeness* (for every $\Gamma \models \varphi$ it is also true that $\Gamma \vdash \varphi$).

The *Logic Theorist*, using the innovative *Information Processing Language* (IPL), a forerunner of the *List Processor* (LISP) artificial intelligence language) converted words and phrases into binary-coded symbols, and by comparing and matching symbol strings in a tree search where the root is the hypothesis, each branch is a deduction founded on symbolic logic, and the objective is at a twig of the tree; the proof is the trajectory from root through branch to twig.

There are many different choices and combinations that one can take along the way to reach the goal. One can try all the possibilities one-by-one, checking the result, and if wanting, backtrack to try the next possibility. Even for restricted domain problems such as the proof of some basic theorems of mathematics and the playing of board games, this *exhaustive search* method would encounter a *combinatorial explosion* of possibilities requiring today's supercomputers to compute.

Good mathematicians of course do not do mathematics solely by trial-and-error exhaustive search, and human chess and *Go* players also do not play in such a pedestrian manner, rather they use knowledge, logic, and heuristics to reduce the number of choices, formulate strategies, and gain experience.

The top-down proponents' idea for *expert systems* was to hard-wire the fundamental operations, collect the knowledge and heuristics of the best practitioners, add *means-end* analysis to feedback information that a process was on the right track, and then working backwards from the desired result, pick the best paths to success.

Altogether this was called *hill-climbing* because a mountain-climber's step up rather than down is generally more likely to contribute to the goal of reaching the summit. However, reflecting the complexity of any endeavor, a step down might lead to an unforeseen lower level roped passage to the top, so the hill-climbing trajectory approach is obviously not absolute; examples in mathematics might be proof by contradiction (*tertium non datur*), and in games, *queen sacrifice* in chess and *tenuki* and *sente* in *Go*.[4]

---

[4] Proof by contradiction is assuming a proposition to be false and showing that this leads to contradiction, tried and true, as formalized in the *Principle of the Excluded Middle* (PEM), but criticized by Dutch mathematician L.E.J. Brouwer for not considering a third "undecided" or "half-right" proposition instead of the rigid "there is no third option". See Hallman, H. 2006, *Great Feuds in Mathematics*, Wiley. *Tenuki* means ignoring an opponent's moves, accepting a possible local loss to gain the initiative later (*sente*).

The Logic Theorist succeeded in proving *Principia* theorems, even in ways different from the *Principia* proofs themselves, delighting Bertrand Russell himself.

From this success, top-down expert systems could break a big problem into smaller sub-problems, tackling each in turn by *if-then* program steps, and integrating all the sub-problems into a core *inference engine* that in principle could solve any problem.

For example, if the problem is to win an American football match, each series of downs is a sub-problem, a traditionally-trained head coach would reason: *if* you are in your end of the field, and *if* it is fourth down and 8 yards to go, *then* punt. However, game strategy and personnel might dictate otherwise; for instance, you have a good fake-punt play, a punter who can run or pass, and a coach whose perceived conservatism would result in surprise. The expert system could objectively take into consideration other options not the least because it can disregard unsubstantiated coaching homilies and accept the assumption of risk (short-time losing the game, and long-term getting fired).

Success in tackling the sub-problems integrated into the total match will more likely result in victory, so an expert system coaching inference engine, due to its logically-organized approach, should perform better than a human head coach.

The ultimate test of the top-down expert system was Deep Blue. Each state of a chess game presents a particular arrangement of the pieces with a player faced with a static array of of legal chess moves that must be evaluated. An evaluation function is used to see if a particular move is probably beneficial to the player; for example, if a move captures an opponent's threatening heavy piece. A *minimax* algorithm with *alpha-beta* pruning to reduce the number of branches, and a *progressive deepening* of the tree search speeds up the evaluations by making decisions at higher (earlier) levels in the tree.

Deep Blue's minimax used a data structure *decision tree* having nodes with a *root node* at the top, and *children* descending from the nodes, and a *branching factor* b that is the number of *children* connected to the node, and the *depth* of the tree d is roughly the number of *nodes* of decision-making from the root down to the farthest leaf node.

In a typical chess game, a depth of $d = 100$ and if $b = 3$ (not a very deep tree), the number of leaf nodes (decisions) is given by $b^d = 3^{100}$ which means that as estimated by the mathematician Claude Shannon there will be about 10^{120} static evaluations to be made in a game. A level of seven layers makes a mediocre player and at least 15 layers are required for a Grandmaster.

Even at a rate of 200 million/second evaluations, exhaustive searches would not be feasible, so the search tree must be *alpha-beta* pruned with up-and-down *minimaxing* with the calculations parallel-processed, and capable of performing uneven tree development using extended *blow-up searches* to take care of special encounters, such as castling or a vulnerable queen.

Alpha-beta pruning is a method based on the minimax theory of eliminating unproductive routes by going up and down from the root through branches to leaves in a tree search to find the optimum route for reaching the goal node, and as such the less effective routes can be eliminated (pruned), and thus reduces the combinatorial possibilities.

Alpha is the best already-explored route for the maximizer and *beta* is the best already-explored route for the minimizer, the possible routes are shown in the simplified search tree shown in the figure below.

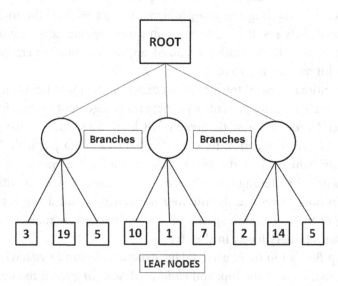

Starting with the *worst case* values for a route, for the maximizer it is $-\infty$ and for the minimizer it is $+\infty$. At the outset, there are no initial values except at the leaf nodes of the search tree which evaluate the "goodness" of a final position before any new moves are made. These leaf node static evaluations can be variously chosen, a simple example for chess could be winning an opponent's heavy piece such that a player's heavy pieces will be greater at that point in the game.

Starting from the root of the search tree, a player goes along the branches one-by-one comparing values, which at first are always $+/-\infty$ allowing no evaluations until a leaf node is reached, at which point a comparison can be made. Then going backwards through all the branches one-by-one back towards the root, when there is a value that is better (more positive for the maximizer and less negative for the minimizer), that branch will be the best choice and all the worse branch choices can be discarded. This "pruning" of the search tree reveals the routes with the least "noise", and all the other branches may be discarded.[5]

Despite being called "progressive deepening" the *iterative deepening depth-first search* (IDDFS) in practice reduces the ultimate tree search depth by earlier iteration of a probably beneficial branch (for example because it is a good move based on some chess heuristic) until a good node is found in that branch.

Deep Blue played by doing the tree search using hardwired *move generators* acting as *evaluators* that alpha-beta pruned based on a Grandmaster's determination of leaf node values in published matches. Opening books and endgames were provided by Deep Blue's Grandmaster advisors and stored for random access.

An example of an evaluator function is the well-known tactic that rooks and bishops could be advantageously placed on or near files where there is an option of early "opening up the files" by removing the pawns on the files (typically by pawn capture) and thereby exerting long-range and long-term pressure on the opponent's heavy pieces. The file of course must not be opened prematurely allowing the opponent to notice and disrupt or challenge. The rooks and bishops rather should be set up on a "potentially open" file and the player should wait for an opportune moment to open the file.

As for overall strategy and in-game responses, board patterns must be recognized. An experiment of champion chess players as subjects found that they could almost immediately memorize *rational* board layouts, but could not memorize irrational layouts, so it was concluded that professional chess players play by the pattern recognition of the disposition of

---

[5] Doing the alpha-beta pruning algorithm is easier than explaining it, and there are canned programs, Abbeel, P., UC Berkeley, "Machine Vision", Spring 2013 online, and Sebastian Lague, "Algorithms explained – minimax and alpha-beta pruning", YouTube April 20, 2018. Minimax is further described in Chapter 28 in relation to game theory. For minimax theory related to chess, refer to Winston, P., "Minimax", MIT Fall 2010 online lectures on artificial intelligence.

the pieces on a board, and through experience, heuristics, and skill, can rationally respond to a logical board. A face screwed-up in confusion during a match is a sure sign of an irrational board disposition contrary to their experience and/or logic. For the computer, its program may be discombobulated by an "unrecognized" pattern, causing some weird responses.

For example, when Deep Blue's predecessor, *Deep Thought*, the first computer to defeat a Grandmaster in a sanctioned game, was presented

with the admittedly not likely to encounter hypothetical board layout shown in the figure at right, it would be clear to a human player that black has an enormous advantage in pieces with two rooks and a bishop, while white has only a king and pawns, but those pawns are arrayed in an airtight defensive line. A draw could easily be achieved by just moving the white king around behind the line of pawns. But be-
cause it was available for material gain with no immediate personal threat, Deep Thought took the black rook with its pawn, and in doing so destroyed the line of pawns defense, resulting in an inevitable defeat.[6]

Even a pedestrian human player, having seen the pattern on the board, would not have made that mistake, but Deep Thought apparently did not recognize the unusual board pattern and was top-down programmed to capture pieces and attempt to checkmate black's king. Deep Thought did what it did, and the expert system in this case was no more than a bungling amateur, proving that although "expert" it could also be stupid.

Deep Blue, with more memory, faster processors, and more chess-playing heuristics, could avoid Deep Thought's naïveté by programming, but the idea that unusual or irrational plays could confuse the computer germinated such that Kasparov for one, believed that this was the key to victory over a machine.

Like all great champions, Kasparov assiduously studied his opponent before-match to find playing proclivities and weaknesses. From his pre-match training with other chess computers, Kasparov evidently realized

---

[6] Deep Thought defeated the "Great Dane" Grandmaster Bent Larsen in 1988. The "pawn-line defence" episode and figure were described in Seymour, J. & D. Norwood 1993, *New Scientist*, 139, No. 1889, 23–6.

that because of the sheer thoroughness of search for good moves that a computer can bring to bear, a straight-up match would be difficult to win, and so devised an "anti-computer" strategy of deliberately playing suboptimal moves that Deep Blue would not recognize, just like Deep Thought and the strange pawn-line defense, he thought that that was the chess computer's weakness that could be exploited.

Therefore in Game 1 even with white advantage, Kasparov abandoned normal openings, and his heavy pieces never left his own half of the board even when Deep Blue's black bishop potential diagonal file was evident as shown in the figure at right. For the first nine moves, the pieces were closed and highly positional, but in a disconcerting *10.e3* move, Kasparov confirmed his suboptimal laying-back strategy, as a normal move would be a *10.e4* offering a pawn exchange.

Deep Blue, however, did not capitalize on this suboptimal move to gain the initiative, because in this instance, its automatic tuning of the evaluation function had increased the weighting for certain types of moves, but in extreme cases the maximum weight was reached, and this saturation meant that Deep Blue no longer distinguished a very bad position from an even worse position. Kasparov believed his strategy was working.

The saturation bug was found and corrected later, but after a few more questionable moves, Deep Blue lost Game 1, but knew why it lost, and Kasparov only gained an expected white victory in the opening skirmish, but in winning, his belief in his suboptimal move lay-back strategy was reinforced.

In Game 2, Kasparov's anti-computer strategy fell apart when Deep Blue, affirmatively responding to the lay-back, pinned down Kasparov's heavy pieces to his back rank utilizing rook and bishop potentially open files and diagonals, taking the offensive and final victory. In light of his success in Game 1, Kasparov did not believe that Deep Blue could adapt and counter his strategy without human operators recognizing the suboptimal moves and changing tactics in-game. He complained after the match,

You know, [the anti-computer strategy] was working, but suddenly it stopped working – suddenly Deep Blue found a way just to break the pawn chains and start a confrontation in a very, very convenient situation.

Deep Blue's last move in Game 2, **Ra6**, deemed a "highly dubious but excellent move" by commentators was sufficiently shocking to end the game with a full point for Deep Blue. Kasparov's suspicions and accusation of cheating no doubt affected his playing, and were likely factors in his missing a substantive chance for a draw in that Game 2 as pointed out in after-game analysis by his seconds, and his black thus had missed a chance for a critical half-point.

Kasparov stubbornly continued his lay-back anti-computer strategy in Game 3, even with white. At the very outset, his **1.d3** was a move that likely had never before been used at the highest levels of chess as an opening. After presumably waiting for Deep Blue to blunder as it had in Game 1, Kasparov allowed Deep Blue to set up an impenetrable defense as shown in the figure at right, and Kasparov offered a draw, losing his white advantage and a half-point, his **1.d3** pawn forlornly still sitting there at the end of Game 3.

In Game 4, after the strange moves in Game 1 attributed to evaluation software bugs were repaired, upon Kasparov's 43rd move, Deep Blue *self-terminated* owing to a piece of code that monitored the efficiency of a parallel search and terminated the program if the efficiency dropped below a given level, which it did, causing Deep Blue to shut down, much to the operator Hsu's chagrin.

Deep Blue had to be rebooted, and according to human vs. computer chess match protocol, the time it took to restart was charged to the computer side. Under time pressure, its subsequent moves were not optimal, and after the 56th move, Deep Blue's *endings ROM* indicated a rook ending draw that Kasparov also saw, and playing black, he expediently offered. Because of the computer coding anomaly, Deep Blue thus only gained a half-point with the white advantage.

In Game 5, Deep Blue had a significant advantage in piece development, and made the controversial **11.h5** move pushing the black h-file pawn forward two squares down from its original position as shown in the figure at right, a move that startled its Grandmaster advisors. However, the move meant to Hsu that Deep Blue was warning the greatest player who ever lived, "if you castle kingside, I will attack you!" It was an audacious threat that no human player would ever dare level at Kasparov.

Indeed, Kasparov post-match lamented, "no computer plays **h5**!" But Hsu knew exactly what Deep Blue's hardware was doing,[7]

> When I saw the move **h5** from Deep Blue, I knew precisely what hardware evaluation features prompted the move. During the last two months of chip design before the rematch, I added drastic changes to the hardware for king safety evaluation. Before the king castles, the hardware computes three sets of king safety evaluations, one for kingside castling, one for queenside castling, and one for staying in the center. The real king safety evaluation is the weighted linear combination of the three, with the weighting based on the relative ranking of the three, and difficulty of making the castling moves. ... In the game position, Deep Blue could always castle queenside safely, and therefore move **h5** was perfectly capable from its point of view.

Although Kasparov later had a passed pawn ready to promote, Deep Blue just marched its king forward and initiated a drawing sequence based on repetition checks, so Game 5 was drawn, with Kasparov's white once again only salvaging a half-point.

After five games, the score was tied 2½-2½ and for the final Game 6, unless Kasparov playing black could defeat a Deep Blue with white advantage, history would be made with a computer tying or beating a reigning world champion.

Before Game 6, the commentators now almost all believed that once Deep Blue had the initiative, it could not be stopped. Indeed, Deep Blue

---

[7] Quote and figures from Hsu, F.H 2002, *Behind Deep Blue: Building the Computer that Defeated the Chess World*, Princeton University Press.

was out of its opening book with **11.Bf4** as shown in the figure below at left, and seeing three pawns worth of positional compensation, it was clearly in attack mode. Spurning material gains for an ultimate king kill, Deep Blue continued its attack and at **19.c4**, Kasparov resigned. History was made with the final board shown in the figure below at right.[8]

Despite a clear loss in Game 6 and the Match, a combative Kasparov refused to acknowledge Deep Blue's superiority, still believing that the IBM team had cheated. He had previously demanded to see Deep Blue's game logs during the Match, but IBM refused on the entirely reasonable grounds that that would be tantamount to revealing match strategy while the match was on-going, akin to a human telling his opponent his strategy and tactics during a match. IBM did agree to provide complete game logs after the Match to show that there was no in-game human intervention.

A rematch was discussed, but Kasparov's demands of further bizarre perquisites for himself and his team, and his proposed three-week match with two- and three-day rest periods (obviously for Kasparov to physically recoup, Deep Blue needed no rest periods).[9]

---

[8] After writing a book about his match with Deep Blue, Kasparov dialed back his pique saying, "I am not writing any love letters to IBM, but my respect for the Deep Blue team went up, and my opinion of my own play, and Deep Blue's play, went down. Today you can buy a chess engine for your laptop that will beat Deep Blue quite easily". He did not add that by logical extension, that chess engine could also easily defeat him as well.

[9] Psychiatrists and social psychologists had a literal field day with Kasparov's well-documented prima donna persona; he and his extremely protective mother Clara demanded all manner of amenities, including a private dressing room with designated furniture, specially-prepared exotic snacks and drinks, bathroom facilities that only he could use, his very expensive match chair, a custom-designed (by Garry) chess clock made by Audemars Piguet, special player timing controls giving the human an advantage, and so on and on. All that might be laid by the psychologists at the door of a quintessential Mama's boy deserving and always getting the best.

Sought-after sponsors felt that such a rematch format was too long to hold public attention and were not forthcoming. IBM, having put up the $700,000/$300,000 winner/loser prize for the Match, paying for the considerable expenses of New York's poshest skyscrapers hotels, and accommodating Kasparov and his entourage every amenity, having already achieved its goal was not enthusiastic.

After leaving IBM, in an effort to dispel all doubts of Deep Blue's superiority, Hsu personally tried to arrange a rematch but was denigrated by Kasparov's manager as "lacking credibility" and having insufficient funds for a prize (at least one million dollars).

Deep Blue's victory over Kasparov demonstrated that a top-down approach could defeat a human in a restricted domain, albeit with hardware and software fixes in-between games, and that Kasparov knew this and thus chose his sub-optimal move strategy.

Unsurprisingly perhaps, but anxiety-inducing nevertheless, if computers are the best players, won't human matches lose their appeal? Will Grandmasters be replaced by computer scientists and their machines playing against each other for chess supremacy?

At least there was still some public interest in a match between the new world chess champion Norway's Magnus Carlsen and American challenger Fabiana Caruana in the 2018 World Chess Championship. It however ended in twelve draws, ultimately being decided by a penalty kick-like rapid chess confrontation (total 30 minutes per player) won by Carlsen.

Carlsen and other GMs nowadays do not play championship matches against computers, but rather use them to hone their skills. The exaltation of a human *World Chess Champion* no doubt has been eroded by computers, and perhaps even worse, because of similar training on them, the computer may also have had a hand in the many stultifying draws of high-level human matches.

Despite the historical significance of Deep Blue vs. Kasparov, the expert system revealed foibles that required human intervention to correct, and attempts to develop broad top-down expert systems would not fulfill their prospective destinies.

JAPAN'S FIFTH GENERATION

The height of optimism for top-down expert systems was on display in Japan in the early 1980s. It was a time of an ascendant Japan threatening to dominate the world economy with its semiconductors, consumer products, and cars. The Ministry of International Trade and Industry

(MITI), in an attempt to minister Japan's *coup de grâce* for advanced technology supremacy, announced a ten-year project to develop thinking machines to translate, converse, and reason for all manner of commercial activities. The culmination of the plan would drive Japan's industry away from manufacturing to an elite position as the fount of *information technology*, making Japan the foremost knowledge-based economy in the world through the widespread utilization and export of expert systems.[10]

This *Fifth Generation* of computing would have powers of reasoning based on symbolic inference systems connected to central knowledge base machines, all connected to each other. The big idea was that natural resources-poor Japan could thrive on exploitation of its formidable human resources, and with the aid of expert systems, solve the problems of resource shortage, environmental damage, ageing populations, education, language differences, and promote more efficient production and communications worldwide through the export of non-depleting and ever-expanding *knowledge*.[11]

In spite of dire warnings of being irrevocably left behind if it did not pursue a similar national plan, after several fits and starts, America's Fifth Generation counter project never got off the ground. And just as well, for the Japanese Fifth Generation Project petered out and was abandoned in 1991after achieving none of its goals, and together with the collapse of the *List Processor* (LISP) artificial intelligence programming language market in 1987, MITI's grandiose plan not only registered the demise of the over-blown pure-play top-down expert systems, but also precipitated the deep freeze of the second *AI Winter*.

LOGICISM VERSUS INTUITIONISM

The problem may have been more fundamental than the lack of computing power, premature timing, and incomplete implementation, the Dartmouth choice of the *Principia* for proof of principle was based on Russell's *logicism* where in effect basic axioms are thrown into the logic machine and after undergoing logical processing, out come mathematical theorems! That is, mathematics depends entirely on the operations of

---

[10] Part of Japan's enthusiasm expert systems to translate and converse likely came from the immense differences between Japanese and Western languages, historically causing the Japanese no little angst, and here perhaps contributing to an overly optimistic belief in the utility of expert systems.

[11] Feigenbaum, E.A., and P. McCorduck 1984, *The Fifth Generation*, Signet. The first four computer generations are designated (1) vacuum tube, (2) transistor, (3) integrated circuits, and (4) very large scale integration (VLSI).

pure logic, and this was the impetus for the search for all the fundamental theorems of mathematics, as pursued by great mathematicians such as Russell and David Hilbert, that came to be called *formalism*.[12]

However, in accord with Plato and Galileo's Heaven-sent "discovery" of mathematical forms, L.E.J. Brouwer and Jules Henri Poincaré believed that fundamental theorems and their associated mathematics are derived from *intuition*: that is, mathematics depends on logical operations which are derived from an intuition that is bestowed by Heaven only upon a very few humans. This so-called *intuitionism* was required because Russell's *logicism* inevitably led to contradictions, for example the paradox "I am lying", which if true is not true because you are lying.

Thus the formalism that an expert system can be developed entirely from logical operations, according to intuitionists, was impossible; a human element of intuition was needed, and although not necessarily from mathematical geniuses, but from the Big Data generated from the intelligence of many humans that can be collated by bottom-up artificial intelligence.

---

[12] The *Principia* famously took 29 equations to prove that 1 is a number and a thousand pages to prove 1 + 1 =2.

CHAPTER 10

Bottom-Up Artificial Intelligence

The mathematical formalists believed that axioms operated upon by pure logic alone would produce theorems that lead to the mathematical *truth*. The intuitionalists invoked the Heavens to bestow certain humans with an intuition that together with logic would create the equations that revealed the mathematical operations *reality*. Top-down artificial intelligence relied on human-constructed expert systems operating to achieve a designated objective. Now bottom-up artificial intelligence relies on the accumulated information of Big Data, that upon undergoing algorithmic logic will find the *ground truth*.

All of these approaches were manifestations of "intelligence", and one man who was endowed with a fearsome human intelligence was to establish the fundamental concept that algorithmically linked the data to the ground truth.

The mathematics prodigy Norbert Weiner graduated from university in mathematics at age 14, further studied zoology and philosophy, could speak seven languages (and was said to be difficult to understand in all of them), wrote his Harvard dissertation on the mathematical logic of set theory, and received his Ph.D. at the tender age of 17.

He was soon a member of the mathematics elite, traveling to Cambridge to learn from the legendary philosopher/mathematician Bertrand Russell and the renowned pure mathematician G.H. Hardy, and thence to the

DOI: 10.1201/9781003214892-13

European citadel of mathematics and physics to study with the great David Hilbert at Gottingen.

With this transcendent résumé, the eclectic Wiener first taught philosophy at Harvard, but then following continually diverging interests, took jobs as an engineer at General Electric and of all things a reporter for the Boston Herald.

With America's entry into World War I in 1917, eager to serve, but failing enlistment because of poor eyesight, Wiener was invited by the mathematician Oswald Veblen to the Aberdeen Proving Ground to work on artillery shell ballistics, something that all governments bade their best mathematicians to do in wartime.

After the Great War and being rejected for a permanent position at Harvard, for which he (and Albert Einstein) blamed on the anti-Semitic views of Professor G.D. Birkhoff, Wiener took a job as an instructor in mathematics at MIT.[1]

In the yeasty environment of Cambridge, Wiener joined regular meetings with intellectuals from many different disciplines, and with his own varied background, he became interested in the study of the boundary between different disciplines, not exactly interdisciplinary studies, but the *nexus* of biology, electronics, the new computers, and finally philosophical ruminations about the mind-body problem.

During World War II, Wiener returned to his ballistics specialty to study the vexing problem of hitting high-flying and fast-moving enemy aircraft with slow-to-respond anti-aircraft guns. The targets were always moving, and for fighters, not necessarily in predictable patterns, and different weather conditions, changing winds, and the proclivities of the anti-aircraft guns themselves, all amounted to a very complicated problem with which the manual-mechanical firing directors of the day could hardly cope.[2]

Here Wiener's own studies in zoology and the many discussions with biologists at the universities in Cambridge, led him to the idea of the *nexus* between all creatures, including humans, to their environment, namely the *adaptive feedback loop* by which information is relayed from

---

[1] Birkhoff, although an admitted right-wing conservative, averred that he was only promoting the advancement of home-grown American mathematicians and physicists in rejecting a position for the European Einstein, but Wiener was an American.

[2] Bombers flew in formation, and even though fighter planes would often stay in wing formations for both attack and defense, once broken off the wing, dog-fight maneuvers were not predictable. See Chapter 32.

the environment to adjust responses in the pursuit of objectives. As Charles Darwin said in his *Origin of the Species*:

> *It is not the strongest of the species that survive,*
> *nor the most intelligent,*
> *but the one most responsive to change.*

It follows that any intelligent machine must be able to adapt, and so he created the discipline of *cybernetics*, the "steersman" of machines, exemplifying the *monism* of the mind-body.[3]

Wiener and colleagues thereupon devised a feedback control system that guided the anti-aircraft guns in response to the movement of the target aircraft's blip on a radar screen; a continually-updated feedback loop to follow and then through heuristics and some rapid calculations, predict the target's trajectory to shoot it down.

The great success, however, came not against human-piloted aircraft but rather against the Nazi V-2 rockets in the second Battle of Britain where reportedly in one incursion nine of ten of the "flying bombs" were shot down by the new fire director antiaircraft guns.[4]

Warren McCulloch was a neurophysiologist graduate from Yale Medical School with a specialty in epilepsy and head injuries. His work led to an appointment as head of the University of Illinois' psychiatric research laboratory, seemingly a long reach from anti-aircraft gunnery. But after attending a lecture on Wiener's machine feedback theories, he was inspired to realize that although a single neuron in the brain when activated has no *sense* in and of itself, rather in response to a stimulus, an aggregate of neurons and their synaptic connections form a pattern that does have a *sense*, and therefore an *artificial neural network* (ANN) in a machine should be able to store sense, and thus gain knowledge, just like a human brain.

With this idea in mind, McCulloch sought the help of the 18-year-old mathematics prodigy Walter Pitts, who noted that since the neurons' activation was either *on* or *off*, they could be binary coded, and the synaptic patterns could follow Boolean algebra to produce logical and desirable outcomes. Upon further fulmination, he surmised that Claude Shannon's two-state on/off electronic switches could be arrayed to

---

[3] Wiener, N 1948, *Cybenetics*, Technology Press and 1950 *The Human Use of Human Beings*, Da Capo Press (1988).
[4] Cf. Chapter 32.

produce cascades of logical patterns to form outcomes that could electronically model the human brain's ability to *reason*.

It was then just a logical step for the artificial neural network to store the reasoning patterns, and *learn* through a feedback loop the best synaptic patterns to reach the desired outcome of that reasoning, thereby endowing the machine with the *adaptive intelligence* to advantageously respond to the changing conditions it encountered in its environment.

In artificial intelligence circles, this came to be called the *bottom-up* approach of modeling the human brain by means of an artificial neural network that constructed synaptic patterns in response to external stimuli, learning bottom-up from supervised training from data sets, heuristics, and experimentation.

In order to improve and hasten learning, McCulloch's basic artificial neural network needed more sophisticated feedback. In the late 1950s in another example of Wiener's interdisciplinary nexus, Cornell psychopathologist Frank Rosenblatt made the two-state artificial neuron more impressionable by attaching a *weight* to the artificial neuron activation level to add nuance to the artificial neural network's response, by "modulating" the feedback to better present observations and data to the ANN, thus promoting more rapid learning of what is significant in the feedback information. Rosenblatt called his weighted artificial neuron a *perceptron*.

The perceptron was first used in *computer vision*. A bank of photoelectric cells focused on particular regions of a test image of two squares. The reflected light photons from the image were converted into analog electrical signals through the photoelectric effect, and those signals were digitized for greyscale-mapping onto a pixel matrix stored in the memory of an IBM 704 computer.

By electronically weighting each pixel's activation level to reflect the intensities of the light and dark patterns of the test pattern, iterative and cumulative repetition would produce an accurate rendition of the target squares on the computer's network of perceptrons, thereby producing the first instance of artificial neural network pattern recognition.

It is important to realize that the IBM 704 has not just reproduced the image to display on a video screen like a TV camera, its artificial neural network has *recognized* the features of two squares for storage in memory, and in principle once having done so, the perceptron network has *learned* to identify patterns of that type to be squares by comparing the pixel patterns of a new viewed image with the stored squares pattern in memory, useful presumably for future identification of objects comprising square conformations.

In his 1969 book *Perceptrons*, MIT's Marvin Minsky however, argued that the perceptrons' combinatory binary circuits could not perform the XOR logical function, and would thus be theoretically limited in application. Minsky's thesis was later disproved by a layered network of perceptrons, but not before it chilled AI neural network research into a ten-year AI Winter that thawed only to encounter the ill-fated Japanese Fifth Generation project begun in 1981, which failure after another ten years triggered yet another AI Winter of the early 1990s.[5]

After Minsky's false Winter, the California Institute of Technology in 1982 rehabilitated the artificial neural network, modeling memory as variable energy levels of artificial neurons in a synaptic pattern, a strong proof-of-concept impetus for the use of perceptrons in artificial intelligence.

AUTONOMOUS VEHICLES

Feedback bottom-up artificial intelligence can be best exemplified by the autonomous car that senses the environment to provide feedback to control the car and *learns* how to drive from a mapping of its motion through the environment, controlling the vehicle using actuators and servos, rewarding good responses and penalizing poor responses, and then storing the driving data for later supervised learning.

The autonomous car is easily identified by its LIDAR tower sweeping out semiconductor diode-produced laser beams to probe and map the surroundings, the microsecond-pulsed Class I low-powered and rapidly rotating 905 nanometer wavelength laser beam is used for shorter range (~50 m) reconnaissance, and is in conformance with the US Food & Drug Administration's eye safety standard and the International Electrochemical Commission's 60825 performance standard. The higher-powered, longer-wavelength 1550 nm laser beam is more commonly used for longer range probing (~200 m) because longer wavelengths are closer to radio waves which can pass through obstacles.[6]

---

[5] Ref. Minsky, M and S. Papert 1969, *Perceptrons, an Introduction to Complex Geometry*, MIT Press. An XOR binary gate outputs *True* when only one of the inputs is *True*, i.e., one or the other but not both.

[6] Lasers are classified 1–4 according to wavelength and maximum output power damage to the eye. The visible wavelength range of light is 400 to 700 nm, so both the 905 and 1550 nm are not absorbed by the retina, but high-powered laser light may cause corneal damage. Electromagnetic waves interact with matter by resonating with lattice molecules in the matter with comparable lattice dimensions. Short wavelength blue light will interact and be absorbed or reflected, long wavelength radio waves have wavelengths longer than most matter lattice dimensions and therefore are able to pass through obstacles unimpeded.

A rapidly rotating electronic device cannot avoid the design problem of winding wires maintaining contact connections, so the laser beam is rotated by reflection from rapidly rotating micro-electromechanical systems (MEMS) mirrors.

The laser beam is reflected by objects in the environment back to the tower where photodetectors pick up the return beams, and in accord with the photoelectric effect, coxnvert the light intensity to proportional electric current. According to the time of the returned light signals, the distance of scanned objects is measured, and in accord with the change in wavelength upon reflection by a moving object, the motion of scanned objects can be computed using the Doppler effect for light.[7]

After collecting all the electromagnetic wave data and performing the necessary wave calculations and mapping, the LIDAR system forms a dynamic 3-Dimensional *point-cloud* image of the car's driving environment.

On-board computers run *simultaneous localization and mapping* (SLAM) software to dynamically follow the car, and actuators and servomotors control the steering, speed, and braking of the car in response to the changing environment as displayed on the point-cloud map and the constraints of embedded traffic rules.[8]

Together with GPS location and local navigation street maps, training sets of actual driver experience responding to the constantly changing environment, the autonomous car learns how to drive in many different environments and situations through numerous training sessions. Clearly, the more training data, the more accurate the response of the autonomous car will be, and just like a human driver, the more driving experience, the more proficient the driving. The self-driving car learns to drive like a human from the bottom up, and gains greater skill by driving more and encountering more different situations.

In the future when sufficient numbers of autonomous cars are on the road, a self-driving *swarm* of cars will all share in and contribute to the entire group's driving skill set, and in principle could never have an accident.

A swarm of bees can unerringly home in on their target, and in the process never bump into each other, or impede the progress of the

---

[7] The Doppler effect is the change in wavelength (or frequency) of a wave source moving away (increasingly lower pitch for sound and redshift to longer wavelengths in the electromagnetic wave spectrum) or towards an observer (higher pitch sound and blueshift to shorter wavelengths).

[8] SLAM is probably not the best acronym for self-driving cars.

whole. Of course, individual cars on their own particular routes will deviate from the swarm formation, but again with larger experience datasets, anomalous behavior such as turning into a parking lot or suddenly changing lanes can be modeled as well in patterns of legal driving activity, while the reckless and drunken driver, can be immediately spotted by the (anti-*bottoms-up!!*) swarm system.

Waymo's new self-driving cars can further improve their driving skills through Darwinian evolution by employing so-called *population-based training* (PBT) originally developed by DeepMind for video-game playing. Driving skill is accelerated by selectively drawing from the "fittest specimens" in the driving population in tune with "survival of the fittest" in a video game to retrain and recalibrate autonomous driving for optimum safety.

Even with an occasional glitch, the autonomous car system will at least reduce the nine deaths and one thousand injuries *every day* in the United States attributable to distracted drivers.[9]

To date, the autonomous car combines a top-down sensing, feedback, mapping, and control systems with bottom-up training for supervised and reinforcement learning; it has not yet employed unsupervised learning to further augment its own driving skills through its own driving actions.

---

[9] Center for Disease Control and Prevention, cdc.gov/motorvehiclesafety/distracted_driving/, March 7, 2019.

CHAPTER 11

Machine Learning Modeling

The functional operations model for a thinking machine can be represented by a simple mapping function,

$$y = f(x)$$

where given the input variables x, the stimulus, the model $f(x)$ maps them onto the output y, the response as schematically shown in the figure below.

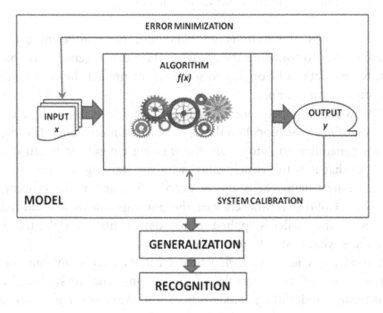

DOI: 10.1201/9781003214892-14

In supervised learning, if the output *y* does not accurately match the labeled input data, the difference between the output and the labeled training data (the error) will be minimized and the adjusted new data fed back into the algorithm as shown in the figure. If after many iterated runs of error minimization, the algorithm still does not produce accurate results, then the algorithm itself may require a *system* calibration.

After supervised training, the Model presumably has learned the common characteristics of the training set data, and is able to generalize those characteristics to recognize new images, probability distributions, or perform classification on new unstructured and unlabeled data presented to the Model.

In artificial neural networks, the mapping function *f(x)* is constructed by training the network on a set of labeled data; that is, by *induction* from the *abstracting of common characteristics* found in the labeled training set data to form a model *generalization* for recognizing newly-presented data by *deduction*, going from the model to a particular case.

A mathematical definition of *generalization* is,[1]

> *There exists a set of elements that possesses common character-istics shared by those elements sufficient to form a conceptual model that can perform deductive inferences*

In other words, the training set data must have sufficient common characteristics to configure the model so its deduced generalizations can classify new data as belonging to some set, or predict the consequences that any new data implies.

How well the model *f(x)* can classify and predict is determined by the *goodness of fit* of the model on the new data. The model *underfits* when it cannot generalize anything from the training dataset, or it can *overfit*, meaning that it is too closely allied with the training set and can only recognize new data that is almost exactly the same as the training set data. Like Goldilocks who chooses the porridge that is not too hot or cold, when the model is applied to new data, it fits *just right*; that is, it recognizes what it should recognize.

A model is said to *underfit* when it cannot adequately capture the abstract common characteristics of the training data. In statistical analysis terms, underfitting models have low variance and high bias,

---

[1] This is the author's definition, following many perhaps better formal descriptions.

meaning that they do not change much in absorbing the training set data (low variance) and the model's assumption about the data is too strong (biased towards itself).

For example, if a very widely distributed set of data points is modeled by a straight line, the model persists no matter how varied the distribution is, and it makes a too strong assumption that the data can be generalized by a simple straight line, whereas for instance a polynomial curve might better fit the data.

Underfitting is easy to detect from the model's poor performance on the training set data; its classifications or predictions do not match the labels on the training data. Underfitting is commonly caused by *under-training* the model, and the remedy is simply to provide more training set data and more *epochs* (runs) through that data. The desired generalizations may then emerge because more training has rendered the model more sensitive, and thus able to more accurately recognize data for what it represents.

Overfitting is the statistically opposite of underfitting in that it has high variance and low bias, meaning that overfitting has included irrelevant data or *noise* into the model (high variance) and thus too closely follows the training set data when presented with new data, so that the model's assumptions are weak (low bias towards itself), with the result that the over-fitted model will not recognize new data that is actually within the purview of the model's desired generalization.

A definition of *overfitting* from the Oxford Dictionary is,[2]

> *The production of an analysis that corresponds too closely to a particular set of data, and may therefore fail to fit new data or predict future observations reliably.*

Again, the machine learning model overfits when the model unwittingly incorporates irrelevant detail or noise in the training set data into its generalization as if those were part of the essential abstracted common characteristics of the training data. Overfitting means that the model has been *over-trained*, and like the diligent but dull schoolboy who has simply memorized the math problem solutions in the textbook instead of learning the abstract generalizations from the problems such that he can apply them to new problems on an examination.

---

[2] Author changed the Oxford definition slightly to reflect modern machine learning usage. For some reason, Oxford does not define "underfitting".

An example of overfitting in bottom-up artificial intelligence is an overly detailed decision tree that includes too many branches and leaves irrelevant to generalized abstraction and contains incidental noise, so much so that in the jumble of extraneous information, it is difficult to recognize new data for what it represents.

The remedy of course is to prudently prune the decision tree, for example by alpha-beta discarding unproductive branches. Prudence is exercised by *resampling*, for instance *k-fold cross validation*, which is just a fancy way of saying take different subsets of the training data, train and test the subsets *k* times, and observe the model performance in regard to the subset test results, and then make appropriate adjustments to the overall model.

Another overfitting cure is to separate a larger subset of the training data to use as a *validation dataset* to test different models trained on the rest of the data and developed from the minimization of the error function in each model. The performance of each model is then tested by the validation dataset to see which model has the smallest error in respect of the labeled dataset. The validation dataset has become an essential tool for promoting machine learning algorithm accuracy.

The model *good-fits* when its performance over time on the training data and validation datasets improves. However, it is important to note that simply doing more training can actually decrease the model's performance through *overtraining* that overfits the training set data. Furthermore, doing too many validation dataset runs may well cause the model to learn the validation as well as the training set data, like the clever schoolgirl who gleans from the quizzes what will be on the final examination.

In this case, a *test dataset* that is independent of the training dataset but follows the same probability distribution as the training data set can be run. If the results are similar to the training data set run, that is an indication that the model does not overfit. This is the case of the brilliant schoolgirl who has learned how to generalize all the subject matter of a course, thereby understanding the essence of the subject.

Finding the optimum training regime can be achieved by observing the rate of improvement of the model in accurately recognizing the labeled training set data over the training epochs, and when the rate of improvement approaches zero, the training should be stopped to avoid overfitting. This is like the able schoolteacher who perceptively introduces more advanced topics to avoid boring the students with routine material.

Underfitting and overfitting are the twin gremlins plaguing artificial neural networks; fortunately in addition to validation and test datasets, there are many ways of dealing with them in machine learning modeling.

Different weights and biases parameter initializations can be employed, such as Bayesian, *Gaussian Mixed Model,* and *Factor Analysis* to tune the artificial neural network to expel the gremlins.[3]

Model underfitting and particularly overfitting both also can be alleviated by *regularization* methods such as the hyperparameters *L1* and *L2, dropout,* and *artificial expansion* of the training data.

Too few neurons in the hidden layers may result in feature maps extracted from the data that miss significant characteristics, seriously underfitting the input data. While on the other hand, using too many neurons in the hidden layers can result in activating irrelevant data and noise, seriously overfitting the data. In this case, the network has so much processing capacity that the data in the training set is too limited to train all the neurons in the hidden layers, and the neurons "find" and falsely interpret extraneous data.

The overfitting of training set data by excess neurons can be alleviated, simply by *dropping out* a randomly-chosen set of activations in a layer by setting them all to zero. This is therefore a test of network perspicuity in that the model should be able to choose the right generalizations regardless of the absence of some activations.[4]

In *dropout,* different sets of neurons are dropped, so it is like training a different neural network after each dropout event, and these different networks will tend to overfit the data in different ways, so taking their average results will curiously alleviate the overfitting. As one of the pioneers of modern AI and a recipient of the 2018 Turing Award Yann LeCun explained,

> *This technique reduces complex co-adaptations of neurons, since a neuron cannot rely on the presence of particular other neurons. It is, therefore, forced to learn more robust features that are useful in conjunction with many different random subsets of the other neurons.*

---

[3] These will be discussed in following chapters.

[4] See Svrisastava, N., G. Hinton, *et al.* 2014, *A simple way to prevent neural networks from overfitting,* J. Machine Learning Res. 15.

To paraphrase Henry Kissinger on Chancellor Gustav Stresemann's astute handling of the very sensitive issue of German disarmament after World War I, "Over time [his] tactics become strategy and the expedient, conviction".[5]

On the other hand, artificially *expanding* the training data can make the artificial neural network model more realistic, for example in improved speech recognition, adding background noise to *best-fit* real-life listening situations.

Overfitting can also be ameliorated by *regularization* techniques, such as *weight decay (L1 regularization)*, which adds a term to the cost function, thereby stabilizing its gradient descent, proving useful when different runs of the artificial neural network result in quite different results. In *L2 regularization*, the cost function is modified by adding the sum of the absolute values of the weights for stabilization of its gradient descent backpropagation.[6]

---

[5] Stresemann placated the victors' demands for demilitarization after World War I by using his knowledge that German industry in the 1920s was not capable of substantial rearmament anyway, a policy of "fulfillment" of treaty terms, all the while *quid pro quo* extracting concessions on war reparations and territorial disputes. See Kissinger, H 1994, *Diplomacy*, Touchstone.

[6] See Chapter 20 Hyperparameterization.

CHAPTER 12

Markov Chain Monte Carlo Simulation

M athematical models of macroscopic natural phenomena and engineering systems almost always take the form of second-order partial differential equations. For deterministic physical systems, those equations are mostly *linear*, meaning that the coefficients of the derivative terms were constants or functions only of an independent variable (and not a dependent variable), and there were no derivatives multiplying each other or themselves squared, cubed or raised to higher powers.

For relatively simple systems, linear differential equations often could be solved in closed form, meaning in terms of the elementary functions of polynomials, sine, cosine, exponentials, natural logs, and combinations thereof, and these solutions would fully describe the physical situation under different initial and boundary conditions, thereby allowing mathematical modeling and prediction.[1]

However, most physical systems in real life are almost always nonlinear, and thereby not solvable in closed form, so using the *finite-differences* first of tiny mechanical turns of cogwheels of the early differential analyzers, and later digitally incrementing the independent variable and correspondingly differentiating the dependent variable, the

---

[1] A differential equation relates a function with its derivatives (rate of change with respect to independent variables) so that its solution can predict outcomes subject to initial and boundary conditions. The differential equations are almost always second-order because the second derivative of position, acceleration, is proportional to force under Newton's second law, and it is force that drives the macroscopic physical systems of interest. Examples are the non-linear ballistic projectile differential equations in Chapter 32.

DOI: 10.1201/9781003214892-15

equations were solved numerically at first very slowly by hand using young women and adding machines, and later very quickly by programming using digital computers, and taking derivatives to hasten convergence.[2]

Adding to the difficulties, the complexities of real world situations involved many factors represented by multiple components and terms in the differential equations, many different independent and dependent variables, and all manner of associated parameters, each situation requiring different initial and boundary conditions.

Newtonian mechanics furthermore did not hold in the world of molecules, atoms, and nuclei, where the quantum mechanical second-order differential equations of Schödinger and the matrices of Heisenberg dealt with the Born probabilities of microscopic wavefunction formation and collapse, rather than the determinism of a Newtonian macroscopic calculation.

MONTE CARLO AND THE ATOMIC BOMB

For many-body systems, however, a statistical *average* could represent the overall behavior of the system in terms of macroscopic characteristics; for example, the *statistical mechanics*-derived pressure, volume, and temperature of a thermodynamical description of gases composed of billions of microscopic atoms.

The Atomic Bomb releases energy because in the splitting of the nucleus of the high fissile rate of radioactive uranium-235 (^{235}U) or plutonium (^{239}Pu and ^{241}Pu) the masses of the fission fragments are less than the mass of the original nucleus. That *mass defect*, according to Einstein's famous mass-energy equivalence equation $E = mc^2$, is equivalent to a release of the *binding energy* of the protons and neutrons in the original nuclei.[3]

The Atomic Bomb explodes when a nucleus is split, protons and neutrons of ^{235}U and are released, and although the positively-charged protons tend to avoid collisions with other protons, the neutral neutrons will collide with other ^{235}U or ^{239}Pu nuclei instigating further nuclear

---

[2] The derivatives are in gradient descent, see Chapter 16.

[3] Uranium occurs naturally as 99.3% ^{235}U so the 0.7% ^{235}U isotope has to be purified for example by high speed centrifuges that spin out the ^{238}U leaving pure ^{235}U, which was used in the "Little Boy", also called "Thin Man", gun-type triggered Bomb on Hiroshima. A nuclear reactor can breed plutonium from uranium fission, a plutonium "Fat Man" implosion-triggered a ^{239}Pu Bomb which was dropped on Nagasaki.

fission and again releasing copious protons and neutrons. When the nuclear fission *effective neutron multiplication factor k = 1*, the amount of ^{235}U or ^{239}Pu has reached a *critical mass* resulting in a spontaneous chain reaction of fission reactions, suddenly releasing all the proton and neutron binding energies in a nuclear explosion.

In designing the A-Bomb, scientists first tried to use second-order differential and integral equations to deterministically follow the neutrons in their collisions with the uranium nuclei and the subsequent release of more neutrons. However, in the spreading cascade of collisions where each collision could produce more than a billion more neutrons, and each neutron could go on to collide with billions of other uranium nuclei, and the collisions would produce even more billions of neutrons in ever-spreading branches of a tree of subsequent collisions, it was clearly not amenable to a deterministic kinematic (study of motion) calculation of each and every neutron.

Furthermore, each collision, fission, and release of neutrons event was quantum mechanical and thus could not be absolutely determined, only the probabilities of collision events were known, and all of the processes were further subject to the initial conditions in the reaction chamber and the boundary conditions of the Bomb casing.

One of those participating in the development of the Atomic Bomb was the mathematician Stanislaw Ulam, an immigrant from a Poland threatened by Germany in 1935, he joined the Los Alamos team in 1943, taking up work on analyzing the neutron flux problem, but with no more success in the kinematics study than others.

Of course, the Manhattan Project ultimately produced a sound design based on the temperature, pressure, and density requirements of the neutron gas flux and the volume of the bomb cavity, and practically engineered through experimentation.

The uranium critical mass neutron flux problem stuck with Ulam, however, and in 1945 when struck with viral encephalitis, he was confined to hospital with nothing to do but play solitaire all day, which he did, over and over again.

Thinking like the mathematician that he was, Ulam wondered if there was any way he could find keys to successfully complete each game, so he began to record the sequence of cards and their play and the game's final layout, and came to believe that if he could just observe a large enough number of games, he might be able to statistically discover some patterns of play that led to success and then model the card layouts analogous to the statistical mechanics of thermodynamic pressure, temperature, and volume describing a gas as a whole, and thus describe the overall behavior of solitaire games.

Because the cards in a 52-card deck can be arranged in more ways than the number of atoms in the our galaxy (about 10^{67}), and a good shuffle results in a completely unpredictable initial arrangement every time, the sequence of cards drawn from the deck will always be random. And although there were only a few placement possibilities for a drawn card, there were different strategic probabilities for each play as to its contribution to a successful conclusion. Furthermore, the card placement choices would depend on the preceding layout state of the cards, and a card placement would change the layout state. All of these probabilities and card layouts would be different for each game, so an astronomical number of games would be required to discover any macroscopic keys to success, if such indeed existed.

Ulam realized all of these conditions would have to be included in any model of the game. He began to think, he knew that a *Markov chain* is a stochastic ensemble of a sequence of random variables X_i (cards) belonging to a finite configuration space (card layout) of separated nodes connected by chains (card placement possibilities) among which an agent can choose to walk but with assigned probabilities P_{ij} of steps to other nodes (card placement possibilities), whereby the probability distribution of states in the process depends only on the present state (card layout) and not on any past states (the *Markovian* property).

A schematic example of a Markov chain is shown in the figure below with the *transition matrix* of probabilities P, where each element of the P matrix represents the probability of a step from A to B and C, B to A and C, C to B and A, and steps in every case to itself.

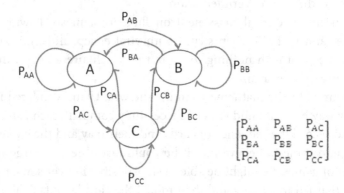

Mathematically, the individual elements of the transition matrix P are given by

$$P_{ij} = Probability\,(X_{k+1} = j|X_k = i).$$

If there is a positive probability, no matter how low, that an agent can move onto any other nodes in the chain, it is *irreducible*; if the agent cannot go around endlessly in cycles of the same nodes, the chain is *aperiodic*; and if the agent can explore every node, the chain is *erdogic*.[4]

The Markov chain was a perfect model for solitaire as it completely satisfied the game's requirements. A deck of cards after shuffling is randomly distributed, but in playing solitaire, there are restricted domains of possible placements of the card in hand that will go towards reaching the final objective. Ulam found that within the domain of possible inputs (the playing of a card), there would be a definite probability for each play commensurate to its efficacy in reaching the objective of all the cards being in the final array, and after a *deterministic* computation whereby the same output is produced given a particular input according to the rules of solitaire, he could model the game using a Markov chain.

As for unpredictability, the random distribution of cards in a shuffled deck could be taken from sampling a random distribution of numbers representing the cards, and then by repeated sampling and aggregating the results, if he could simulate a sufficient number of games, he could discover the keys to success, such that existed.

A simulation employing a random distribution is called "Monte Carlo" after the name of a casino in Las Vegas itself named after the gambling capital of Europe, evincing the gambling industries' propaganda of a completely random chance at winning, something that does not include the assured profits of the casino, based as that is on the *Law of Large Numbers*. Also called *Bernoulli's law*, it is the ultimate regression to the mean of any activity after a very large number of trials (the mean in gambling is always with the house), and is the foundation of the efficacy of a Monte Carlo simulation of a complex system[5].

---

[4] For a mathematical description of a Markov chain, refer to Richey, M 2011, *The evolution of Markov chain Monte Carlo methods*, American Mathematical Monthly, Vol. 117, No. 5, online. The Markov chain schematic was adapted from intechopen.com.

[5] Casinos make 65–80% of their profits from slot machines based on the low probability of a random combination of symbols that is a reward much less a jackpot, so most players will win some, but lose more before they reach any jackpot. In card games, high rollers betting big money will not play long enough to regress to a far-off mean winnings, and the zero and double-zero of roulette gives the House a 5.26% edge. Ref. *Finance Monthly*, "Here's how casinos make money".

As the size of a statistical sample N approaches infinity, the *variance* σ^2, which as the average squared standard deviations σ is a measure of the variability of data from the arithmetic mean μ, will approach zero, and the regression to the mean probability will approach the true probability of any activity. The standard deviation σ measures the dispersion of the data, and is just the root mean square of the variance,

$$\sigma^2 = \frac{1}{N}\sum_i (x_i - \mu)^2 \text{ and } \sigma = \sqrt{\frac{1}{N}\sum_i (x_i - \mu)^2}$$

The variance as the *square* of the difference will always be positive, and squaring furthermore will highlight the outliers from μ, and regress to the mean (if an absolute value is used instead of squaring, it will regress to the median rather than to the mean).

The variance will approach zero as the number of trials approaches infinity, so in the example of a fair coin toss, the probability of heads or tails will eventually proceed to the mean probability of 0.5, with a variance of zero as the number of trials approaches infinity as shown schematically in the figure below.

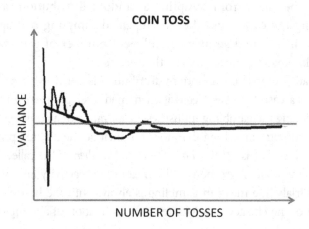

COIN TOSS

VARIANCE

NUMBER OF TOSSES

The detonation of an atomic bomb could be similarly simulated using Markov chain Monte Carlo simulation (MCMC) because there is a domain of possible interactions in fission reactions and neutron collisions that depend on the probabilities of the particles' *elastic scattering* (change direction but not energy), *inelastic collisions* with nuclei (change of direction and energy), *absorption* by the nuclei, and possible *fission* of the nuclei, analogous to the choice of card placement in solitaire.

As a simplified example, a source of neutrons is passing through a cavity containing uranium-235 and they may either be scattered or absorbed by the uranium nuclei with the latter possibly resulting in fission depending on the energy of the neutrons and the accumulating neutron flux density. The problem thus is one of neutron diffusion and fission multiplication of neutrons, the probabilities of which depend on previously derived experimental results. The mean distance that the neutrons will travel without being scattered or absorbed (*mean free path*), and the probability of a neutron collision with a uranium nucleus (*collision cross-section*), is also dependent on the kinetic energy of the neutrons.

It is known (and completely believable) that the probability density P of a neutron traveling a distance x before being scattered or absorbed (free path) decreases exponentially depending on the density of nuclei ρ and their collision cross-section ζ, the infinitesimal probability for an infinitesimal travel distance dx thus is given by,

$$dP = \rho\sigma e^{-\rho\zeta x} dx$$

Integrating this equation will give the density of the neutron flux (number of neutrons passing per unit square area) as,

$$Neutron\ Flux = \frac{Number\ of\ Neutrons\ Passing\ Through}{Number\ of\ Constructed\ Trajectories}$$

Now x_i the free path length for trial i, which is over the interval $(0, \infty)$, can be represented by a computer-generated sequence of *pseudorandom numbers* ξ_i uniformly distributed in the interval $(0, 1)$ by making the transformation,

$$x_i = -\frac{1}{\rho\sigma} \ln(1 - \xi_i).$$

That is, the neutron free path can be expressed by pseudorandom numbers through this variable transformation. For example, if experimental data for neutron collisions with uranium isotope nuclei shows a 0.9 probability of scattering and only 0.1 probability of absorption leading to fission, and if the ξ_i interval (0, 1) is segmented into two groups (0, 0.1) and (0.1, 1), if say the pseudorandom number generated by the computer for example is 0.2, then it belongs in the second larger group (0.1, 1) meaning that the neutron has been scattered. Repeating for more and more sets of pseudorandom numbers will give better and better approximations for the *Neutron Flux* equation above.

If a neutron passes through, it is given a "score" *s = 1* and if absorbed *s = 0*, so the probability of contributing to the neutron flux is given by the mean score $\bar{s}$ where the error is measured by the variance.

Performing the same type of transformation and scoring for scattering angle, the directions of the scattered neutrons can also be simulated, although the possibility of neutrons scattered back into the neutron flux must also be considered, which complicates matters and must be considered in more detailed calculations.

For more complex situations considering protons, different cavity designs and initial conditions and so on included, the situation can be modeled through previously experimentally-derived cross-section and mean free path parameters for different types of reactants and cavity configurations, and entered into the MCMC simulation.[6]

From this example, it can be seen that the neutron's travels are not merely a random walk; that is, there are different probabilities for the steps taken to succeeding nodes, and so just given the relevant event probabilities, any system of many interacting entities can be simulated.

Now after sampling from a normal probability distribution and after many runs of the MCMC simulation, the vast number of particles in atomic bomb neutron diffusion flux (10^{15}–10^{25}) can be modeled by sampling of only 10^5–10^8 trajectories, and the conditions for critical mass represented by a function $f(X)$ with sequences of random samples X_i to approximate a desired probability function $P(X)$, where $f(X)$ is proportional to $P(X)$.[7]

The desired probability $P(X)$ for critical mass can be thought of as a *probability density* that is reached by $f(X)$ stepping through the Markov chain in steps commensurate with the greater probability (generally towards the peak of a random distribution), iteratively pushing $f(X)$ closer to $P(X)$, and consistent with Bernoulli's law, the MCMC simulation in

---

[6] For more detail, see Hendricks, J.S. 1994, *A Monte Carlo code for particle transport*, Los Alamos Science, Number 2.

[7] The $f(x) \propto P(x)$ proportionality is sufficient for the calculation obviating the difficulty to determine a normalization factor.

aggregate will regress to the mean probability of attaining a critical mass of uranium nuclei to produce a neutron diffusion flux sufficient to form a self-sustaining chain reaction and subsequent detonation.

A large number of neutron trajectories are constructed by sampling from the experimental probability distributions of parameters as the neutrons travel through the bomb cavity. The chain reaction therefore depends on the aggregate outcomes of the total set of trajectories.

The random distribution ensures that the actual probability of a chain reaction will be "covered" by the 10^5–10^8 trajectories, and with the ever-increasing computational capabilities of computers, including the super-computers used for nuclear weapons research, the number of trajectories can be increased to better satisfy the law of large numbers.

Running the Monte Carlo simulation over the atomic bomb Markov chain many, many times will drive the variance of outcomes to zero and thereby reveal the mean probability of attainment of the chain reaction required for producing the detonation of the Bomb.

If the probability is low, then the thermodynamic and bomb cavity engineering parameters can be adjusted and the simulation run again and again until critical mass is attained and the process conditions for Critical, Super- and Sub-Critical situations are known.

It is paramount to know the conditions for detonation so that the bomb will detonate when desired and not in the laboratory, so a simplified plot of Mass/Energy vs. Time must be calculated from the MCMC simulation of neutron diffusion, as shown in the figure below.

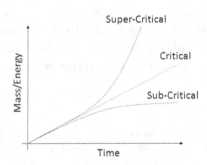

The MCMC was developed too late for the atomic bomb, but beginning in 1951 the development of the hydrogen bomb required fission reactions to generate the radiation to trigger the fusion of the hydrogen isotopes deuterium and tritium.

Ulam first ran the Metropolis-Hastings MCMC algorithm for a system of many interacting particles on John von Neuman's MANIAC computer (derived from the IAS computer at Princeton) and later successfully completed the simulation on the ENIAC computer at the University of Pennsylvania.

The H Bomb detonated based on the idea of *radiation implosion* instead of only neutron flux to produce fusion, with controversy over whether it was Edward Teller or Stanislaw Ulam's proposal, but Teller's insight regarding Ulam's Markov chain Monte Carlo simulations was spot-on,[8]

Take advantage of the statistical mechanics and take ensemble averages instead of following detailed kinematics

In summary, the Markov chain is a finite ensemble of connected nodes each having an assigned probability of choice whereby the probability distribution of nodes depends only on the present state of nodes and no past states. The Monte Carlo simulation depends on a transformation of variables allowing pseudorandom numbers generated by a computer to represent agents in a complex process, with the law of large numbers ensuring that repeated trials will drive the system to the mean, thereby revealing the ground truth of the process; in the example, instead of the benign outcome probability of a fair coin toss, the horrific detonation of an atomic or hydrogen bomb.

An analogy with the bombs can be made for a presidential election prediction. Survey samples from the general population are constructed from demographics such as party affiliation, gender, economic class, ethnicity, and so on, providing in effect event probabilities just as the mean free path and collision cross-sections for neutrons and uranium isotope nuclei have probabilities for scattering or absorption and subsequent fission.

---

[8] Ulam was a principal scientist in the development of the Hydrogen Bomb; the crucial idea of radiation pressure from a fission explosion to ignite fusion has been attributed to either him or the "father of the H-Bomb" Edward Teller, or both or others in an on-going controversy kept alive by the top-secret classification of H-Bomb development documents. Ref. author's book, Chen, R.H. 2017, *Einstein's Relativity, the Special and General Theories with their Cosmology*, McGraw-Hill Education and Rhodes, R 1986, *The Making of the Atomic Bomb*, Simon & Schuster and 1995 *Dark Sun, the Making of the Hydrogen Bomb*, Simon & Schuster. Plot figure adapted from Gunzi, A., "Monte Carlo analysis and simulation", towardsdatascience.com. Quote attributed to Teller by Marshall Rosenbluth shortly before Rosenbluth's death in a 2003 presentation "Genesis of Monte Carlo algorithm for statistical mechanics" at the Los Alamos National Laboratory.

Aside from nuclear weapons and the risks inherent in democratic elections, Monte Carlo simulation has been used in the more beneficent areas of weather prediction, turbulent airflow around jet planes, expansion of the Universe, biological systems, ecology, stock market and sales predictions economics, and in any operations research problem such as traffic control and airport passenger flow. Monte Carlo simulation has been gainfully employed in almost all science and engineering, both natural and social, and particularly in simulations of the results of the Big Data of artificial intelligence.

IV

Structure and Operation

CHAPTER 13

Artificial Neural Networks

I n humans, vision is generated from light focused by the eye's lens onto a *retina* at the inside posterior of the eye, the retina converts the light into electrical signals which are received by an *optic nerve* behind the eye that transmits the signals through the *lateral geniculate nucleus* (LGN) relay pathway to an aggregation of neurons at the posterior region of the brain called the *visual cortex,* as shown schematically in the figure below. The visual cortex receives, processes, and integrates the vision signals to form a pattern for the brain to cognitively process by means of a network of neurons, one neuron of which is schematically illustrated in the figure below.[1]

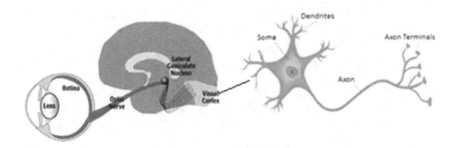

The *soma* of a cortical neuron is activated if the sum of the signals from other cortical neurons at the neuron's *dendrites* is greater than

---

[1] Vision system image of adapted from cs231n.github.io.

DOI: 10.1201/9781003214892-17

some threshold value. The neuron's activation is transmitted to other neurons through *axons* whose *axon terminals* are connected to the dendrites of the other neurons, and in accord with the neuroscience maxim,

Neurons that Fire together, Wire together,

synaptic firing patterns of activated neurons are formed within the visual cortex which are then resolved by the brain to form images for cognition.

In computer vision, a camera's lens receives pixels of light reflected from an object and an array of sensors converts the light into electric signals by means of the photoelectric effect. The signals from this artificial retina are amplified and relayed in analogy with the optic nerve and LGN, and transmitted to an artificial neural network (ANN) that is modeled after the visual cortex.

The ANN is a network of layers of arrays of artificial neurons. An example of a four-layer deep artificial neural network (with *layers* being the vertical columns) has an *input layer* to receive stimuli to the network, followed by two succeeding *hidden layers*, and an *output layer*, each column layer having four row neurons organized in a 4×4 array with node connections from each neuron in a given column layer to all the neurons in the succeeding column layer, as shown in the schematic the figure below.

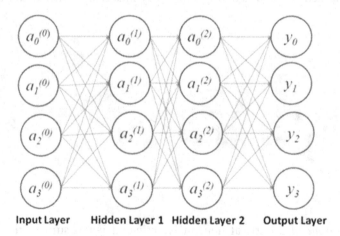

| Input Layer | Hidden Layer 1 | Hidden Layer 2 | Output Layer |

The activation of an individual artificial neuron is represented by the elements in the network as designated below,

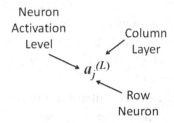

where *(L)* is the layer number, the subscript *j* denotes the row neurons in the layer *L*, and the y_j in the ANN structure figure are the elements of the decisional output vector.

The artificial neural network's layers are held in computer memory as volume matrices (second-rank tensors) with the artificial neuron activation level as elements, typically with two dimensions for spatial distribution and one for color, and vectors (first-rank tensors) for decisional output. The elements can be binary-activated as either "on" or "off" as in the biological neural network or gradation-activated with levels reflecting the intensity of the light from the viewed image as in digital cameras.

Artificial intelligence algorithms are executed by basic mathematical matrix operations on the ANN's matrix layers, including addition, subtraction, multiplication, convolution, inner and outer vector products, thus incarnating an artificial neural network's "thinking" process, while parameterization and gradient descent backpropagation effectuates the ANN's "learning", and how well it learns and recognizes will be a measure of its "artificial intelligence".

The number, size, and type of hidden layers are determined by the recognition task. Generally speaking, an artificial neural network with two or more hidden layers is considered to be a *deep neural network* (DNN). If all the artificial neurons in a succeeding layer are connected to each of the neurons in a preceding layer (as shown in the figure), the layers are said to be *fully connected*; if only some of the neurons in the preceding layer are connected to a succeeding layer, they form sub-matrix *windows* (called *filters* or *kernels*) in a *convolutional layer* whereby sectors of a preceding layer are selected for specific, finer or coarser, and positional *feature extraction* in *convolutional neural network* (CNN) computer vision.[2]

---

[2] For CNNs see Chapter 19.

In *feedforward* mode, the activated neurons connect the artificial neurons in succeeding artificial neurons in the network to form synaptic patterns of artificial neuron activation, just as in a biological neural network. However, in an artificial neural network the importance of each artificial neuron's activation level towards forming a pattern is artificially modulated by weighting and biasing the activations in a procedure called *parameterization* that helps to distinguish the features of the pattern.[3]

The weights and biases are initially arbitrarily assigned, forming a blank canvas for the artificial neural network to perceive patterns by enhancement of significant features and diminution of insignificant ones (such as noise or background). In *supervised learning*, the ANN is presented with a labeled training dataset, it attempts to match the dataset by adjusting the initially random values of the weights and biases to minimize the difference (*error*) between its activation pattern and the labeled training dataset by *gradient descent* and *backpropagating* that error through its network layers. When the error approaches zero (converges), the distinguishing features of the training set data has been learned, to be used for future recognition tasks.

Generally, the first hidden layer detects "high-level" features such as edges from clear shifts in neuron activation level, for example the triangular edges of a cat's ears, the second hidden layer detects "low-level features" such as the color of fur, and succeeding layers pick out or refine features like patterns in the fur in a process of *hierarchical feature extraction*. After delineating the features by parameter adjustment commensurate with minimizing the error with the training set, the combined result will provide characteristic features of a cat to be stored for later recognition of viewed objects.

Adding more hidden layers and employing convolutional layers for finer feature extraction and relative position should result in a more refined composite array of features, but additional layers of course carry a greater computational burden.

There are many *hyperparameters* that can be added and adjusted to fine-tune the artificial neural network's recognition capability, and the backpropagation gradient descent can be hyperparameterized for greater stability and speed of convergence.[4]

---

[3] Cf. Chapters 15, 16, and 17.
[4] For hyperparameterization, see Chapter 20.

After the supervised training, if the ANN wants to play chess, *Go*, or video games, it can further undergo *reinforcement learning* (RL) wherein rewards and punishments are given based on the ANN's moves in the games being helpful or unhelpful in reaching a goal commensurate with success.

A *deep belief neural network* (DBN) fuels the ANN probability distributions rather than objects or data, providing the ANN with a prior *belief* based on those probabilities about which it may be trying to ascertain. For example, in automatic speech recognition, a *Hidden Markov Model* employs a Markov chain to provide statistical probabilities to infer letters, words, or speech sequences whose occurrences are more probable than others, in cases such as vowels after consonants and figures of speech.

Since speech recognition is strongly dependent not only on acoustic patterns, but also on the timing of utterances, a *recurrent neural network* (RNN) delays, activates, or deactivates selected artificial neurons for temporal characterization of the speech and for identifying inferences based on prior patterns of speech (recurrence).

In *unsupervised learning*, the ANN learns from scratch by training against different improving versions of itself in a process of self-strengthening from the bottom up to ultimately develop into a pure-play *inference engine* such as AlphaGoZero which dominated human champions in chess, *Go*, and video games without *a priori* knowing the rules of the games, and is capable of learning pattern and speech recognition directly from actual speech without supervised training.

All of these different types of artificial neural networks, the parameterization, gradient descent, backpropagation, and hyperparameterization will be described in more detail in the following chapters.

CHAPTER 14

Pattern Recognition

A child upon seeing a cat for the first time, and being told by her parents what it is called, creates an image with the prime features of fur, four legs, a long tail, pointy ears, big round eyes, whiskers, and a small pink triangular nose, all arranged in an appealing configuration. The child's visual cortex forms the compound image, labeling it as a "cat" and stores it in memory.

In computer vision, light reflected from an object is picked up by a camera's lens and transmitted through an optic nerve-like relay to retina-like photodetectors that convert light to proportional electrical signals. Those signals are then analog-to-digital converted by sampling the signals at regular intervals and assigning each sample a number representing the level of brightness in a range from 0 to 1, called *greyscale* for digital entry into an array of pixels.

The array of pixels is represented in a computer as a two-dimensional matrix of pixels of different light intensity with a third dimension holding the primary colors typically red, green, blue (RGB) in proportions that can together generate any color, much like a television camera does in reproducing images on a liquid crystal display (LCD) screen.

Computer vision, however, does more than just reproduce an image of the object for viewing, the computer's three-dimensional volume matrix, in analogy with the human visual cortex, constitutes an artificial neural network (ANN) that can form and store *feature maps* of objects by artificial neuron synaptic connection patterns just like the biological visual cortex forms a mental image.

DOI: 10.1201/9781003214892-18

ANN then, just like a child learning to recognize objects, can undergo supervised training on labeled datasets. The difference between ANN's synaptic patterns and the training dataset is minimized by adjusting weight and bias parameters applied to the artificial neuron brightness levels to more closely match the training set brightness level patterns, iteratively reducing the "error" in the artificial neural network layers to create synaptic pattern *feature maps* of the viewed object to be stored and labeled in ANN's memory for subsequent recognition.

In *classification* pattern recognition, when an object is presented to ANN for recognition, ANN's labeled feature maps are compared with the viewed object and the object is classified. In *clustering* pattern recognition, unlabeled data is presented to ANN, who then groups the data in accord with feature similarities.

The data can be represented by vectors with the components being the features such as size, shape, color, and so on, and their "closeness" determined by the inner (dot)product of different vectors. Most pattern recognition algorithms "recognize" based on statistical inference, and output layers list the probabilities of the recognition of specific features.

Labeled template recognition can be used for identifying relatively simple, well-defined whole objects, such as printed digits and letters of the alphabet, and clearly specified component parts for robotic assembly, but objects that are even only slightly different may not be classified accurately using templates.

For pattern recognition of more complicated objects and scenes, edges are easiest to detect as they are an abrupt greyscale change in transitioning from the background to the object, for example a cat's ears; likewise for abrupt color changes like an orange cat lying on a blue rug.

However, even abrupt changes can be obscured by *noise* in the form of variations in texture, scratches or electronic instability in the recognition system. Such noise can be *smoothed* by replacing the pixel brightness value with the average or median of itself and its neighbors, thus eliminating the noise but preserving the contrast.

Depth perception is gained by two separated cameras for stereographic imaging, but this requires correlation of the corresponding points of each detector's image. This can be done by reducing the greyscale arrays to edge maps, scanning the maps for similar appearances to identify the corresponding points, then measuring the distance to each camera's image plane, and from those differences, reconstructing a three-dimensional image point-by-point.

A seemingly very involved process requiring almost instantaneous multiple computations for every pixel in an image, but this is just what a computer can do, in this case almost as well as two biological eyes.

An important feature for recognition is an object's *texture*; that is, regular patterns of pixel brightness, such as the *structural analysis* of *tokens* (salient features) like kernels in an ear of corn, and *statistical analysis of directional coherence* like a cat's fur. Tokens and coherence can be relatively easy to detect by means of the statistical probability that a pixel's intensity level will be similar to that of its near neighbors.

A camera needs only three *primary* colors ("primary" meaning no one color of the primary three can be made from mixtures of the other two), typically red, green, and blue (RGB), because the admixture of components of each primary color can produce *any* color. This can be represented by a simple equation,

$$Any\ \ Color = rR + gG + bB$$

where *r, g,* and *b* are the component amounts of each primary color. So in a three-dimensional coordinate system with red, green, and blue axes, any color can be represented by a point in the *3D color space* from the value of its RGB components.

One of the main difficulties of color recognition is that its three independent attributes, *hue, intensity,* and *saturation,* depend critically on the type, angle, and intensity of illumination on the object. To recognize hue, computer vision must first determine the intensity and saturation; the intensity can be taken as the average of the three RGB intensity values and the saturation is the ratio of color to illumination, however the accurate distinction of colors in computer vision may still be difficult under different lighting conditions.[1]

Combinations of shape, texture, and color called *features* can be *extracted* for classification of, for example, strawberries and bananas in a basket of fruits based solely on their different shape and color, but separating strawberries from tomatoes would require size scale and texture analysis.

For more complex objects, *structural relationships* must be employed for recognition, for example the legs, tail, pointy ears, fur, big round eyes,

---

[1] For details on color reproduction, see *Time-Life* 1989 series *Understanding Computers,* and the author's book, Chen, R.H. 2011, *Liquid Crystal Displays, Fundamental Physics and Technology,* Wiley.

and triangular nose must be to be identified as a cat, but different poses, such as sitting serenely and lying on its back with legs akimbo, must still be classified as a cat.

Suppose an artificial neural network was presented with a cute little orange shorthair puppy, but its training set, in the dog classification primarily consisted of large dogs such as great danes and German shepherds, and its cat classification included many cute small orange shorthair kittens, then ANN may well misidentify the dog as a cat.

If after many more training runs to enlarge and refine the dog feature maps, our puppy is still misidentified as a cat, it will be incumbent on ANN to undergo more supervised learning on puppy dog training sets.

Alternatively, ANN could recalibrate the cat feature maps to emphasize the apparently distinguishable differences, for example a cat's pink nose as opposed to a dog's black none, so the third dimension color matrix element pink for the nose should be more heavily weighted or a pink nose-color bias hand-engineered for cats.

By more training sets including say dog lookalike floppy-eared Scottish Fold cats and cat lookalike Samoyed dogs, plus more training epochs with hand-engineered weights and biases (for example a greater bias towards cats in response to their pink noses, then progressively finer distinctions can be made, and ANN will be better able to classify dogs and cats.

CHAPTER 15

Parameterization

The hidden layers in an artificial neural network conjunctively extract distinctive features by feedforward artificial neuron activation from one layer to the next for hierarchical feature extraction. In biological vision systems, cortical neurons are believed to be binary activated (on/off) and only activation levels above some threshold will instigate a synaptic connection to other neurons. In artificial neural networks, the initial activation levels can be proportional to the input signal intensity, providing scaled information, but the activation levels usually are randomly selected, providing a blank canvas that when modulated by *parameterization*, better reflects the training set data.

Parameterization provides greater significance to distinctive features by enhancing artificial neuron activation levels, or conversely diminishing the indistinguishing neuron activation levels, by multiplying the activation level by a weighting factor and adding a bias to the sum of activation levels in a given layer.

A *perceptron* is an artificial neuron that takes multiple binary (*0* or *1*) inputs x_i and produces a single binary output a (*Yes* = 1 or *No* = 0). Each x_i input is multiplied by a weight w_i reflecting the significance of that input, the weighted inputs are summed, and if the weighted sum is less than or greater or equal to some chosen threshold bias b, the decision a to activate (*yes*) or not (*no*) is made, as illustrated by the schematic figure,[1]

---

[1] Ref. Rosenblatt, F. 1958, *Psychological Review*, Vol. 65, 6. Example adapted from Nielsen. M., *Neural Networks and Deep Learning*, academia.edu online pdf. Perceptrons can be implemented as NAND gates, so they can be programmed in integrated circuit (IC) design.

DOI: 10.1201/9781003214892-19

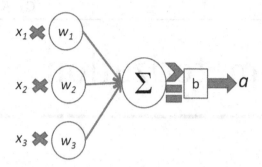

For example, you are trying to decide whether to attend a piano re-cital; there are a few decisional factors but it is a binary decision, *yes* or *no*. Say the input factors are:

x_1 = *close by so can walk,*
x_2 = *girlfriend goes with you,*
x_3 = *girlfriend's little brother comes too.*

You analyze the situation: You like piano music, the recital is close by, and you think your girlfriend would like to go with you, *but* she may bring her little brother along. In that case do you still want to go? Is any one factor decisive? If not, then a deeper analysis is required.

The relative importance of each input factor can be determined by attaching a weight to it; for instance, having no car and little money, within walking distance is important, so $w_1 = 3$, your girlfriend coming is very important, so $w_2 = 5$, but her little brother also coming is a definite negative, so $w_3 = -4$. You like piano music so the threshold for attending is a low (for biases) $b = 6$.

Therefore, if you can walk to the concert and your girlfriend will come without her little brother, the weighted sum is $1 \times 3 + 1 \times 5 + 0 \times (-4) = 8 > 6$, and so the decision will be to go, you can walk with only her to the recital. If she (and presumably her little brother) will not come with you, then you won't go even if you can walk to the recital since $1 \times 3 + 0 \times 5 + 0 \times (-4) = 3$ is below the threshold. If she will go but brings her little brother, your decision is more difficult, but the perceptron will decide for you. The weighted sum is $1 \times 3 + 1 \times 5 + 1 \times (-4) = 4 < 6$, so you will not go if her little brother comes along.

Parameterization clearly helps decision-making, but the perceptron has also identified a critical factor, namely little brother. Your decision can be helped along by finding some ground truth, for instance if (hopefully) little brother has violin lessons that night. The worst case is of course your girl-friend does not come with you, but her little brother does, you have to pay for an Uber ride, and the pieces played at the recital are all atonal.

Interestingly, in addition to deciding for you whether to go or not, the perceptron also reveals an *inference* that piano music may not be all that important to you; that is, your girlfriend's unfettered accompaniment is likely more important than any cultural pretensions you may have.

If you find out that the recital will have pieces by composers that you particularly like, you can lower the threshold towards attending; that is, the bias towards attending is increased, perhaps even to the extent of little brother tagging along being worth it.

The perceptron therefore is a sophisticated decision-making device operated by assigning weights that signify the relative positive and ne-gative significance of decisional factors, with a threshold bias reflecting the importance of the decision.

This kind of *parameterization* in artificial neural networks is done by treating the artificial neuron layer as a perceptron, weighting each neu-ron's activation level and biasing the sum in a layer to enhance or di-minish the effect of that neuron layer on the activation of the succeeding layer's neurons to ultimately form synaptic patterns in the network re-presenting features in the training set data.

In the perceptron example above, the weights and biases were assigned according to an individual's preferences, but just how are the weights and biases determined for any given situation by a machine which ostensibly has no preferences?

The *initial* values of the weights can be *arbitrarily* assigned because they will be tuned by a parameterization that will iteratively adjust the values of the weights for matching a labeled training data set, thereby constituting a learning process. Random values of a Normal (Gaussian) distribution are typically used in *initialization* so as to avoid subsequent learning of different objects being similar because of the same initial weightings.

Described mathematically, the weighted activation levels of all the neurons in layer (0) of the network are connected to every neuron in the succeeding layer (1) of the artificial neural network and modulated by weights; for example, the activation of the 0th neuron in the succeeding layer (1) is given by the sum of the ith row and j^{th} layer weights $w_{i,j}$ times the activation levels of the preceding 0th layer's j neurons,[2]

---

[2] For an excellent video description of parameterization, see *3Blue1Brown* YouTube, October 5, 2017.

$$a_0^{(1)} = w_{0,0} a_0^{(0)} + w_{0,1} a_1^{(0)} + w_{0,2} a_2^{(0)} + \ldots$$

The weights thus are like a measure of the strength of the connections between the neurons in adjacent layers in the network. As such, it can be seen that the first synaptic connection strength pattern in the input layer, based solely on random activation levels are refined by adjusting the weights and biases in accord with minimization of differences with the training set data. Hidden layer hierarchical feature extraction will further dovetail the characteristic features and their surroundings.

To further improve image feature discrimination capability, different biases (b_0), can be added to the sum of weighted activation levels, for instance positive biases to ensure that the weighted sum in a neuron layer will meaningfully contribute to the feature extraction of distinct features, or conversely negative biases to downplay or totally ignore irrelevant features and noise,

$$a_0^{(1)} = w_{0,0} a_0^{(0)} + w_{0,1} a_1^{(0)} + w_{0,2} a_2^{(0)} + \ldots + b^{(0)}.$$

Instead of the binary "on" (1) or "off" (0) of biological cortical neurons or the unlimited linear increase of light intensity in the interval (0, ∞), optical displays use a greyscale of *decimal* values between 0 and 1 for activation intensities. Because the decimal fractions within a range can be infinitesimally small, the artificial neuron activation level can be extremely fine yet still distinguishable (particularly by a computer). Furthermore, small changes in weights and biases will properly produce small changes in the feature maps, and will not inadvertently cause the derivatives in gradient descent to flip in reversals of significance, nor will large changes in weighted sums and biases cause the gradient descent backpropagation to diverge.

Greyscale is generated by the *sigmoid function* (also called the *logistic function*) that restricts variables x to the domain (0, 1) to produce a countably infinite number of possible values between the asymptotic 1 and 0,

$$Sigmoid\ Function = \sigma(x) = \frac{1}{1 + e^{-x}}$$

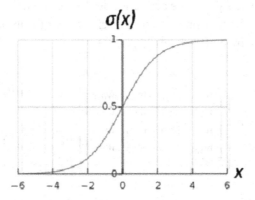

To express the probabilities used in pattern recognition, the sigmoid function output must be positive because there is no such thing as a negative probability; so since the exponential function e has no negative values, it is ideally suited to provide positive greyscale values.[3]

The sigmoid function can also represent a smoothed version of a step function, so it can also "*Yes/No*" differentiate, depending on the value of x as either negative or positive as can be seen by the plot of $\sigma(x)$ in the figure above, and thus objects can be separated into the left and right sides of the graph, and so can be used for object classification, such as distinguishing cats from dogs, germane from spam emails, and classifying hip-hop and classical music aficionados in social networks.

The sigmoid function for one neuron in one layer operates on the neuron activation level weights and biases as

$$\sigma\left(w_{0,0}a_0^{(0)} + w_{0,1}a_1^{(0)} + w_{0,2}a_2^{(0)} + \ldots + b^{(0)}\right) = \frac{1}{1 - e^{-\left(w_{0,0}a_0^{(0)} + w_{0,1}a_1^{(0)} + w_{0,2}a_2^{(0)} + \ldots + b^{(0)}\right)}}.$$

There are multiple neurons in each layer of a neural network, so a given neuron receiving synaptic greyscale activation from a preceding layer's neurons itself has an activation level that can be represented by a multiplication of a weights matrix times the preceding layer neuron activation level vector, plus the bias vector, and then the whole kit operated on by the sigmoid function.

---

[3] Like the sigmoid function, *fuzzy logic* expresses degrees of truthfulness by assigning values between *0* and *1* instead of the binary *0 or 1*.

For example, the greyscale activation levels for the neurons in layer (1) as a function of the neuron activation levels of layer (0) in our simple 4×4 neural network in matrix form is given by,

$$a^{(1)} = \sigma \left\{ \begin{bmatrix} w_{0,0} & w_{01} & w_{0,2} & w_{0,3} \\ w_{1,0} & w_{1,1} & w_{1,2} & w_{1,3} \\ w_{2,0} & w_{2,1} & w_{2,2} & w_{2,3} \\ w_{3,0} & w_{3,1} & w_{3,2} & w_{3,3} \end{bmatrix} \begin{bmatrix} a_0^{(0)} \\ a_1^{(0)} \\ a_2^{(0)} \\ a_3^{(0)} \end{bmatrix} + \begin{bmatrix} b_0^{(0)} \\ b_1^{(0)} \\ b_2^{(0)} \\ b_3^{(0)} \end{bmatrix} \right\}$$

where $a^{(1)}$ is a column vector representing all the weighted neuron activation levels in layer *1* expressed in terms of the sigmoid function of the weights matrix times the previous layer's neuron activation levels plus the biases for each weighted vector sum. The equation then can be written compactly as,

$$a^{(1)} = \sigma(Wa^{(0)} + b^{(0)})$$

where W is the *weighting matrix*, and b is a column vector of biases in layer (0), with the sigmoid function operating on the vector $Wa^{(0)} + b^{(0)}$ to produce the weighted greyscale activation $a^{(1)}$ of the neurons in layer 1. This elegant equation explicitly shows the dependence of succeeding layer neuron activations on the weighted neuron activation levels and their biases of all the neurons in the preceding layer.

Seen in this way, each neuron layer is a perceptron arrayed in a multilayered network called appropriately enough a *Multilayer Perceptron* (MLP) model, the earliest modern artificial neural network. Each neuron has an input comprised of the weighted and biased neuron activation levels from the preceding layer, and a resultant activation of its own, which will be subsequently modulated by weights and biases for input to the neurons in the next succeeding layer in the so-called *feedforward* mode.

The activation of layer (1) neurons in terms of the sigmoid function is,

$$a^{(1)} = \sigma(Wa^{(0)} + b^{(0)}) = \frac{1}{1 - e^{-(Wa^{(0)}+b^{(0)})}}$$

The activation of every layer's neurons then must be processed as above, and since artificial neural networks may have many layers and neurons, together with voluminous training set data, even though computationally burdensome, such a network is eminently programmable because computers are very good at the linear algebra of matrices, and computations are fast using massively-parallel graphical processing units (GPUs) which can compute the matrix operations simultaneously.

Such daunting calculations show why artificial intelligence could not really take off until the advent of mass-storage, ultra-fast parallel-processing computers, and the creation of efficient learning and recognition algorithms taking advantage of that hardware.

In addition to the new hardware and innovative learning algorithms made possible thereby, artificial intelligence has been developed more rapidly and comprehensively by free open source computational software from *MatLab, Octave*, and *Numpy*, freely accessible training sets such as *ImageNet*, and the free public use and inclusive system development of host-computer coding platforms such as *GitHub* and *RedHat*, all conveniently available to anyone on the Internet.

With the 21st Century's decentralization (democratization) and sharing (communization) of artificial intelligence resources, rapid widespread AI development could proceed vigorously after the *AI Winter* of the 1990s.

The sigmoid function and the hyperbolic tangent function (*tanh*) were commonly used in early AI systems, but more recently-developed systems use the simpler *Rectified Linear Unit* (ReLU) function defined as,

$$f(x) = max(0, x),$$

which is just a straight *45°* line that changes all the negative activations to *0*, and with a *softmax* function in the network, will provide greyscale. This simple function is obviously easier to compute than sigmoid and hyperbolic tangent and therefore faster to process while making no significant differences in accuracy compared to other greyscale functions.

Furthermore, since the learning gradient approaches zero when the sigmoid and tanh neurons activation level outputs are near either *0* or *1*, learning will severely slow down or stop (saturate). An open-ended ReLU neuron will not saturate, so the learning will not slow down, however if the final weighted input to a ReLU neuron is negative, the gradient vanishes (goes to zero), and so the ReLU neuron will also stop learning altogether. These imperfections have spawned a plethora of alternate greyscale conversion functions which can be employed *ad hoc* as needed for particular AI tasks.[4]

Choosing among sigmoid, tanh, ReLU, and others thus is an exercise in first addressing the task at hand in its simplest implementation, and then as problems arise, finding the best corrective functions and procedures, usually by trial and error. When improved classification and prediction accuracy are required, algorithm tuning, different cost functions to enhance convergence, hyperparameteration, and so can be called on, all the while keeping in mind computational burden. Procedural choices often are made by just going with what works best and not necessarily completely understanding why something works better than something else.

The parameterization of the artificial neuron activation levels provides a means for dynamic adjustment of synaptic patterns for feature extraction, but how exactly are the weights and biases adjusted so that the artificial neural network can learn, and thus exhibit artificial intelligence?

---

[4] ReLU alleviates the sigmoid function vanishing gradient problem because the deeper layers train very slowly due to the exponential gradient decrease to values so small that they do not change the weights. Other greyscale conversion functions are CUBE, ELU, HARDSIGMOID, HARDTANH, IDENTITY, LEAKY RELU, RATIONAL TANH, RRELU, SOFTMAX, SOFTPLUS, and SOFTSIGN.

CHAPTER 16

Gradient Descent

A n artificial neural network (ANN) must be trained to recognize objects and data, young ANN is learning how to recognize by being presented with training sets of images and data. The neuron activation levels have been parameterized initially by a Normal distribution of weights and biases, her neural network is thus a blank canvas, she is ready to *machine learn*.[1]

The difference between her initial random artificial neural activation level distribution and the training set data naturally will be quite large, her learning task then is to reduce that difference in order to extract features characteristic of the training set images and data to store in memory in order to recognize images and data presented to her. That difference is quantified by a *Loss Function*, expressed by the sum of the squares of the differences between the outputted activation levels of the decisional row vector neurons in layer L and the training set y vector,[2]

$$Loss\ Function = (a^{(L)} - y)^2.$$

As employed in artificial intelligence, taking the average of all of the Loss

---

[1] A Normal (Gaussian) distribution takes random noise into consideration and the bias parameter considers systematic error.

[2] The reason for taking the square of the difference in the Loss Function is that if the goal is to have the difference approach zero, and since a negative loss (profit?) is just as bad as a positive loss, taking the square of the difference considers both. Squaring also renders outliers more pronounced, eliminates the possibility of negative values, and is a measure of the statistical variance; furthermore, the derivative of a squared expression is also easy to calculate, leaving the difference intact as a factor. The absolute value of the difference is not used because it regresses to the median instead of the mean, and it is undefined at the origin, causing unneeded computational problems. Refer to any book on statistics for details, for example Navidi, W 2019, *Statistics for Scientists and Engineers*, McGraw-Hill Education.

DOI: 10.1201/9781003214892-20

Functions over all the m samples in the training set gives the *Average Cost Function*; it comprises all the weights and all the biases in the network averaged over all the samples i in the training set.

The Average Cost Function $\bar{C}$ is a term taken from economics as the cost of inefficient production, thus C can be thought of just the *Cost of Being Wrong* in regard to matching the training set, so the minimization of the Average Cost function will reduce the differences between ANN's neuron activation patterns and the training set.

Calculating the Average Cost Function will not be as computationally burdensome as calculating the Loss Function of each training set example in turn, and it is noted by some that taking the average will beneficially average out noise and irrelevant factors that may be in the data.

The Average Cost Function then is defined as,[3]

$$Average\ Cost\ Function = \bar{C} = \frac{1}{2m} \sum_{i=1}^{m} [(a^{(L)} - y)^2]_i,$$

where recall from Chapter 15 that

$$a^{(L)} = \sigma(Wa^{(L-1)} + b^{(L-1)}).$$

In elementary calculus, minimization of any continuous and differentiable function of a single variable is easily done by taking the derivative with respect to that variable and setting it equal to zero to find where the slope is horizontal (that is zero slope), which is the minimum point of a concave curve.

Taking C to represent any Cost Function, a quadratic C is continuous and differentiable, so it can be minimized, for example with respect to a weighting factor variable w,

$$Set \frac{\partial C}{\partial w} = 0.$$

To find the minimum point with respect to a weighting variable w, randomly choose a point on the curve, and determine what direction to move in order to reach the minimum point on the C-w curve. This direction is

---

[3] The ½ factor in the Cost Function equation is for convenience as it cancels out during calculations because the derivative of a squared variable gives a factor of 2, rendering the form of the subsequent equations simpler.

given by the sign of the slope of the curve at that chosen point; the analogy is a ball rolling on the Average Cost Function curve, it will roll left if the slope is positive and right if the slope is negative, and with a speed depending on the severity of the slope. If not rolling too fast, it will stop at the horizontal slope minimum, thereby determining a minimum *Cost*.

This gives the clue that this operation would be best described using a vector since it has both magnitude and direction. From a randomly chosen point on the Average Cost Function versus weighting variable curve, as the minimum point is approached, since the absolute value of the slope decreases and the rolling ball slows down, the learning algorithm can accordingly reduce the step size of the ball to prevent inadvertently overshooting the minimum point.

Unfortunately, the Cost curve with respect to the variable w may have many concavities and therefore multiple *local minima* and also include convex curve maxima (that also have zero slope) as shown in the figure below at left, and the Cost will not be minimized with respect to a particular weighting variable unless the *global minimum*, meaning the absolute minimum of the Average Cost Function, and not just a local minima, is found. The problem of encountering local minima in the search for the global minimum has plagued artificial intelligence research since its inception.

If the minimization of the Cost Function for two variable weights is to be determined, instead of C-w curves there will be a three-dimensional contour of Cost Function versus weights as shown in the figure below at right, with a rolling ball searching for the minimum of the contour,

COST

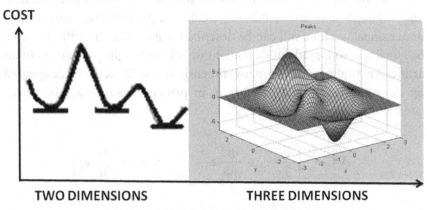

TWO DIMENSIONS   **THREE DIMENSIONS**

GRADIENT DESCENT PROGRESSION

Local and global minima for two-dimensional and three-dimensional models can be found by simply looking at the computer-generated C-w plots, but artificial neural networks usually have many, many weight and bias parameters, so the Cost will be a function of many, many variables, and any contour of greater than three-dimensions is impossible to visualize.

Although humans cannot physically visualize in greater than three dimensions, they can conceptually view with the mind's eye, and fortunately the computer can operate in almost infinite dimensions, and so the computation of Cost Function minimization with respect to any number of variables can be performed by finding the *gradient* of vector analysis. The gradient is a vector representing the direction of steepest *descent*, with a magnitude that is a measure of the steepness of the multidimensional contour, and for finding a minimum it will be a *gradient descent* and thus a *negative* gradient vector,

$$\text{\textit{Vector of Steepest Descent}} = -\textbf{grad}C = -\nabla C.$$

The gradient operating on the Cost Function C in an example for just the weighting variables in three dimensions is,

$$-\nabla C = -\left(\frac{\partial C}{\partial w_x} \textbf{\textit{i}} + \frac{\partial C}{\partial w_y} \textbf{\textit{j}} + \frac{\partial C}{\partial w_z} \textbf{\textit{k}} \right)$$

where $\textbf{\textit{i}}, \textbf{\textit{j}}, \textbf{\textit{k}}$ are the unit vectors in the x, y, and z directions respectively and w_i are the weights in those directions respectively.

A ball rolling on the Cost Function contour will roll towards minima, and although it is impossible to visualize, a greater than three multi-dimensional contour still can be described mathematically with the same ball analogy, so a gradient dependent on all the weight parameters in an artificial neural network of many dimensions j in "directions" designated by the unit "directional" vectors $\textbf{\textit{e}}_j$ in principle can always be calculated as,

$$-\nabla C = -\left(\frac{\partial C}{\partial w_1} \textbf{\textit{e}}_1 + \frac{\partial C}{\partial w_2} \textbf{\textit{e}}_2 + \frac{\partial C}{\partial w_3} \textbf{\textit{e}}_3 + \dots + \frac{\partial C}{\partial w_j} \textbf{\textit{e}}_j \right)$$

Multivariate calculus is a good example of how mathematics can broaden one's mind beyond what can be perceived by the senses. That is, "seeing is believing" is helpful, but neither necessary nor complete in mathematics where "seeing" really means conceptual contemplation.

This is one of the reasons why *doing mathematics* may indeed be the touchstone of intelligence, for no one can doubt that the construct and comprehension of the complex conjugate vector calculus of infinite-dimensional *Hilbert space* requires no little grey matter.[4]

The algorithm to compute the minimization of the Cost Function in multivariate calculus computes the gradient vector at a point on the multidimensional contour by taking a step in the gradient direction, and repeating the calculation of the gradient vector over and over again until you find a minimum. The size of the step is called the *learning rate*, a large step for fast learning will hasten the process to convergence and reduce computational burden, but too large a step may overstep a minimum.[5]

The gradient descent of the Cost Function will involve taking the derivatives of the sigmoid (or other greyscale conversion) function σ, the weighting matrix W, the previous layer activation levels $a^{(L-1)}$, and the previous layer biases $b^{(L-1)}$, altogether giving the values of the weights and biases that will cause the most rapid minimization of the Cost Function. The calculations are shown in the next Chapter for backpropagation.

The sign of the resulting adjusted weights and biases promoting Cost minimization indicates a higher (+) or lower (−) adjustment, and the relative magnitudes of the weights and biases reveal which of the adjustments will have the greatest impact in reducing the Cost, in other words, how sensitive the Cost is to a particular parameter adjustment.

The gradient descent therefore amazingly encodes the relative significance of each weight and bias towards minimizing the error and accurately reflecting a labeled training sample, in effect teaching the artificial neural network how to properly regard the training set data for what it represents.

Since the derivative of the gradient shows how the gradient is changing, as its absolute value decreases, it must be nearing a minimum, so the second derivative of the Cost can be arrayed in a *Hessian matrix*,

---

[4] Hilbert space is an infinite dimensional generalization of the Euclidean space of three dimensions that expands vector analysis to the measurement for instance of *distance* as a multidimensional vector inner (dot) product, and although that distance cannot be visualized, it is among many other invariant physical quantities based on the very abstract idea of symmetry in Nature, and very useful for mathematical physics calculations, particularly for the covariance requisite of Einstein's relativity, see the author's book Chen, R.H. 2017, *Einstein's Relativity, the Special and General Theories with their Cosmology*, McGraw-Hill Education.

[5] The learning rate will be described in Chapter 20 on Hyperparameterization.

from which the determinant of a second-order partial differential equation with respect to the scalar field of weights and biases can be calculated. Because the determinant is positive definite, it can be used to test for extrema; a minimum if the Hessian determinant is positive, and if negative, it is a maximum, and if zero, a saddle point of a hyperbolic paraboloid.

The fearsome burden of calculating second derivatives thankfully has some labor-saving techniques such as the gradient descent acting to change the *velocity* (already a derivative) instead of *position* which avoids the large second-order derivative calculations by taking a *momentum* with *friction* reducing the velocity as minima are approached in small steps from different points on the curve in a physics-oriented approach.[6]

Gradient descent and/or the Hessian will find the first minimum encountered, but will stop when the slope at that minimum is zero, essentially stopping the learning process, once again foundering on a local minimum hollow. At this point, it will be necessary to start the calculation from that point once again to find the next minimum, hopefully a *global* minimum instead of just another provincial local minimum.

---

[6] Nielsen, M. 2019, *Neural Networks and Deep Learning*, adademia.edu pdf.

CHAPTER 17

Backpropagation

The process of gradient descent to minimize the Cost Function employs the simple minimization calculus. But the artificial neural network (ANN) is forming synaptic connection patterns at each layer and passing them on to the succeeding layer. Therefore, gradient descent must operate throughout the layers of the artificial neural network with reference to preceding layers. This is done by performing gradient descent going backwards through the network, in a process called *backpropagation*, essentially a feedback loop adjusting the weights and biases to minimize the Cost Function through calculation of the gradient descent at each layer in terms of the preceding layer.

The significance of the activation level of each artificial neuron towards matching the training set data can be increased or decreased by changing their weights and biases, and since the activation levels of the preceding layer neurons will affect the activation levels of a given layer's neurons, going backwards through the neural network layer-by-layer and recursively adjusting the weight and bias parameters in each preceding layer in accord with minimizing the Cost of Being Wrong, in principle will ultimately match the ANN synaptic pattern to the training set data pattern.

Since every run requires considerable computational power, the training data typically is divided into *mini-batches* and run in turn as iterative *stochastic gradient descents* with validation and test sets to enhance the network's accuracy in matching the training set data.

Gradient descent backpropagation is based on the Gauss-Newton numerical analysis computation of non-linear partial differential equations

DOI: 10.1201/9781003214892-21

called *Newton's Method* where "Newton" refers to numerically taking the derivatives which Isaac Newton conceived. The process of backpropagation is based on the fundamental *chain rule* of differential calculus, as will be seen.

The *Loss Function* for a given artificial neural network layer L was given in Chapter 16 where $a^{(L)}$ is the activation vector of the row neurons in layer L and y is the training set vector,

$$Loss\ Function = (a^{(L)} - y)^2$$

Since this will be the *Cost of Being Wrong* for each layer L, to avoid confusion with the L designating the network layer, and further to be in accord with the AI literature, we will use C for the Cost Function per layer. It is understood that the Average Cost Function over all the training set examples of Chapter 16 is designated by $\bar{C}$.

As is often done in mathematical derivations, a change of variable makes life easier, so define a new variable $z^{(L)}$ in terms of the weights $w^{(L)}$ and the biases $b^{(L)}$ in layer L, and the activation level of the neurons $a^{(L-1)}$ in the previous layer $(L-1)$,

$$z^{(L)} = w^{(L)} a^{(L-1)} + b^{(L)}$$

Recall that the neuron activation level of a neuron, its weight and bias in layer L is converted to greyscale by operation of the sigmoid function,

$$a^{(L)} = \sigma(z^{(L)}) = \frac{1}{1 + e^{-z^{(L)}}}$$

To first compute the sensitivity of Cost to the change in weighting factor variable, $\partial C/\partial w$, the fundamental chain rule of calculus is used, which is the mathematical basis of the idea of backpropagation, we can write,[1]

$$\frac{\partial C}{\partial w^{(L)}} = \frac{\partial z^{(L)}}{\partial w^{(L)}} \cdot \frac{\partial a^{(L)}}{\partial z^{(L)}} \cdot \frac{\partial C}{\partial a^{(L)}}$$

---

[1] The logic of the chain rule of calculus can be made eminently clear by just cancelling each partial derivative numerator with the denominator of the following partial derivative.

Taking the derivatives of each term starting with the last term (with a prime on the sigmoid function σ means taking the derivative as shown),

$$\frac{\partial C}{\partial a^{(L)}} = 2(a^{(L)} - y),$$

$$\frac{\partial a^{(L)}}{\partial z^{(L)}} = \sigma'(z^{(L)}) \equiv \frac{\partial}{\partial z^{(L)}}\left(\frac{1}{1 + e^{z^{(L)}}}\right),$$

$$\frac{\partial z^{(L)}}{\partial w^{(L)}} = a^{(L-1)}.$$

The last equation says that the change in $z^{(L)}$ with respect to the weight $w^{(L)}$ in layer L depends on the activation intensity of the neuron in the preceding layer, $a^{(L-1)}$; that is, as in the synaptic patterns of biological brains, the neurons that fire together are wired together, and in the backpropagation of artificial neural networks, the artificial neurons that fire together are chained together. So,

$$\frac{\partial C}{\partial w^{(L)}} = a^{(L-1)} \cdot \sigma'(z^{(L)}) \cdot 2(a^{(L)} - y).$$

Now average the Costs with respect to the weights in a given layer L over the m training set examples,

$$\frac{\partial \bar{C}}{\partial w^{(L)}} = \frac{1}{m}\sum_{k=0}^{m-1}\frac{\partial C_k}{\partial w^{(L)}}$$

This gives the average of a dataset for one element of the gradient descent vector which includes all the partial derivatives of the weights of a given layer.

Repeating the process for the rate of change of Cost with respect to the biases $\partial C / \partial b$ gives,

$$\frac{\partial C}{\partial b^{(L)}} = \frac{\partial z^{(L)}}{\partial b^{(L)}} \cdot \frac{\partial a^{(L)}}{\partial z^{(L)}} \cdot \frac{\partial C}{\partial a^{(L)}}$$

But from the definition of the new variable $z^{(L)}$ given before,

$$\frac{\partial z^{(L)}}{\partial b^{(L)}} = 1$$

and since the other terms have been determined above,

$$\frac{\partial C}{\partial b^{(L)}} = \sigma'(z^{(L)}) \cdot 2(a^{(L)} - y),$$

and recall that

$$\sigma'(z^{(L)}) = \frac{\partial}{\partial z^{(L)}} \left(\frac{1}{1 + e^{z^{(L)}}} \right).$$

Now just repeat the process iterating backwards through all the layers, one-by-one to minimize the Cost with respect to the weights and biases of the layers in turn.

To consider each and every neuron in the layers, just add row subscripts to the a's and two subscripts (for row j and column k) to the w's in the terms so that[2]

$$z_j^{(L)} = \dots + w_{jk}^{(L)} a_k^{(L-1)} + \dots$$

$$a_j^{(L)} = \sigma(z_j^{(L)})$$

and the Cost over the j rows of neurons will be the sum over m training set examples,

$$C = \sum_{j=0}^{m_L - 1} (a_j^{(L)} - y_j)^2$$

---

[2] In keeping with the notation formalism used in the AI literature, j denotes the row (output) and k the column (input) instead of the more natural i row (input) and j column (output) used earlier in describing the artificial neural network because the latter would require replacing the weight matrix with its transpose, thereby messing up the application of the weight matrix on the activation level. Ref. Nielsen. M 2019, *Neural Networks and Deep Learning*, academia.edu pdf, p. 41 footnote.

The chain rule expression is now,

$$\frac{\partial C}{\partial a_k^{(L-1)}} = \sum_{j=0}^{m_L-1} \frac{\partial z^{(L)}}{\partial a_k^{(L-1)}} \cdot \frac{\partial a_j^{(L)}}{\partial z^{(L)}} \cdot \frac{\partial C}{\partial a_j^{(L)}}$$

Then sum the above expression over L for all the different layers. This is the same as for the single neuron example, except for the Cost with respect to the activations in Layer L-1; that is, the L-1 neurons influence the Cost through multiple different paths because of the multiple neurons in the layers, and they must be all added up.

Performing these derivatives for a given layer will adjust the weights and biases in relation to the preceding layer in accord with minimizing the Cost, and the activation levels of the artificial neurons (hopefully) will converge to match the training set data.

Ostensibly a great deal of computation, all these calculations can be efficiently performed by freely accessible software computational programs such as those found on GitHub.[3]

In summary, the chain rule gives expressions for the derivatives that determine each component of the gradient descent vector by repeatedly stepping downhill through the network layers on the steepest slope towards the minimization of the Cost by adjusting weights and biases in each layer in turn by going backwards through the network.

For understanding today's artificial intelligence, it is critical to realize that the artificial neural network *was not specifically told what features of the training set data to learn or how to learn* those features, the network learned *all by itself* because it knows calculus; that is, the AI machine knows the minimization techniques and how to apply the chain rule of calculus for backpropagating an error.

This is the essence of bottom-up artificial intelligence, the AI machine was not programmed to perform specific tasks or recognize particular things from the top-down; rather within its hidden layers and through its algorithms, gradient descent and backpropagation, the machine can perform and arrive at conclusions based on images and data. In other words once trained, the AI machine can act *autonomously*, and then through reinforcement and unsupervised learning, it can learn more and improve its capabilities on its own.

---

[3] For a simple example of a manual calculation, refer to Mazur, M., "A step-by-step back propagation example", mattmazur.com.

CHAPTER 18

Convolutional Neural Networks

T he human visual cortex is segmented into small clusters of neurons that are responsive to specific features or sectors in the visual field, these so-called *receptive fields* are then merged to constitute the entire mental image in the neural network.

In analogy with the visual cortex, a computer vision artificial neural network receives light reflected from the object of interest and converts the photon to electrical signals that activate artificial neurons in the network's input layer matrix.

In a multilayer perceptron (MLP) neural network, all the neurons in adjacent layers are *fully connected*, and therefore cannot directly pick out and focus on specific areas of the visual field for closer examination.

The hidden layers of a *convolutional neural network* (CNN) are not fully connected, but rather are interleaved with smaller windows of matrix *filters* akin to the receptive fields of the human visual cortex. In a typical CNN, a first *convolutional filter* sweeps over the input matrix layer, and succeeding convolutional filters stride over the preceding hidden layer picking out features to help constitute a *feature map* of the viewed object.

A *convolution* is simply a mathematical operation of two functions to produce a third function that represents how the functions are conjoined. In two dimensions, a mapped function $f(x, y)$, is *convolved* by figuratively placing a *convolving* filter $h(x, y)$ over $f(x, y)$, spatially stepping through it and integrating the result,

DOI: 10.1201/9781003214892-22

$$Convolution = \iint f(x, y)h(x + 1, y + 1)\,dxdy.$$

The double integral is over the filter's x times y area spanning a layer sector of the same size, the displacement shown is a $+1$ step (typically starting from the upper left-hand corner and first to the right, then down) of the $h(x + 1, y + 1)$ filter over the $f(x, y)$ as it strides step-by-step over successive same-sized sectors of the input matrix $f(x, y)$, extracting feature map matrices of the same size as the filter. The filter type, size, starting point, and step size can be chosen to fit the mapping task at hand.

The convolution process combines taking the *inner product* of the vector rows of two adjacent matrices and then integrating, which is a measure of the degree of *confluence* of vectors within the matrix.

The inner (or dot) product of two vectors is defined as the magnitudes of the vectors times the cosine of the angle θ between them. The dot product can be illustrated for those who like basketball by the trajectory vector of the ball approaching the basket from the top of its arc with θ being the angle between the vector of the ball and the vertical axis vector through the hoop. So if the ball is coming vertically down along the axis of the hoop ($\theta = 0°$ and $\cos\theta = 1$), it "sees" the full circular area of the hoop and thus has the maximum-sized target for a score. If the ball comes in horizontally ($\theta = 90°$ and $\cos\theta = 0$), it sees only the edge of the basket, and there is no possibility of a score. If the ball comes in at an angle of 60° (a relatively "flat" shot), $\cos\theta = 0.5$, it sees only half the area, so it has only half the chance of a vertically-falling shot. Generally, the smaller the angle of the ball with the vertical, the more likely the ball will go through the hoop as measured by the cosine of the angle that determines the size of the target hoop as "seen" by the basketball.

Of course, shooting a ball almost straight up so it falls almost vertically through the net takes inordinate strength and because of the long trajectory is more difficult to control, so trading-off, an angle of say 45° will give a 0.707 hoop area which is much better than a flat trajectory of say 75° which gives only a 0.26 hoop area target.[1]

---

[1] Premier players like Kobe Bryant and LeBron James with relatively flat jump shots are so talented that their percentage is still pretty good, but the high-percentages of high-arcing 3-point shooters like Steve Nash, Ray Allen, Stephen Curry, and the improbable Steve Kerr (whose very high shooting arcs resulted in his record for highest percentage of 3-point shots made in the NBA) are proof of the efficacy of the dot product for long-range shooting in basketball. Incidentally, the backspin of a shot helps to keep the ball on the desired trajectory, so Klay Thompson's high-arcing, tight backspin 3-pointers are not only beautiful to watch, but designed for maximum probability of a score.

From this, it can be seen that the dot product is a measure of the magnitude of the *union* of the two vectors as a scalar value. The inner product is a generalization of the dot product to multidimensional vector space, obtained by multiplying the corresponding elements of the row vectors in a multidimensional matrix and summing the products to produce a scalar measure of the union of the multiple vectors constituting a new matrix.

Taking the double integral over the inner product of the matrices produces a *confluence* over area that measures the converging of the vectors in the matrices, just as in the merging of two flowing rivers, from whence the term came.

A convolutional filter striding over an artificial neural network matrix layer can be seen as a *sliding* inner product that extracts the confluences between the filter and the matrix layer, detecting, augmenting, or dampening, and thereby extracting *features*.

As a filter matrix (also called a *kernel* or *window matrix*) glides over a matrix layer like a flashlight beam, it convolves the activation levels of the "illuminated" regions of the matrix, row by row. Prominent features will be enhanced because the elements of the *matrix layer* having higher-weighted activation levels will be affirmatively convolved by the inner product confluence and the higher-weighted activation level elements of the *filter*. Weaker features will be negatively convolved because of the inner product of small or negatively-weighted activation levels of the low-weighted activation levels in the matrix layer and the filter will be small or negative.

The double integral produces a sum calculated by adding the inner products of the row vectors of the filter matrix and the covered sector of the layer to produce a single activation level having *shared weights* and a *shared bias* registered in a single *destination pixel* that is positioned in the center of the registered section of the newly *convolved layer*. The weights and bias sharing scheme greatly reduces the computational burden, and may also reduce noise because of the convolution of all the shared weights and biases of the convolved area to a single destination pixel.

The process for one filter acting on an input matrix layer with the row vector inner product computation to produce a destination pixel on a new convolved layer is shown schematically in the figure below.[2]

---

[2] Figure and further explanation is available from the excellent article by Conelisse, D., *An intuitive guide to convolutional neural networks*, freecodecamp.org.

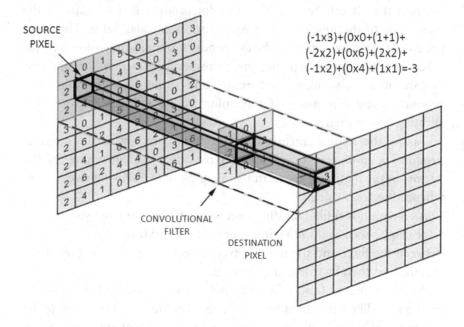

SOURCE PIXEL

$(-1\text{x}3)+(0\text{x}0+(1+1)+$
$(-2\text{x}2)+(0\text{x}6)+(2\text{x}2)+$
$(-1\text{x}2)+(0\text{x}4)+(1\text{x}1)=-3$

CONVOLUTIONAL FILTER

DESTINATION PIXEL

Many different filters may be employed one after the other to produce many feature maps, and all of the feature maps can be combined by producing the destination pixels in new convolved layers one by one, producing a final convolved layer matrix that can be flattened into a decisional vector.

A convolutional neural network thus delineates and positions prominent features, retrocedes specious features and dampens noise using filters to produce a series of convolved layers, allowing a faster and more refined feature extraction.

In supervised learning, a typical training set input might be a two-dimensional *480 × 480* pixel image presented to the CNN's initially "blank" input layer of random weights and biases. A *3 × 3* window matrix filter scans the training set input matrix for specific features such as edges, curves, and colors.

The filter can be composed of a sector of the input layer matrix itself, a specific feature filter such as the *Sobel Gx* edge filter, or a Normal (Gaussian) or other random distribution of element values that itself will be trained through multiple slides over the input layer matrix. However different filters should use different kinds of initialization to avoid increasing the probability that the filters extract the same features.

As the CNN runs through the training sets, just like the artificial neuron layers, the filters also learn from training sets. As such, the filters can provide bottom-up feature information that hand-engineered filters (likely expressing preconceptions) may not be able to extract or locate, particularly in the case of objects or images with unusual or unexpected features.

Because of the translational or rotational invariance of a specific feature (move or rotate a cat, and it's still a cat), filters can map specific features into different positions on succeeding convolutional layers, thereby providing spatial relationship among the features.

Furthermore, if an image is modified by crops, flips, rotations, color changes, blurring, and the like, and compared with the original, significant features can be enhanced and extracted with noise deleted.

For example, *Google Brain's simple contrastive learning* self-supervised algorithm (*SimCLR*) together with a downstream classifier was applied to identify the covid-19 virus in medical imaging of lungs.

When the hierarchical feature map is completed, it is projected onto a final convolutional layer which is *flattened* (the matrix is *vectorized*) into a *fully connected* decisional column vector. Flattening a matrix is achieved by successively stacking the matrix column vectors elements end-to-end to form a (very) long column vector.[3]

A *softmax* function, true to its name, is a *max* function that *softens* a ReLU by taming monotonically increasing integers into the interval (0, 1) to provide greyscale,

$$Softmax = \xi(z)_i = \frac{e^{z_i}}{\sum_{j=1}^{K} e^{z_j}}$$

where z_i is the ith element of the vector z, and $\xi(z)_i$ is normalized by dividing each exponential function by the sum of the exponential functions to ensure that the values are between 0 and 1 as required for probabilities; $\xi(z)_i$ cannot be negative because the exponential function cannot be negative.

The fully connected output layer is an N-dimensional column vector, wherein each element represents the probability that the input image is of a certain class, for instance in the classification of pet images, it will have high values in the feature maps that show round eyes, pink

---

[3] A matrix may be flattened into a column matrix automatically by for example numpy.matrix.flatten.

triangular noses, and pointy ears. The fully connected column vector displays probabilities for instance for the classification of household pets arrayed in the output vector as,[4]

$$[\text{cat, parrot, canary, dog, hamster, rabbit}]^T,$$

and suppose the decision vector is

$$[0.6, 0.05, 0.03, 0.2, 0.1, 0.2,]^T,$$

then the image presented to the CNN is most likely a cat.

Conv2D filters are typically used in the first few convolutional layers to extract high-level features, and are usually stacked in each convolutional layer. An *inception* layer convolves different sizes in parallel, from the most accurate (*1 × 1*) detailing to bigger (*5 × 5*) filters, thereby accessing fine detail while covering a larger area.

Inception layers were used for example in Google's cancer tumor diagnosis and in *GoogleNet's* winning the computer vision *ImageNet Large-Scale Visual Recognition Challenge*.

Detecting, segmenting, and locating an object in a scene requires distinguishing the object through the noise of other objects and the immediate surroundings. In these more complicated information transmission problems, using techniques such as *bounding boxes* to isolate, and *rich feature hierarchies* for multiple class recognition, allows more accurate re-construction of the entire scene.[5]

There is of course a trade-off, multiple filters and many convolutional layers greatly increase the size of the artificial neural network and the computational burden. However, all of these calculations for convolutional neural network feature extraction can be performed very efficiently by packaged computational software freely accessible from, among others, Python TensorFlow and PyTorch.

---

[4] The output layer neurons are arrayed in a column vector, which is conveniently represented in text by its row vector transpose $[0.8]^T$, with the superscript T denoting the transpose of matrix elements from row to column and vice versa.

[5] There are many other methods for detection, segmentation, and position of objects, including for example, RCNN, Fast RCNN, Faster RCNN, MultiBox, Bayesian Optimization,Multi-region, RCNN Minus R, Image Windows, Semantic Seg, Unconstrained Video, Shape Guided, Object Regions, and Shape Sharing, See Adeshpande3.github.io,Girshick, R., *Rich feature hierarchies for accurate object detection and semantic segmentation*, Tech Report (vol. 5), arXiv 1311.2542v5[cs.CV], 22Oct2014.

V

Progression

V

Progression

CHAPTER 19

The Cross-Entropy Cost Function

A common problem encountered in the minimization of the Cost Function is that the gradient descent at times will suddenly slow down and even stop altogether while backpropagating through the hidden layers, never minimizing the Cost, and therefore ceasing to learn.

Learning by minimizing a quadratic cost function may be slow because when the neuron activation is very wrong, the Cost is very high, and the weights and bias parameter adjustments will take time, or because the minimization method has gone beyond the pale when confronted with a massive error, never able to iteratively overcome the error to lower the Cost to match the training set.

To overcome this problem requires a cost function that can accelerate gradient descent when encountering a large error. The *Cross-Entropy Cost Function* is based on a "measure of surprise" in information theory; that is, if a neuron's activation level is determined by an artificial neural network to be $a^{(L)} = 0$, and the labeled target is $y = 1$, the cross-entropy registers a "surprise" that is dealt with as *information entropy* that must be rapidly reduced in order for a network to converge to accurately reflect the training set data.

Thermodynamical entropy is a measure of disorder or uncertainty in a system, and for spontaneous changes (what happens when a constraint on the system is removed), the disorder of the system will always naturally increase. This is encountered in everyday life as for example

DOI: 10.1201/9781003214892-24

while walking, if your shoelaces loosen and start to disengage, they have been released from the constraint of being securely tied, and as you continue walking, your shoelaces will further unravel as your walking system continues to add energy. Your laces will never miraculously re-tie themselves as you walk, returning to a more ordered state, but rather the longer you walk, the looser your shoelaces become. Within your walking system, the shoelaces have gone from the more-ordered tied state to the more disordered untied state, and the entropy of your walking system has increased.

Entropy in action can be directly observed for instance in an array of computer cables below your desk; no matter how carefully initially arranged, at the next observation, they have all somehow mysteriously deteriorated into a hopeless tangle of high entropy disorder.

This spontaneous increase of entropy can be explained by the probability of occurrence of states in statistical mechanics. To illustrate, if five coins are tossed, the probability of coming up all heads or all tails is very low, but the probability of four heads and one tail (or vice-versa) is five times larger because five different arrangements of heads and one tail satisfy the criterion (since there are five different coins which can be the odd-out). For three heads (tails) and two tails (heads), there are ten cases each that satisfy the criterion (3-2 either way) and thus each is ten times as likely to occur. So the highly-ordered state of all heads or all tails has only one state, and the more disordered state of three heads and two tails has ten possible states. Therefore, the high-disorder state is much more probable because there are more available states.

If 100 coins are tossed, the total number of different combinations of heads and tails is about 10^{30}, and thus the probability of coming up all heads is practically nil at $1/10^{30}$. For typical molecular systems of one mole (6×10^{23} molecules) of gas, the possible *degrees of freedom* of the system are correspondingly enormous and the molecules will naturally spread out to where there are more available positions. That is why one never sees the molecules of a gas in a container spontaneously congregate in a corner all bunched together.

And that is also why your untied shoelaces will not re-tie themselves as you continue walking and your computer cables are always in a tangled mess. The tied shoelace and the separated, parallel cables are more ordered states with fewer degrees of freedom, while the untied shoelace and tangled cables have many possible different unordered states and are thus overwhelmingly more probable.

This also explains the frustration of never finding what you are looking for in places where you expect something to be; the possible places where your sunglasses might be is much greater than the one place where it happens to be.

Of course, re-tying your shoelaces and disentangling your computer cables makes them more orderly, but the price to pay is increasing disorder in your body system (including the heat of psychic anguish) from having to expend energy to reorder those systems, and they will never be exactly back to the same original state (thermodynamic irreversibility). The result is that even if you re-order the system, the total entropy of the coupled systems (you and the shoelaces and cables) has still increased.

The direction priority of the natural spontaneous transfer of heat (energy) is popularly expressed by the Second Law of Thermodynamics as "the direction of energy transformation is always from a hotter place towards a colder place"; for example, putting a kettle of cold water on the stove burner will not result in what little heat the water has being transferred to make the burner flame hotter; the truth of the Second Law is heralded by the kettle whistle.

With every spontaneous event, the thermodynamical arrow of time flies only forward, and as natural events are deemed irreversible, they always proceed towards the greater disorder; for example, if your freshly baked apple pie slid off the kitchen table and splattered on the floor, you will not see it spontaneously reconstitute itself and fly back up to the tabletop.

Entropy therefore is present in any system, natural or artificial, and in particular communications. *Information entropy* is the average rate at which information is produced stochastically from some source of data; the amount of information conveyed by an event is a random variable whose difference from its expectation value is determined by its amount of information entropy. A low information entropy means that the information conveyed is close to the expectation value, for example a clean voice transmission over a near-by wireless base station.

When a low probability event is found in an element of a high probability target vector, the error is large, and that event carries more disordered information than when a high probability event is found because the latter event more closely matches the target element; that is, correctly predicted events carry less information entropy, and unexpected events are more disordered and carry more information entropy.

This information entropy can be quantified in units of *surprisal*, with high information entropy registering a surprise to the observer so that first of all it will be noticed as an anomaly, and secondly that its entropy must be decreased by gradient descent backpropagation in order to match the expectation value.

For example in baseball, a pitcher hitting a home run, and in football, a goalie scoring a goal, are low probability events with a high information entropy surprisal that goes against expectations.

Information theory was conceived from electronic communications where clean signals are the expectation values. "Communication" means "the identification of data from a source by means of the transmission of an encoded signal"; information entropy provides an absolute limit on the shortest possible average length of accurate expression of the data in the encoded signal, and if the entropy of the source is less than the transmission channel's entropy capacity, the information is deemed a "lossless" communication.

For artificial intelligence, learning the correct recognition of an image or interpretation of data by an artificial neural network is just an exercise in performing lossless communication. Therefore decreasing the information entropy in a neural network results in more accurate recognition of input data, and this is just what the cross-entropy cost function is designed to do.

The of cross-entropy cost can be simply described, although the detailed mathematical theories are complicated. For an $M = 2$ binary classification (*Yes, No*) the cross-entropy cost function is,

$$Cross\ Entropy|_{M=2} = -[y log\,(p) + (1 - y)log(1 - p)]$$

where y is the resultant binary indicator *(0, 1)* and p is the predicted probability with the expression in square brackets being just the sum of the resultant times the predicted probability and its only alternative in this case, the probability of the only other possibility. The minus sign in front of the square brackets indicates the negative for cost (or signal loss).

For multiclass classification $M > 2$ (for example, classifying cats, dogs, goldfish, and horses), the cross-entropy cost function is the sum of the separate cost for each class label c per observation o,

$$Cross\ Entropy\ Cost = -\sum_{c=1}^{M} y_{o,c} \log(p_{o,c})$$

where $y_{o,c}$ is the binary indicator $(0, 1)$ if the class label c is the correct classification for the observation o, and $p_{o,c}$ is the predicted observation probability that o belongs to class c.[1]

The cross-entropy cost function's information theory entropy underpinnings may appear complex, but as in many artificial intelligence constructs, the implementation just involves writing a simple program representing the above equations or downloading canned software, such as *XENT Cross Entropy*, letting it run, and seeing how well things progress, if at all.[2]

In many cases of artificial intelligence development, the engineering ethos of "if it works, go ahead" trumps the "knowing why and how" of physics. However, it is still true that if one wants to invent something new, or fundamentally improve something old, the theoretical bases of the technique will have to be understood.

But it is a fact that many of the recent successes of artificial neural networks have come about simply through experiment, trial-and-error, and heuristics, in a completely utilitarian manner that can be generalized, as expressed by the artificial intelligence pioneer Yann LeCun:[3]

You have to realize that our theoretical tools are very weak. Sometimes, we have good mathematical intuitions for why a particular technique should work. Sometimes our intuition ends up being wrong .... The questions become: how well does my method work on this particular problem, and how large is the set of problems on which it works well.

---

[1] Ref. Shannon, C. and W. Weaver, 1971, *A Mathematical Theory of Communication*, University of Illinois Press.

[2] Software packages for cross-entropy include XENT Cross Entropy: Binary Classification, MCXENT: Multiclass Cross Entropy, and RMSE_EXENT: RMSE Cross Entropy.

[3] *Convolutional Nets and CIFAR-10: An Interview with Yann LeCun*, "No Free Hunch". December 22, 2014.

CHAPTER 20

Hyperparameterization

A convolutional neural network can be tuned to accelerate convergence and avoid overfitting or underfitting data by utilizing *hyperparameters* such as *learning rate, stride, padding,* and *pooling*; the computational burden can also be reduced by adjusting the resolution and dimension size of the convolutional layers. In practice, experience is often the best guide in choosing hyperparameterizations and combinations thereof.

A *learning rate* η adjusts the speed of gradient descent by specifying the size of the steps of the gradient descent; bigger step sizes produce speedier learning, but too big a step size may skip over a minimum.

The transposed (superscript T) gradient vector of the Cost function with respect to a number of m weights w_k,

$$\nabla C = \left[\frac{\partial C}{\partial w_1}, \frac{\partial C}{\partial w_2}, \ldots, \frac{\partial C}{\partial w_m} \right]^T,$$

if a small change in the variable w_k with respect to the gradient is factored by the learning rate η,

$$\Delta w_k = -\eta \nabla C$$

and the weights are iterated as,

$$w_k \rightarrow w_k - \eta \nabla C,$$

DOI: 10.1201/9781003214892-25

this then is just the process of gradient descent with an adjustable learning rate factor η specifying the descent step size. Adjusting the step size and thus the speed of convergence can also be used to *stabilize* the gradient descent of the cost function to avoid slowdown or stoppage. Trial and error is most often used to find the best gradient descent step size for optimal learning.

The *stride* is the step size of the convolutional filter as it slides over the matrix, it can be increased to reduce receptive field overlap and produce faster coverage over the matrix layers while concomitantly reducing computational burden. However, if the stride is too large, the filter may skip over or misinterpret some features.

Since the feature maps are the same size as the filters, they will be smaller than the size of the input layer, so the feature map matrix can be *padded* with zeros around the borders of the matrix to ensure that the filter and stride will successfully register with the convolved layer matrix.

The output size in height/length dimensions of a convolutional layer in terms of these hyperparameters is given by,

$$Output\ Size\left(\frac{height}{length}\right) = \frac{(W - K + 2P)}{S} + 1$$

where *Output Size* is the height/length of the layer output matrix, W is the input matrix height/length dimension, K is the filter dimension ratio length/height, P is the padding and S is the stride.

The choice of hyperparameters and filter dimensions will depend largely on the computer vision task at hand and considerations of computational burden.

With this in mind, a *pooling* (also called *downsampling* and *subsampling*) *layer* reduces the dimensions of a convolved feature by matrix multiplying an input layer matrix by a 2×2 pooling matrix of stride 2 which outputs either the maximum value or the average value in the sector that the filter convolves, thereby achieving significant dimensional reduction to reduce the computational burden.

Pooling is based on the idea that if a specific feature is known to be in the input matrix by having a high activation level, its exact position is not as significant as its position relative to other features. The resulting down-sampled feature maps are more robust with regard to changes in the position of the feature in the image, so its dimensions can be reduced;

this is called *local translation invariance*. Pooling may also help to extract positionally and rotationally invariant dominant features, reduce noise, and avoid overfitting.

For an example of a convolutional neural network and its hyperparameterization, the AlphaGo policy network that defeated Lee Sedol comprises 12 hidden layers of convolution filters with *zero* padding and stride *1* to maintain the spatial dimension. The network takes $19 \times 19 \times 48$ input features to represent the 19×19 board. The input layer uses $5 \times 5 \times 49 \times 192$ filters while the hidden layers all use $3 \times 3 \times 192 \times 192$ filters, and all the layers are rectified by a sigmoid or other greyscale function. The last convolutional layer is a $1 \times 1 \times 192 \times 1$ filter with different biases for each location followed by a *softmax* function. The value network is similarly constructed, but hidden layer *12* is an additional convolution layer, layer *13* is a $1 \times 1 \times 192 \times 1$ filter and layer *14* is a fully connected layer with 256 rectifiers. The output layer is a fully connected layer with a single *tanh* output. AlphaGo altogether uses 192 filters.

From this example, it is clear that a deep convolutional neural network can be an extremely complex structure embodying many different hyperparameterization techniques all of which will require a significant computational burden.

DCNNs for example are used in assembly line manufacturing, medical diagnostics, *Facebook* to tag photos, and of course by self-driving cars, as well as many other uses now, and in the future particularly for robot computer vision.

CHAPTER 21

Big Data

B y age three, children have already seen millions of objects, and can learn to name them to classify and store in their memories. Thus the first task of computer vision artificial intelligence is to similarly learn to recognize objects, classify them and store in computer memory. The objects are identified by their particular features, for example the four legs, black nose, fur and so on of dogs, and even though objects may have vastly different individual features, viewed in different poses and aspects, they must still be classified as dogs; for example, the genus *dog* includes the tiny short-hair Chihuahuas to gigantic shaggy Sheepdogs. However, they are also subject to further classification as in the zoological class of mammals, the societal class of domesticated pets, and working guide, watch, search and rescue, retriever, and customs inspector dogs, just to name a few. Cats however although being mammals and domestic pets just like dogs, will never deign to work for humans.

Even an inanimate object like the very common hammer a can be separated into the species claw, ball pein, cross pein, straight pein, pin, club, mallet, joiner's mallet, soft-faced, nail-punch woodcarver, veneer, upholstery, sledge-, bench-, power-, and spring-hammers, all belonging to the genus *hammer*. Humans furthermore can identify the hammer from only a small segment appearing in a toolbox, for instance the edge of the claw, and from the size of the toolbox distinguish the claw hammer from a crowbar.

So even though they belong to the same genus, species can be vastly different as to appearance, character, and utility. From this, one with a

DOI: 10.1201/9781003214892-26

mathematical bent might believe that the theory of sets and groups could form the basis of expert system top-down classification algorithms. However, such algorithms would be faced with a tangled web of *if-then* branching steps and taxonomic overlapping.

The migration from top-down to bottom-up classification for computer vision began when Princeton's Li Fei-Fei realized that since infants cannot innately recognize objects and scenes, the algorithm should learn through experience just as humans do. For a machine to be able to classify *something*, it would first have to be exposed to almost *everything*; that is, it required training on a very large dataset with every kind of example and detailed identification and distinguishing annotations regarding its particular classification; in other words, computer vision needed *Big Data*.

An object database for computer vision recognition project was begun where Princeton undergraduates collected and labeled images for $10/hour, but Professor Li quickly realized that utilizing student power for the project would take at least 90 years and cost millions of dollars to complete even for a rudimentary database.

Despairing at the apparent demise of a good idea for want of a practical implementation, just at this time, a graduate student told her about the new *Amazon Mechanical Turk* crowdsourcing website that attracted tens of thousands of denizens of the Internet Universe to participate in individual project tasks on their own computers to earn extra income, albeit at a very low per unit rate.

Professor Li immediately saw the Mechanical Turk as a data-gathering tool that could scale, and accessing the crowdsourcing website, she and her team supervised some 50,000 participants in 167 different countries to collect, classify, label, and manually annotate nearly one hundred million images for her project, including 62,000 images of cats alone.

Her *ImageNet* project took two and a half years to complete, however when announced in 2009, it was rejected as a *Computer Vision and Pattern Recognition* (CVPR) research report talk and relegated to a humble poster presentation in a corner of the convention hall.[1]

Moving to Stanford to become the Director of the AI Lab and to Silicon Valley to be the Chief Scientist at Google Cloud, Professor Li

---

[1] Professor Li had difficulty obtaining research grants for the ImageNet project, with comments such as "it was shameful that Princeton would research this topic" and "the only strength of the proposal was that Li was a woman". Gershgom, D., *The data that transformed AI research, and possibly the world*, Quartz, qz.com.

sought to test the efficacy of her Big Data approach to computer vision by proposing the idea of a contest for the accuracy of computer vision machine recognition of 1.2 million *ImageNet* images drawn from 1,000 different categories in the *ImageNet Large-Scale Visual Recognition Challenge* (ILSVRC).

In 2012, *GoogleNet*'s deep convolutional neural network (DCNN), split into two parts and partitioned across two GPUs, won the ILSVRC, and two years later, its 22-layer, 9-inception module DCNN defeated not only the competitor machines, but also routinely performed better than human beings at image recognition.[2]

This amount of data and the care of detailing classifications required for any useful recognition brings to mind Charles Darwin, who did just that for Earth's geological formations, flora and fauna.

On the toll of decades of observing, and analyzing, collecting specimens, classifying, generalizing, recording, and ultimately formulate a theory, Darwin in his *Autobiography* lamented,[3]

My mind seems to have become a kind of machine for grinding general laws out of large collections of facts such that neither music or literature nor appreciation of fine scenery held any pleasure any longer

Indeed Darwin was the ultimate human manifestation of a deep convolutional neural network algorithm for searching, classifying, and generalizing huge amounts of data. As the recognition capability of DCNNs grows, such a machine can do all the above without want of human pleasures, so academia can look forward to many Darwinian robots tirelessly performing observational science on flora and fauna, and indeed on any genus of matter.

Darwin's epochal 1859 book *Origin of the Species* set forth the induction, deduction, and generalization that established the Theory of Evolution, one of the greatest scientific achievements of mankind.

Darwin first established the branching patterns of flora and fauna evolution based on his theory of natural selection; he later turned to human

---

[2] *ImageNet* is a large scale hierarchical image database designed by Jia Deng, Wei Dong, Richard Socher, Li-Jia Li, Kai Li, and Li Fei-Fei in 2009; Alex Krizhevsky, Ilya Sutskever, and Geoffrey E. Hinton of the University of Toronto won the 2010 ILSVRC. Two CPUs were necessary because the *Nvidia GeForce GTX 580* had insufficient on-chip memory.

[3] *The Autobiography of Charles Darwin*, John Murray III publisher (1887).

evolution in two books, *The Descent of Man* (1871) and *The Expression of Emotion in Man and Animals* (1872). He thus amalgamated the classification of biological objects and their emotive expression (emotional knowledge).[4]

Particular traits either innate or nurtured of different nationalities, for example relatively reserved Germans and Japanese compared to more expansive Italians and Nigerians could also form a class (although fraught with the dangers of stereotyping) for deeper and more extended recognition. Woe to the Italian negotiator who believes she has closed the deal with a Japanese company because its representatives all nodded in seeming assent to her proposal, their response actually being no more than polite acknowledgment that they had heard what she was saying.

The enormity of variations of expression in diverse cultures would require huge amounts of extremely subtle facial expression and body language data, all analyzed and minutely annotated yet still fraught with ambiguity.

The human visual cortex has 140 million neurons and billions of connections; by adulthood a person can easily recognize billions of objects and scenes in many different guises and settings.

To achieve this ultimate capability, the human brain operationally has a *frontal lobe* for thinking, emotion, and behavior; the *motor cortex* for movement; the *sensory cortex* for sensation including visualization; the *parietal lobe* for perception and mathematics; the *temporal lobe* for memory and language; and the *cerebellum* for balance and coordination, as shown in the schematic figure below.[5]

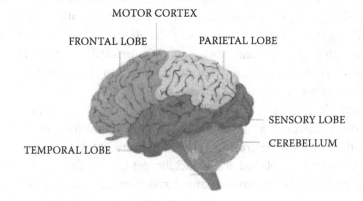

MOTOR CORTEX

FRONTAL LOBE   PARIETAL LOBE

SENSORY LOBE

CEREBELLUM

TEMPORAL LOBE

---

[4] Refer to the definitions of intelligence in Chapter 3 which included the perplexing "emotional knowledge".

[5] C

Can artificial intelligence mimic these biological constructs and be as perceptive as humans are, and be able to resolve the ambiguities?

A deeper artificial neural network and larger training sets can produce more accurate image recognition, classification, and inference, but DCNNs can also improve their range of discernment by *augmenting* data to form a broader group by including other image representations while keeping the image label the same. By emulation of the biological brain's *parietal lobe* for recognition of rotational and translational invariance, segment identification and association group expansion, together with simple image pixel shifting, horizontal and vertical flips, random crops, color jitters, translations, rotations, and so on, the original feature characteristic is maintained, but the class is expanded several-fold to include variations of the same, without the need for fresh data.

If a trained network with already tuned parameters is concatenated to a new network with relevant objectives, the new network can "fine-tune" the pre-trained network with only *relevant* new data that is fed to the new network to enhance a specific recognition capability.

This so-called *transfer learning* is implemented by freezing all the gradient descent parameters of all the layers of the trained network, removing the fully connected layer, and replacing it with the input layer of the new training network, and then proceeding with training of the new network with data more relevant to the task at hand. In this way, the features already extracted by the *pre-trained network* do not have to be newly identified by the concatenated network, they just are transferred to the new network and the concatenated network can be taught new, more specific, and more subtle data.[6]

---

[6] For example, Yosinski, J, *et al.*, *How transferable are features in deep neural networks?* arXiv.1411.1792v1[cs.LG] 6Nov2-14.

CHAPTER 22

Massively Parallel Processing

T he von Neumann computer architecture is serial; a central processing unit (CPU) processes the programs and data that are fetched from a memory storage unit through a bus connected to the central processing unit (CPU). Each piece of information is assigned a memory location with a unique address, and after fetching, is processed sequentially by instruction cycles in step with a timing clock. Because all fetched information shares the bus, the CPU must always wait for instructions and data before it can proceed, which can considerably slow down operations.

Many speed-up techniques have been employed to decrease the *latency* (time between procedures), including adding an input/output processor, partitioning memory into banks, installing fast data caches, adding a coprocessor to perform some slower functions faster, pipelining for multiplex operation, and multiple CPU cores.

With these additions, von Neumann machines can handle most of today's routine computing tasks using multi-core serial architecture organized as in shown in the figure below, where the LN's designate layers, LLC is the last layer cache and is shared among the cores, and if the data is not in the caches, it will be fetched from the DDR-4 memory.

DOI: 10.1201/9781003214892-27

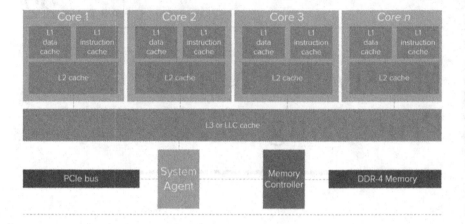

The multiple cores naturally led to the idea of a vector architecture where the processor treats information as a vector of data elements instead of individual scalar data points, and instead of a single or multi-core processor, an *array* of processors.

Machine learning's voracious appetite for very large data sets meant processing speed was a paramount concern, and although advances were made, the serial *von Neumann bottleneck* seriously limited artificial intelligence machine performance.

While some operations which require knowing a result of one step in order to process the next step are inherently serial, for example conventional cryptography algorithms, other operations such as ray tracing in computer games and the matrix operations of machine learning can be performed by simultaneously fetching and running in parallel.

Originally designed for the graphical images of computer games where an array of pixels (a *raster*) defines the images, and animation of the images is the change in the image attributes (including textures and shading) with time. *Ray tracing* generates an image by tracing the path of light through the pixels in an image plane producing realistic 2D renditions of 3D objects from the different ray paths; the pixels are stored in a matrix and a *graphical processing unit* (GPU) comprising multiple core CPUs perform the calculations in parallel, as shown schematically in the figure below.[1]

---

[1] Ref. Multicore and GPU descriptions and images with kind permission from Hagoort, N., "Exploring the GPU Architecture", nielshagoort.com.

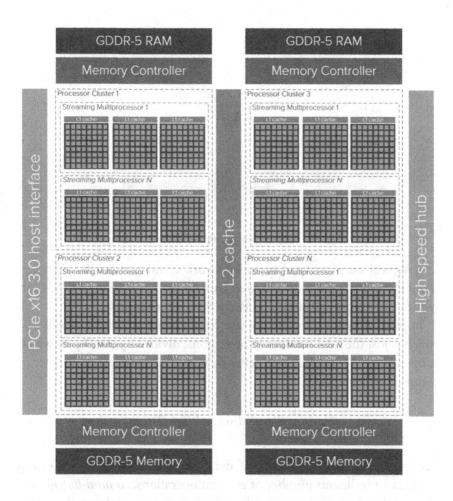

Each processor cluster (*PCle*) has multiple streaming multiprocessors (*SM*) and each SM has a layer-1 instruction cache layer. One SM will fetch from a dedicated layer-1 cache and a shared layer-2 cache before using the global GDDR-5 Memory; the cache layers in GPUs are generally fewer and smaller as GPUs are less concerned with memory latency as long as the processing is going on steadily. In this way, the GPU parallel-processing architecture can clearly increase computer throughput.[2]

Looking at the exemplary artificial neural network structure from Chapter 13 shown in the figure below, it is easy to see why parallel processing by GPUs would be superior to serial architecture CPUs, as each hidden layer's activation level change could be handled in parallel by a single graphics core processor.

---

[2] GDDR-5 is a "graphics double data rate type 5 synchronous random access memory".

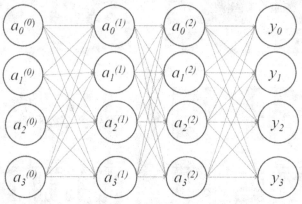

| Input Layer | Hidden Layer 1 | Hidden Layer 2 | Output Layer |

A typical deep artificial neural network could handle 30 GBytes of elements and has millions of nodes. Utilizing GPUs instead of CPUs can reduce the number of nodes by two orders of magnitude.

In parallel-processing, the *average parallelism* is defined as the *Work*, which is just the total number of operations, divided by the *Depth*, which is the number of layers in the network, and gives the average number of computing elements,

$$Average\ Parallelism = Work/Depth.$$

Because of the huge amounts of data, deep learning data processing requires a prodigious number of element operations, so *mini-batches* are processed in turn. Taking mini-batches will also promote greater accuracy because noise will be filtered out on average over the mini-batches. Finding the right size for the mini-batches is an exercise in just seeing what works best for the particular problem at hand.[3]

It should be evident that there should be a limit to how much a computation can be speeded up by parallel processing; it is given by *Amdahl's Law*,

$$Maximum\ SpeedUp = S = \frac{1}{1 - P + \frac{P}{N}}$$

---

[3] Hoefler., T 2019, *Demystifying Parallel and Distributed Deep Learning*, Swiss High Performance Computing (HPC) Conference.

where P is the proportion of the system that can be made parallel (and $1 - P$ is the proportion of the system that remains serial) and N is the number of processors. As the number of processors $N \rightarrow \infty$, $S = 1/(1 - P)$, so the *SpeedUp* ultimately depends on the proportion of the system that cannot be parallel processed; this can never be zero as it is unavoidable that some operations depend on computations that came before.

The deep convolutional neural network *GoogLeNet* that won the 2014 ImageNet Large-Scale Visual Recognition Challenge has 6.8 million parameters and is 22 layers deep, running on the Nvidia Tesla V100 with 80 Streaming Microprocessors each with 64 cores. Software to run the Teslas includes *VMWare VSphere ESXI* that dedicates a GPU to a Virtual Machine using *DirectPath I/O*.

Google's *tensor processing unit* (TPU) AI accelerator ASIC is architecturally the same as a GPU but does not perform the graphical rasterization or texturization; it is specifically designed for machine learning neural network operations using *TensorFlow* software mundanely in high volume, low precision processing such as GooglePhotos, RankBrain search, computer vision, and sensationally in AlphaGo's match with Lee Sedol.

The TPU has progressed from a simple 8-bit matrix multiplier chip manufactured in a 28 nm process, to adding 600 GB memory bandwidth with performance each reaching 45 teraFLOPS arranged in four-chip modules, and thereupon doubling the processing power using 16 chips per module.

The world's biggest AI chip *circa* 2020 is the Cerebras *Wafer Scale Engine* (WSE) with 1.2 trillion transistors, 400,000 cores, 18 GB on-chip memory one clock-cycle away from the cores, and 100 petabits/second memory bandwidth (rate at which data read from and stored to memory) comprising a low-latency, high bandwidth input/feedback chip specifically designed for machine learning. The WSE is 56 times larger, has 3000 times more memory, and 10,000 times the memory bandwidth of Nvidia's largest GPU, and purportedly will reduce the interconnection transmissions latency from weeks to minutes, and increase processing speed with massive numbers of computation cores alongside memory, ideally providing distributed computing power for more data-intensive machine learning.[4]

---

[4] The "Wafer" indicates that instead of the size of semiconductor chips cut from a pure silicon wafer, the WSE is the size of the wafer itself.

High performance computing competitions are nothing new. For years America or Japan held the title for world's fastest computer, but recently China's Sunway and Tianhe claimed the title, but in this big power technology leadership race where national prestige at stake, America had retaken the lead in 2020 only to see Fujitsu's *Fugaku* in 2021 surpass it with a 442 petaFLOPS machine. The back and forth among the three computer powers can be expected to continue well into the future.

The Summit supercomputer located at Oak Ridge National Laboratory in Tennessee was built by a consortium of IBM and Nvidia/Mellanox for the US Department of Energy; it is a parallel processing system covering the size of two basketball courts, employing 9216 IBM Power9 CPUs, 27,648 Nvidia Tesla V100s GPUs, 2.41 million cores, and 250 petabytes (PB) of memory with a speed of 148.6 petaflops (peak 200 petaflops). It is currently used for cosmology simulations, climate modeling, and medical research.

Summit's sister supercomputer the Sierra was built for the National Nuclear Security Administration, and is located at Lawrence Livermore National Laboratory in California. With a design similar to the Summit, it has 8640 CPUs, 17,280 GPUs, and 1.38 PB of memory with a peak speed of 125 petaflops. It is currently used almost exclusively for nuclear weapons simulations and its efforts therefore understandably highly classified.

Japan's Fugaku located in Kobe, was built by Fujitsu and Japan's National Research Institute *Riken,* and strangely does not use GPUs for speed but rather 158,976 ARM 48-core system on chips (SOC) for the artificial intelligence analysis of automobile collisions, Big Data processing, and covid-19 protein-folding.[5]

QUANTUM COMPUTING ARTIFICIAL NEURAL NETWORKS

In addition to the purely scaling up of components to produce greater computational power, the esoteric physics of quantum mechanical wavefunction superposition and entanglement has also entered the artificial intelligence fray with the ever-faster and almost infinite bandwidth of *quantum computers.*

---

[5] Specs for supercomputers can vary according to how architecture is configured and speed is measured; the peak speed is theoretical and operational speeds are typically 30–50 petaflops slower. A petaflop is 10^{15} floating point operations per second, a petabyte (PB) is 10^{15} bytes. Chip-linking technology company Mellanox was acquired by Nvidia.

When driven by n *qubits* that can parallel process 2^n possible super-position states between the classical *1* and *0* bits simultaneously, the quantum computer collapses the wavefunction of a process to observable probabilistic states of n bits. In this way, an almost unlimited number of entangled unobservable quantum states on the way to collapse into ob-servables may be processed or communicated to other quantum com-puters using quantum encryption; that encryption would be theoretically impossible to decipher because of the process of entanglement of states before observation cannot be known with certainty. For example only $n = 50$ qubits means $2^{50} = 10^{15}$ possible states; from this the potential for supermassive parallel-processing quantum computers is clear.

By networking an array of high-n quantum computers, tremendous computational power can be used in chemical process prediction, ma-terial science simulations, pure mathematics, and the very deep artificial neural network matrix computations of artificial intelligence.

The operations of quantum mechanics depend on representing and storing large complex tensors (scalars, vectors, and matrices); performing linear algebra operations on the tensors requires exponential amounts of neural network memory storage and processing power.

A quantum perceptron model using *qubit neurons* can exploit the huge quantum information storage capability of quantum computers by encoding an *m*-dimensional input and parameterization on quantum hardware using N qubits $(m = 2^N)$.[6]

In September 2019, Google and NASA announced the attainment of "quantum supremacy" by the superconducting metal 54-1qubit quantum processor *Sycamore* that solved the *random circuit sampling problem* in just 200 seconds, a calculation that the present world's fastest super-computer Summit would take billions of years to complete.[7]

---

[6] Ref. Tacchino, F 2019, *et al. An artificial neuron implemented on an actual quantum processor.* npj Quantum Inf **5**, 26 (). https://doi.org/10.1038/s41534-019-0140-.

[7] NASA/TP-2019-220319. The random circuit sampling problem used for claiming quantum su-premacy involved a circuit to model the entangled 2^n states; this required using gates just as in integrated circuit design, but as the number of gates increases (the circuit *depth*), the error in-creases because every gate operation foments a relatively high possibility of the error endemic to quantum mechanical processing, reaching in this case to about 0.5% for a 10-deep circuit (compared to a classical computer's error rate of 10^{-17}). A random distribution like Monte Carlo is employed to start simulation. Google-NASA, IBM, and Rigetti employ superconducting solid-state circuits, IonQ uses trapped ions, Harvard uses rubidium atoms, and Microsoft goes to the esoteric extreme with topological qubits. Cf. *Quantum supremacy ...*, quantamagazine.org.

In December 2020, the China University of Science and Technology in Hefei announced that their *Jiuchang* optical photon processor also achieved quantum supremacy by performing *Gaussian Boson Sampling* (GBS) in 3 minutes, what the Sunway Taihu supercomputer would take 2 billion years to compute.[8]

The problems chosen to demonstrate quantum supremacy, however, are endemic to quantum computing itself, rendering "proofs" of quantum computing speeds somewhat contrived. Nevertheless, the potential of $2^{high\ number}$ simultaneous parallel computations augers well for a bright albeit minatory vision of the future of artificial intelligence computation.

---

[8] Photons belong to the class of Boson particles in high-energy physics. *GBS* samples from the probability distribution of identical bosons are scattered by an interferometer. An optical circuit of N modes is injected with M indistinguishable single photons ($N>M$), then the boson sampling generates single-photon measurements at the output of the circuit. The probability distribution sampled is related to the *permanent* of of complex matrices (a sum of products that lie in rows and columns, but whereas a determinant weights each of these products with a ±1 sign, the permanent weights them all with a +1 sign, an extremely involved computation that a conventional computer would take almost forever to achieve.

VI

Powers of Prediction

CHAPTER 23

Predictive Analytics

P redictive analytics deduces correlations in data to predict future performance from past behavior. For example, if a veteran NBA player with a lifetime 3-point shooting average of 35% has made all of his six 3-point shots in the first half of a game, the opposing coach will tell his shell-shocked team, "Don't worry, he can't keep that up!"

If the coach means that because the shooter has made six straight shots, he more likely will miss the next shot, he is engaging in the *gambler's fallacy*, for any given 3-point shot is *stochastic*, meaning that shot success does not depend on the success or failure of the previous shot; if the coach means that the shooter will cool off in the second half, he is only slightly more accurate, but if he means the shooter will *regress to the mean* over the whole NBA season or for the rest of his career, he is correct in his assessment by *the law of large numbers*.

That is, the shooter may remain *on fire* throughout the game, and although of scant comfort to the opposing coach of this game, with a confidence interval as measured by the standard deviation in the 90% range, the veteran 35% shooter will never perform in the larger sample size of whole seasons at greater than a standard deviation from his average, meaning that no player, however great, can escape the regressive clutches of *Bernoulli's law*.[1]

More practically, predictive analytics is useful for predicting hardware and vehicle breakdowns in manufacturing and transportation, personal

---

[1] Some misguided coaches (and commentators) will exhort the team to step up their defense on the shooter in the second half, but from predictive analytics, he will naturally either start to regress to the mean in the second half and miss some shots or remain on fire no matter the intensity of the defense against him. A preferable tactic would be to assiduously avoid fouling him on his 3-point attempts.

DOI: 10.1201/9781003214892-29

health problems, epidemics, and any correlation with a causal relation-ship because "there is no causation without correlation", but of course "correlation does not *imply* causation, it might be just coincidence", and *coincidence* to the technologist is just *noise*.

In an important game, the stars' performances, role players' con-tributions, the coach's strategies and tactics certainly are factors in the game's outcome, but many players, coaches, and owners also believe that the hotels where the teams stay, what the players wear before the game, the color of their sneakers, the songs in their pregame music headphones, and all manner of superstition are also factors in the game's outcome.

They believe that there are correlations because of some coincidences they have noticed, and who among us have not had the same beliefs, even in the knowledge that they are unwarranted. The problem here is to separate the significant factors from the insignificant "noise" and dis-cover the principal *correlations as causes*. This can be done by collecting large samples of data over long time periods and allow the law of large numbers give you your answer.

In this sense, the real value of predictive analytics lies not in simple correlations such as the end of Summer and the increased sales of school supplies, which are readily apparent and demonstrated by years of retail statistics, but in discovering *latent* factors and inferences from the statistical data.

The simplest regression model is to fit a straight line that best bisects the data points as shown in the figure, a data set with one independent variable *x*, and one dependent variable *y*, in a linear regression model defined by the equation of a straight line,

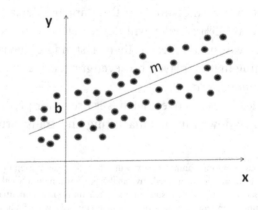

$$y = mx + b$$

where m the slope of the straight line, and b the y-axis intercept.

Once the slope and y-intercept are determined from the data, from any input of a new independent variable x, the y output can be predicted, not necessarily completely accurately for that value of x, but a value that will equal an average over many x inputs.

A linear regression model can also help to quantify the strength of the relationship between the independent and dependent variable by the variance of data points from the straight line; that is, if almost all the points are close to the line (as in the figure above), a strong dependence is indicated, and if the points are randomly scattered relatively far away from the line, a weak dependence is indicated.

Linear regression typically uses the *least squares* method, which minimizes the *variance* which is the sum of squares of the errors, to find the slope and y-intercept. This is done by first calculating the mean of the x values and the mean of the y values from the data plot above,

$$\bar{x} = \frac{\sum_{i=1}^{n} x_i}{n}$$

$$\bar{y} = \frac{\sum_{i=1}^{n} y_i}{n}$$

finding the slope m from,

$$m = \frac{\sum_{i=1}^{n} (x_i - \bar{x})(y_i - \bar{y})}{\sum_{i=1}^{n} (x_i - \bar{x})^2}$$

and the y-intercept from,

$$b = \bar{y} - m\bar{x}$$

If there are more correlations depending on more independent (input) variables, *multiple linear regression* (also called *multivariable linear regression*), produces for a particular dependent variable y (output), a linear sum of the multiple input variables x_i each of which is factored by a *regression coefficient* β_i that weights the significance of that variable, and a *residual error* term ε which distribution function is used to adjust the values of the β_i,

$$y = \beta_0 + \beta_1 x_1 + \beta_2 x_2 + \ldots + \beta_i x_i + \ldots + \beta_k x_k + \varepsilon$$

For more complicated correlations, higher powers of the independent variables x_i, such as x^2 and x^3, or the interaction of the independent variables, such as $x_1 x_2$, or even elementary functions of the independent variables, such as $sin(x)$ and $cos(x)$, can also be used to fit the data. However, fitting regression curves too closely to the data points can lead to overfitting and a loss of a predictive model's generalization capability.[2]

If there are n observations on the $k + 1$ independent variables, then for the ith dependent variable,

$$y_i = \beta_0 + \beta_1 x_{i1} + \beta_2 x_{i2} + \ldots + \beta_i x_{ij} + \ldots + \beta_k x_{ik} + \varepsilon_i$$

This can be written in compact vector/matrix form as a *general linear model*,

$$y = X\beta + \varepsilon$$

where y is a column vector holding the y_i elements, X is a matrix arraying the independent variables x_{ij}, β is a column vector holding the regression coefficients β_i, and ε is a column vector holding the error terms ε_i.

For example, a company wants to optimize the time expended in the delivery of soft drinks to vending machines; the independent variables are (1) how many bottles to stock (x_1) and (2) distance driven by the deliverer (x_2) in each run to the machines. Employing statistics software packages such as SPSS, a plot command to produce a matrix of scatter plots can assess if there are linear relationships among the data. If there are, then the regression coefficients β_i and error ε_i can be calculated by Gaussian elimination (typically by means of the determinant of the matrices) using canned systems of simultaneous equations solver software. The linear relation of delivery time as a function of number of

---

[2] Even with higher powers and functions of the independent variables x_i there is still a *linear* dependence on the regression coefficients β_i so the dependence is still called a "linear" regression.

bottles and driving distance then can be found in a fitted regression model equation with calculated regression coefficients such as,

$$y_{est} = 2.341 + 1.616x_1 + 0.0144x_2$$

where y_{est} is the estimated delivery time, and it can be seen that the delivery time dependence on the number of bottles x_1 is much greater than the driving distance x_2.[3]

After presumably optimizing the process by reducing the number of bottles stocked per machine and driving to more machines in a delivery run, if after many runs there is no significant improvement in the company's overall delivery time, then there may be hidden correlations at work, such as the refill percentage requirement of each vending machine, and the number of bottles delivered for each brand of soft drink. These factors then can be included in the analysis to see it there is any decrease in the overall delivery time, and if so, this correlation should be included in the model as new independent variables.

The general linear model can be expanded to handle the effects of interdependent multiple correlations in a *multivariate linear regression* model,

$$Y = XB + E$$

where the dependent variable Y is a matrix with each column having a row of estimations of each of the dependent variables y as functions of the weighted independent variables, and the independent variable X is a matrix with each column being a set of observations on one of the independent variables x which is a function of the other independent variables, B is a matrix of parameters to be adjusted for fitting the data, and E is an error (noise) matrix that is assumed to be uncorrelated across observations and follows a *multivariate normal distribution*.

For an example, a medical researcher collects data on the measurable independent health variables: weight, blood pressure, and cholesterol level of a cohort population, and further data on red meat, fish, milk, and alcohol consumed by the cohort per week. A multivariate linear regression model can determine the interrelated correlations among each of the health and diet independent variables, and the errors (such as false reports of low alcohol consumption) are assumed to follow a normal distribution.

---

[3] Bremer, M., *Multiple Linear Regression*, Math 261A, mezeylab.cb.bscb.cornell.edu.

Simple linear, multiple linear, and multivariate linear regressions can be distinguished by the scalar, vector, and matrix representations respectively as shown in the equations above, and the coefficients of the terms will reveal the inter-relationships.

Of course, parameter calculations, hypothesis testing, analysis of the models and the extraction of further information from intermediate steps can become quite complex, and are the subjects of on-going research.

Linear regression is widely used in science and engineering data analysis, and in the biological, medical, behavioral, economic, and social sciences in predictive analytics. Common applications are *trend estimation* where curve movement data can represent a trend, for example in epidemiology, a linear regression model found a direct negative correlation between a cigarette smoking independent variable and a smoker's lifespan dependent variable. In finance, the *capital asset pricing model* uses linear regression and *beta* (whether the stock is more or less volatile than the market as a whole) to quantify the systematic risk of an investment. In economics, linear regression is widely used in almost all areas of prediction from economic downturns to inflation. And in artificial intelligence, linear regression is one of the fundamental learning algorithms used in supervised machine learning.

CHAPTER 24

Restricted Boltzmann Machine

A *Restricted Boltzmann Machine* (RBM) is an early artificial neural network with only an input (visible) layer composed of vectors *v*, one hidden layer composed of vectors *h*, and no output layer. There are no node connections among the artificial neurons *within* the layers (hence the "restricted" adjective in its name). An RBM learns probability distributions (the probabilities of many different possibilities at once) based on the *free energy* of distributions to determine the ground-truth probability distribution of unstructured input data.

The RBM structure is a Markov chain random field of connected nodes where the *joint probability* of the neuron activations in the layer vectors "*h* given *v*" and "*v* given *h*" can be represented by that free energy, which is a measure of the stability of the probability distribution; that is, the less free energy in the system, the more stable the system, meaning for artificial intelligence, the closer it is to the ground truth.

The *Gibbs free energy* of physical chemistry is a measure of the thermodynamic potential of a state of matter. For example on Earth, H_2O has three phases: liquid, solid, and vapor; at room temperature and atmospheric pressure, although there is some water vapor in the air (the humidity), the liquid state of H_2O has the lowest free energy and is the most stable of the three states, so as ice cubes in an ice tray on the kitchen table melt, free energy is released in a phase transition of ice to liquid water, and as water liquid in the air evaporates, free energy is released in the phase transition of liquid to vapor, and the free energy of the system is decreased.

In other words, under standard temperature and pressure (STP) conditions, liquid water is the most stable state of H_2O, meaning that it has the highest probability compared to the other states, which exist but have more free energy and are less stable and therefore less probable.

If the temperature is considerably higher than 100°C or considerably lower than 0°C, or the pressure is not atmospheric, vapor and ice respectively could have less free energy and be more stable, meaning that if conditions change, the ground truth probability distribution will be different.

An RBM, starting from a random initial distribution, compares its distribution with the distribution of the input data; the difference (error) is just the free energy of the candidate distribution, so just as in other artificial neural networks, minimizing that free energy by back-propagation will cause the RBM-generated probability distribution to converge to the probability distribution of the input data, and thus reveal the ground truth probabilities and the latent inferences hidden therein.

The Gibbs free energy of a pair of Boolean vectors (v, h) representing the visible v and hidden h layers is given by the RBM *energy function*,

$$E(v, h) = \sum_i a_i v_i + \sum_j b_j h_j + \sum_{i,j} v_i h_j w_{ij}$$

where a_i is the activation energy of the ith neuron, v_i the binary state of the neurons in the visible input layer, and h_j the binary state of the neurons in the hidden layer; b_j are the elements of the bias vectors, one for each layer, and w_{ij} the elements of the weights matrix W.

The thermodynamic probability P_i of the ith state of a system having an energy E_i at temperature T is given by the well-known Boltzmann distribution (hence the name of the RBM machine),

$$P_i = \frac{e^{-E_i/k_B T}}{\sum_{j=1}^{M} e^{-E_j/k_B T}} = \frac{e^{-E_i/k_B T}}{Z}$$

where M is the number of all possible states in the system, k_B is the Boltzmann constant (relating temperature and energy), and Z is the *canonical partition function* that normalizes the equation to values between *0* and *1* as required by probability.

For an RBM, the joint probability $P(v, h)$ of v given h, and of h given v depends on the RBM energy function $E(v, h)$, and is given by,

$$P(v, h) = \frac{e^{-E(v,h)}}{\sum_v^M \sum_h^M e^{-E(v,h)}} = \frac{e^{-E(v,h)}}{Z_{rbm}}$$

where Z_{rbm} is the canonical partition function sum over all possible pairs of visible and hidden states.

At a given point in time, the RBM-generated probability distribution is in accord with the RBM energy function $E(v, h)$, which energy is determined by the parameterized activation levels of neurons in the visible and hidden layers. In feedforward mode, the RBM thus is acting as an *autoencoder*.

The calculation of the possible probabilities of all the states of v and h is prohibitively dense, so instead the *conditional joint probabilities* of h given v and v given h are employed,

$$p(h \mid v) = \prod_i p(h_i \mid v)$$

$$p(v \mid h) = \prod_i p(v_i \mid h)$$

Since each neuron activation level by itself is binary, it can only be *1* or *0*, the weight and bias parameterization are factors, and of course are effective only for the case that the neuron activation level is *1* and not *0*. For given neuron activation levels of the visible layer v, the probability that a single neuron in the hidden layer h is an activated binary *1* with level adjusted by the shared weights w_{ij} modulating the visual layer neurons v_i is,

$$p(h_j = 1 \mid v) = \frac{1}{1 + e^{-(b_j + \sum_i v_i w_{ij})}} = \sigma\left(b_j + \sum_i v_i w_{ij}\right) \qquad (24.1)$$

where σ is the sigmoid function. There are two biases b_j in the RBM autoencoding, the *hidden layer floor biases* that activate some neurons regardless of any lack of relevant data points, and the *input layer biases* that accelerate learning on the backpropagation passes.

In the same fashion, the probability that for given neuron states of a hidden layer, a visible neuron is an activated binary *1* with level adjusted by the shared weights w_{ij} modulating the hidden layer neurons h_j is,[1]

$$p(v_i = 1 \mid h) = \frac{1}{1 + e^{-(a_i + \Sigma_j v_i w_{ij})}} = \sigma\left(a_i + \sum_j h_j w_{ij}\right) \qquad (24.2)$$

Equation 1 determines the activation probabilities of the hidden neurons (so-called *Gibbs sampling*) for **h** given **v**, where **v** is initialized by a random Bernoulli distribution (binary *yes* or *no*, *1* or *0*, as in a fair-coin toss). Equation 2 determines the activation probabilities of the visual neurons for **v** given **h**; together the equations produce the *joint probabilities* of **h** given **v** and **v** given **h**.

The difference between the initial random Bernoulli probabilities and the input data likely will be large. Feedforward runs and iterative back-propagation adjusting the weights w_{ij} and biases b_j will minimize that difference to produce *reconstructions* of the probabilities that will be better approximations of the unknown input data probability distribution.

In unsupervised learning, the RBM performs forward and backward passes between the visible and hidden layers where the activations of the hidden layer are the inputs to the input layer in a backward pass, multiplied by the same weights, and the sum is added to the input layer bias at each input layer node, and thus constitutes iterative reconstructions of the input layer.

The parameter adjustment is best performed not by gradient descent as in artificial neural networks but rather by so-called *contrastive divergence*. After k iterative runs, the adjusted input values vector v_k is iteratively reconstructed from the original input vector v_o, and used to determine the activation levels of the hidden vectors changing from h_o to h_k. The update matrix ΔW is the difference between the *outer products* $\otimes$ of the vectors v_o and v_k,[2]

$$\Delta W = v_o \otimes p(h_o \mid v_o) - v_k \otimes p(h_k \mid v_k)$$

---

[1] Equations 1 and 2 can be derived by applying the Bayes formula (Chapter 30) to the conditional probability equations and expanding. Interestingly, the sigmoid function can be derived from the *unrestricted* Boltzmann machine from the differences between energy states as expressed by the Boltzmann factor $E_i = -k_B ln P_i$. This shows that artificial neural network probability classification of objects is mathematically analogous to the phase changes of matter (solid, liquid, gas) as functions of free energy differences and temperature.

[2] The outer product is a matrix multiplication of two vectors to form a matrix, $[a \otimes b]_{ij} = a_i b_j$.

The new matrix is calculated using *gradient ascent*,

$$W_{new} = W_{old} + \Delta W.$$

The RBM-generated probability distribution can reveal latent inferences from "features" displayed by the neuron activation levels h_j in the hidden neuron layer h.[3]

For example, suppose the RBM is presented with a dataset of a survey of ages 18–29 users of an on-demand movie website comprising millions of data points. The users have chosen among the movies *Star Wars, the King's Speech, the Kissing Booth, the Matrix, Harry Potter,* and *the Three-Body Problem,* rating the films as to whether they like (*1*), do not like (*0*), or have not seen (*−1*) the movie.

For this particular group, the RBM finds that the probability distribution shows high ratings for *Star Wars* and the *Matrix* indicating a strong *like* inference for science fiction films, but the hidden layer feature neurons also show that those who like *the Matrix* also like *Harry Potter* in a cross-correlation revealing a *latent factor in collaborative filtering* inference for fantasy.

Now the *Three-Body Problem,* a new movie which no one has yet seen, has no-rating (*−1*) in the survey, but since the RBM discovered a preference for *science fiction* with a *fantasy* inference, it is highly probable that a specific user from that age 18–29 group will like *the Three-Body Problem,* and if inferences are further based on that particular user's data, the new movie may be confidently suggested to the user.

Whereas regression models estimate a continuous dependent variable based on the independent variable data input, and ANN classification models compare features extracted from the data with the features in labeled datasets, RBM reconstruction is attempting to model the *probability distribution* of the original input data through generating better and better probability distribution approximations to the input data by iteratively minimizing the error, and thus is a form of *generative learning.*[4]

---

[3] This mathematical description of an RBM has been simplified following Oppermann, A., *Ðeep learning meets physics, restricted Boltzmann machine, Part I,* towardsdatascience.com, which is based on the original paper, Salakhutdinov, R., A. Mnih, and G. Hinton 2006, *Restricted Boltzmann Machines for Collaborative Filtering,* University of Toronto.

[4] The RBM was invented by Geoffrey Hinton, one of the 2018 Turing Award winners. RBMs are one of the earliest ANNs and the forerunner of the more recent *generative adversarial networks* (GANs). In 2019, a GAN based solely on clothing contours could probabilistically reconstruct the body beneath the clothing; needless to say, the website was taken down soon afterwards, refer to MIT Technology Review, The Algorithm.

For example, if the unknown input data probability distribution $p(x)$ and the reconstructed probability distribution $q(x)$ are both normal distributions but have slightly different shapes and only partially overlap, the difference is the *Kullback-Lieber Divergence* that measures the diverse areas under the two probability distribution curves, as shown in the figure below.[5]

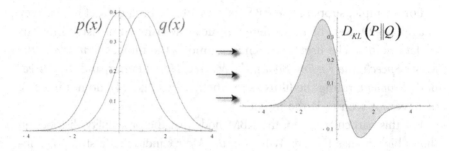

RBM contrastive divergence minimizes the diverse areas by adjusting the weight and bias parameters to model the unknown data probability distribution iteratively using the reconstructed probability distributions.

The integrated difference is shown at right in the figure is the Kullback-Lieber Divergence $D_{KL}(P\|Q)$ of the unknown probability distribution P and the reconstructed probability distribution Q.

Probability distributions are based on the probabilities of a set of outcomes. For example in rolling dice, out of a total of 36 possibilities, the probability of a lucky "7" is six time higher that the probability of snake eyes "2" since there are six ways of the dice adding to 7 and one for a snake eyes. The probability distribution will be revealed as a Normal distribution curve with the "7" at the peak and "2" and double six "12" on the wings of the Gaussian bell curve.

For different conditions, just as in the non-STP conditions for the phases of H_2O, for say speech recognition, the *e*, *t*, and *a* are the most commonly used letters in the English language, while in Icelandic, the most common letters are *a*, *r*, and *n*, so the probability distribution curves for the alphabet letter occurrence in speech are substantially different. Therefore using an English alphabet probability distribution on Icelandic speech will result in a large free energy, and the reconstruction will require several contrastive divergence runs to minimize the Kullback-

---

[5] Image from Mundhenk, T.N. 2009, Ph.D. thesis, University of Southern California.

Lieber Divergence to produce a better Icelandic alphabet distribution for speech recognition.[6]

An RBM is typically used in unsupervised learning initially to first model the unknown input distribution, and RBMs can be stacked to deep learn. The RBM hidden layer can act as a preprocessor, substituting its input layer with its hidden layer distribution and feeding its final reconstructed input layer to the input layer of a feedforward artificial neural network so that the ANN will have a generative-learning head start on determining the input data ground truth distribution.

An RBM can serve as a preprocessor for convolutional neural networks performing image and text recognition, and in conjunction with recurrent neural networks, also do speech recognition. But the RBM's main claim to fame is with regard to *latent factors in collaborative filtering.*

---

[6] Ref. Skymind.ai/restricted-boltzmann-machine.

CHAPTER 25

Latent Factors in Collaborative Filtering

R egression analysis and the restricted Boltzmann machine can reveal the overt and hidden features and correlations in raw input data, but deeper latent tendencies may remain buried and hidden in the data. Stanford University's *Parallel VLSI Architecture Group* has employed machine learning to analyze artificial intelligence neural networks' *hidden layers* to draw "inferences from inference at the data center", meaning obtain hidden information by delving more deeply into not only what the original network reveals, but also what can be further inferred from those revelations and their implications.[1]

Further processing of cloud-based artificial neural network results can reveal *latent factors* that improve the type of machine recognition that requires a great deal of inference to be accurate, for example in speech, translation, facial expression, body language, and precepts of human behavior.

In marketing, it is well known that purchasing decisions are not necessarily made on the ostensibly rational bases of price, quality, and utility, but for instance rather on the latent factors of fashion and prestige. Conformance to common fashion trends implies steadily lower pricing and thus less regard for quality so that more people will follow the trend, whereas high fashion implies a prestige that warrants over-pricing to maintain the exclusivity that a high price ensures. In neither case is utility a factor.

---

[1] Ref. *Spectrum*, IEEE, January 2017.

DOI: 10.1201/9781003214892-31

The inference for the luxury goods seller is that, unlike a common goods retailer, they should never lower prices or engage in discount sales promotions, for that would be contrary to the buyer's desideratum of exclusivity.

So what does the luxury goods seller do when a product just does not sell or is going out of fashion and unsold inventory is piling up? Big luxury brands' dirty little secret is that they will allow their employees upon sworn secrecy to buy unsold inventory at bargain prices. In this way, prices are never publicly lowered, inventory is cleared, and the employees who have acquired luxury items at discount hardly have incentive to reveal the secret as that would be detrimental to their own image.[2]

In the marketing of high-priced luxury items, advertisements and commercials in high-class settings populated with the stylish upper class are overtly placed to attract new customers, but covertly designed to mitigate the buyer's *post-purchase dissonance* that overpriced items invariably engender by reinforcing the wisdom of the buyer's original choice, with the inference of promoting future purchases.

At the other extreme, online purchasing is largely utility-oriented, and decisions made after price comparisons and online comments from previous buyers' regarding quality, so price-cutting on useful goods and peer reviews are critical to sales. Indeed, customer ratings and comments are even more important in regard to the purchase of common goods and the more subjective promotion of a song to listen to or a movie to watch.

The on-demand video website Netflix has found that factors such as age, gender, level of education, and demographics, or even the browsing history of the user, although useful, by themselves are inadequate precursors of movie choice.

Artificial intelligence has revealed that movie streaming decisions are often based on number of upvotes (likes), ratings, shares, and peer reviews, *in toto* the online *buzz* generated by a film.

Based on this buzz factor, which is a form of an online survey, Netflix has classified users into *taste clusters*; for instance, appreciative viewers of the film *The King's Speech* may not be interested in the high school film series *The Kissing Booth*, but nevertheless, based on latent inferences, teenagers with real or imagined speech impediments may like both, and Netflix will recommend "you may also like" films outside your designated cluster that have been flagged by the latent inferences of collaborative filtering.

---

[2] Personal communication with the Chief Executive of a famous French name brand.

Because there is a limit to how many movies a person can view in a given period of time, Netflix must ensure that users are happy with their choices, so for example using a restricted Boltzmann machine to predict inferentially what they will like, Netflix can recommend "twenty movies that are guaranteed to make you cry" to empathetic users, with further differentiation based on love, death, animal and pet stories, and thereby further present some "out of the box" recommendations to entice new interests, all to maintain Netflix's all-important churn rate at below 4%.

Netflix's successful use of inference surveys and artificial intelligence is a prime factor in its potential to disrupt the entire entertainment industry. The television movie-dominating HBO has 150 million subscribers, but they were acquired through the TV cable companies, so HBO had no direct access to viewer data on which to perform artificial intelligence predictive analytics, but with the acquisition by AT&T, HBO will become the telecommunications giant's subsidiary *WarnerMedia*'s on-demand movie hub, and now with data for predictive analysis, presumably make up ground on the online streaming video business dominated by Netflix.

In response, Netflix's Chief Content Officer Ted Sarandos, who bought the rights to the *House of Cards* series that launched Netflix's take-off into the online media world, posed the question very cogently to the future of the industry at large, "Will we become HBO before HBO becomes us?"[3]

The complexity of consumer behavior has spawned an entire academic discipline of artificial intelligence marketing psychology, and an enterprising *Adtech* service industry that employs machine learning and Big Data to go beyond intuition to delve more deeply into consumer behavior. Indeed, Adtech's discovery of latent factors driving the deeper psychology of purchasing decisions may be the genesis of some ostensibly very unusual advertisements and commercials.

Predictive analytics performed by restricted Boltzmann machines and artificial neural networks' generative learning can reveal the latent factors of decision-making through so-called *collaborative filtering*, which is based on the hypothesis that "people like things similar to other things they like, and things that are liked by other people with similar tastes".

Seemingly an utterly obvious premise, the similarities and tastes however are *latent* in the collation, and still must be discovered as

---

[3] Quote is from *The Economist*, November 3, 2018.

second-degree inferences from the first-degree inferences. Predictive analytics first seeks the low-hanging fruit of surveys, concert and box office receipts, DVD store sales, and so on; and then from music and movie websites, collect further data on online browsing, "likes", "shares", comments and social network discussions. The minimization by contrastive divergence then reveals the second-degree "inferences from the inference center". This more sophisticated data analytics can be used to predict the success of new, yet unheard songs and unseen movies that then can be utilized in *recommender systems* to generate buzz and concomitantly produce more data for more and perhaps deeper latent factors filtering.

Everyone now is aware that the surveys and constant requests for comments are not only meant to impart the feeling that the website has your interests at heart and strives to best serve your needs, but also to contribute your choices to their Big Data. Sales of consumer data by certain websites and analytics firms are proof of the data's commercial value.

In addition to the ostensible factors of romance, action, biography, fantasy, science fiction, and animation preferences of film choice, assume that a latent "redemption theme" is collaboratively filtered out, the members of a taste cluster then may find redemption-themed film recommendations on visiting the website, a predilection of which the viewers themselves might not have been wholly aware.

Some time ago in 2005, Netflix held an open competition for the best collaborative filtering algorithm to predict the attractiveness of new, yet unseen films. The analysis was based on the hard data of film buzz, and the soft data of collaborative filtering; the winning algorithm was performed on a restricted Boltzmann machine.[4]

EXOMOON DISCOVERY

The esoteric discipline of exoplanet-hunting by astronomers using space telescopes also depends on the latent factors in collaborative filtering of periodic dips in stellar light from faraway Galaxies as inferences of the signatures of putative exoplanets, possibly bearing intelligent beings, orbiting a star.

---

[4] Salakhutdinov, R., A. Mnih, and G. Hinton, 2007 *Restricted Boltzmann Machines for Collaborative Filtering*, University of Toronto, Proceedings of the 24th International Conference on Machine Learning dl.acm.org.

The nuances of an orbiting planet's periodic effect on a star's light was revealed by the deep artificial neural network *AstroNet-K2* that automatically removed instability and noise from the star's light signals by extracting brightness-over-time light curves for the star in question to find anomalies that betrayed the existence of an orbiting exoplanet. By autonomously filtering out other periodic light variations, thereby deleting false positives, AstroNet-K2 claimed a 98% accuracy on training datasets of found exoplanets, priming it for the inference of the existence of new exoplanets.

Periodic instabilities in the light signal from the star as disturbed by the exoplanet have revealed a latent filter collaboration that has been conjectured be an *exomoon* orbiting an exoplanet that is orbiting the star.

Astronomers have long believed that since for instance Saturn alone has 82 moons, large and small, it would be entirely reasonable that other planets around other stars would also have moons. Researchers sifting through brightness data from 284 exoplanets found by the Kepler Space Telescope indeed spotted the telltale smaller secondary brightness dip following an exoplanet's signature dip while transiting the star, and after confirmation by the Hubble Space Telescope, the inference was established that exoplanet K-1625b has a moon as massive as the Earth and four times its diameter.[5]

In July 2019, researchers using the *Altacama Large Millimeter/ Submillimeter Array* (ALMA) in Chile inferred from fuzzy splotches in millimeter wave patterns 370 light years away that the young planet PDS 70 c orbiting the T Tauri star PDS 70 has a circumplanetary disk one-fourth the mass of the Earth's Moon. Further studies have found numerous exomoons not so far from Earth.

Computer vision pattern recognition by a DCNN and data analytics could be employed on the images of giant radio telescope arrays in Chile and China to search for more exoplanets and exomoons.[6]

AstroNet-K2 could only spot the type of exoplanets that it had learned to recognize, but with reinforcement learning and self-supervision it

---

[5] Teachy, A., *Evidence for a large moon orbiting K-1625b*, Science Advances, 03 October 2018. Saturn's 20 new moons were discovered after long observations on the Mauna Kona telescope in Hawaii and reported on October 9, 2019.

[6] Refer to Isella, A., *et al.* 2019, *Detection of Continuum Submillimeter Emission Associated Candidate Protoplanets*, Astrophysical Journal Letters, Vol. 879, No. 2. Unfortunately, the Arecibo radio telescope in Puerto Rico collapsed in December 2020 just after de-commissioning Twice the size of Arecibo, China's Five hundred meter Aperture Spherical Radio Telescope (FAST) began operations in 2019.

could begin to think for itself to discover exoplanets with different signature characteristics, and like AlphaGoZero and the AI Video Gamer in their pursuits, could outperform even the most expert human astronomers in finding exoplanets and exomoons.

In doing so, the AI Astronomer will be assisting humankind in what is perhaps its ultimate undertaking, finding other intelligent beings in the Universe. It has been estimated that in our Milky Way Galaxy alone, almost every star has some orbiting planets and that there are therefore more than one trillion exoplanets and even more exomoons to be discovered.

Thus, humankind can either create intelligent beings here on Earth in the form of thinking robots, or find them in our own Galaxy as developed by superior beings. For the one trillion exoplanets developing during the 14 billion years of the Universe, taking the Earth as instance, intelligent beings will surely evolve on some of those exoplanets, and like us, they will surely develop artificially intelligent machines.

In the two trillion galaxies in the Universe and one trillion exoplanets per Galaxy, two trillion trillion (2×10^{24}) exoplanets have had and will have billions of years to develop some form of life, so by the sheer dint of numbers and time, there is little doubt that intelligent beings and their intelligent creations are on exoplanets and exomoons in the far reaches of all of the Galaxies.[7]

In this sense, the development of intelligent robots appears inevitable in some galaxy, and in spite of its threat to humankind's dominance on Earth, it is incumbent on us humans to do the same, if for no other reason than our own or our electromechanical progeny's advancement to maintain relevance in the Universe.

---

[7] The number of Galaxies is determined by telescope deep exposures of a sector of the sky and then extrapolation over the entire sky. The 1995 Hubble Space Telescope Deep Field two-week exposure by Robert Williams and subsequent deep field exposures by the Wide Field Camera 3 on the HST and the Subaru and Keck Telescopes taking exposures of different wavelengths together with the Doppler effect redshift provide depth, and the total number of Galaxies could be calculated from the Galaxies' known Gaussian and Power mass distributions. Conselice, C.J. 2017, *Our trillion-galaxy universe*, Astronomy, June.

CHAPTER 26

Support Vector Machines

C lassical statistical analysis such as regression analysis relies on the law of large numbers, which means that as the number of observations tends to infinity, the empirical probability distribution function inevitably converges to the ground truth distribution function. The recent successes of artificial neural networks have largely rested on today's unprecedented Big Data that provides the large number of numbers as training sets for machines to learn to classify and predict with ever greater accuracy.

There are, however, many disciplines that just do not have sufficient data to meet the requirement of the law of large numbers, so AI machines were devised to provide classification in cases of limited data.

A *Support Vector Machine* (SVM) takes subsets of data organized into *data vectors* and separates those *vectors* of data into classes by producing a demarcation that best divides the data vectors into classes on opposite sides of the demarcation; for two-dimensions, the demarcation is simply a line or curve, for three-dimensions the demarcation is a plane, and for higher-dimensions, the demarcation is a non-visualizable *hyperplane.*

By focusing on the data vectors closest to the dividing demarcation, called the *support vectors*, because they most significantly "support" the demarcation. Other data vectors in the assigned class but farther away from the optimal hyperplane do not define the classification and will

DOI: 10.1201/9781003214892-32

have little influence on the position of the optimal hyperplane, but they will be accurately classified.

The distance of the support vectors away from the hyperplane is called the *margin*; it that can be thought of as the width of a "street" running through the data vectors; the goal of an SVM is to find the demarcation that creates the maximum margin of the support vectors (the broadest street), thereby providing the optimal (most clear-cut) hyperplane separating the data being correctly classified on the appropriate side of the street margin(s).

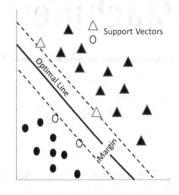

The figure at right depicts a two-dimensional space of data vectors to be classified with the different class vectors represented by circles and triangles, and classified by the *optimal line* whose margin is a measure of the severity of the separation in the vector space. The clear circles and triangles vectors represent the "support vectors" that are closest to the optimal dividing line and thereby delineate the margin (width) of the dividing classification; that is, they are the front-line "supporters" of the classification.

If a simple two-dimensional line cannot be found to distinctively separate the data vectors, for instance as in the case where the circle data vectors are bunched up and surrounded by triangular data vectors as shown in figure below at left, the data vectors can be mapped by a process called *kernelling* onto a three-dimensional space with the now "floating in 3D space" circle and triangular data vectors being separated by figuratively stretching out the classifying demarcation line to form a *flat plane*, and rotating the plane in space so as to best separate the circle and triangular data vectors and find the optimal plane with the margin of the support vectors as shown schematically in figure below at right. In physics terms, the expansion to three-dimensional space has created one more degree of freedom for the segregation of the data vectors into different classes.[1]

---

[1] The basic SVM algorithm was formulated by Vladimir Vapnik in 1963 and extended in 1992 to higher dimensions. "Distances" and "widths" in hyperspace are defined by vector inner products and are invariant in any dimension and in any coordinate system. For a marvelous mathematical derivation of SVM, see Winston, P. 2014, *Artificial Intelligence*, MIT 6.034, online, which is an excellent demonstration of how to do mathematical physics.

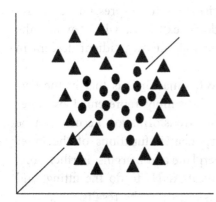 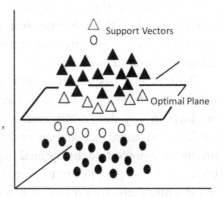

If the three-dimensional planar separation of the data vectors still does not clearly segregate the data vectors into classes, the space can be expanded into the higher dimensions of *hyperspace*, to provide more degrees of freedom for segregation of data vectors by finding *hyperplanes*. This kernelling of the space to four, five, six, and higher dimensions (in principle even to an infinite-dimension Hilbert space), although not visualizable, can be continued until the classification separation reaches a clearly definite *optimal hyperplane* (which in some cases may not be realizable).

The margins in any dimension can be calculated by the inner product of the support vectors and vectors orthogonal to the hyperplane producing scalar invariant margin "widths". These are the extent in *hyperspace* of the optimal hyperplane margins; that is, the minimum distances of the support vectors away from the hyperplanes. Clearly, the wider the margins, the more definite the classification.

The *Euler-Lagrange equation* and *Lagrange multipliers* can be employed to find the function that minimizes the margin extent under the constraint that the support vectors must be the vectors closest to the hyperplane (see the Appendix for the Euler-Lagrange equation and Lagrange multiplier).

The resulting optimal hyperplane expression, unfortunately in nonlinear form, produces a decision vector from a group of samples, and the optimization equation must be solved using numerical analysis, but since all of these computations are being done by a computer anyway, this is just another step in the SVM algorithmic process.[2]

---

[2] For the sampling algorithms and examples, see Ludicky, L. & P.H. Torr, 2011, *Locally Linear Support Vector Machines*, Conference Paper, January, available at researchgate.com, pdf.

It also can be shown that the decision vector expression is always concave so that there is only one global extremal, which avoids the problems of local minima and maxima endemic to gradient descent in artificial neural networks.[3]

The marvelous aspect of support vector machines is that in the kernelling transformation, the *kernel* can be simply represented by inner products in any dimension, and various transformation kernels can be tried, for example polynomial and exponential functions of the inner product vectors to find the optimal hyperplane and margins. Furthermore, there are fewer parameters than in typical ANNs to do the fitting, and significantly there are no local extremals to plague the results.

Support vector machines are typically used for text classification, spam filtering, image recognition, colors classification, and currently for handwritten digit recognition currently used in post office automation.

COMPUTATIONAL CHEMISTRY

An example of support vector machines use in the chemical sciences and engineering can highlight the research approach and the solutions that can be achieved by SVMs.

Experimentation, analysis of the data obtained, and an organizing hypothesis for making predictions for process engineering and new discoveries based on the analysis of those discoveries have been the general procedure of scientific and engineering research in chemistry, chemical engineering, materials science, environmental science, and pharmacology.

The analysis and predictions of chemical reactions has been done largely by classical statistical methods such as regression analysis performed on reactions data. However most of the reaction processes are complicated, non-linear, multivariate, with copious noise, all of which have made the efficient and accurate extraction of useful chemical research information extremely difficult.

Chemical reactions are influenced by temperature, pressure, concentration, catalytic activity, solvents, initial and boundary conditions, and myriad situational factors. The character and behavior of the materials involved are also affected by their chemical composition, phase, particle size, impurities, and other factors. Pharmaceutical drug design depends on the shape and charge of large organic molecules to complement the biomolecular target and is so complicated that it can only be done by computer modeling.

---

[3] Fung, G., *Concave Minimization for Support Vector Machines Classifications* PowerPoint, research.cs.wisc.edu.

Chemical and metallurgical engineering processes in industrial man-ufacturing involve heat transfer, mass transfer, fluid flow, chemical re-actions, reaction series, and typically more than five or six simultaneous processes that must be *feature selected* from dozens of possibilities, and all optimized for efficient plant operation.

Because of the many determinants relevant to *sui generis* chemical reactions and material processes, and then even more particulars to consider for industrial processes *in situ* operations, the solution to a practical problem involving a bewildering montage of disparate chemical agents, plus the necessity to separate the relevant factors from the irre-levant noise (which because of the complexity of the processes is always considerable) altogether render the predictions of any model fraught with difficulty and uncertainty.

For example, in a typical petroleum plant, the incoming crude oil from different countries is essentially and compositionally different, the crude oil composition from different tankers carrying oil even from the same source can substantially vary, and within the transport and storage holds, the temperature and pressure conditions are different for different con-tainers and change with time, the catalytic activity also changes over time, so there are on-going exothermic chemical reactions that can induce chaotic chemical and physical changes, and so on *ad infinitum* an en-ormous number of constantly changing factors affecting the chemical and thermodynamical processes of the plant. These factors render predictions regarding the chemical composition of the oil at delivery and during processing extremely uncertain.

Even being able to manage in the midst of all the vagaries of chemical reactions, different physical states, environmental and industrial plant conditions, the separation of relevant process factors from noise can further even vary with just the size of the sample.

A linear relationship certainly makes the hypothetical organizing re-gression function life simpler, but almost all the complicated chemical reaction processes of research interest are non-linear, and the simple straight line of linear regression considers *all* non-linear data as noise, so a simplistic linear model has the risk of underfitting the data, while the use of more complicated functions with many terms and adjustable parameters to fit non-linear data can result in too many adjustable parameterizations that will overfit the data.

The use of multivariate regression, because of the large number of variables and their often very complicated non-linear interactional

228 ■ Artificial Intelligence

relationships, typically results in a model having too many parameters, rendering its predictions and theoretical implementation results too variable to have much use.

If the organizing function is changed to a polynomial regression model based on the fact that any continuous function can be represented by a series of polynomials with an infinite number of terms (*Weierstrass' theorem*), and appropriately truncating the series may adequately approximate the function if multi-term polynomials of various degree with different coefficients can better fit the data. But this requires many more terms and parameters, again bearing the very real risk of overfitting the data and loss of generalization for prediction and practical implementation.[4]

Any continuous function can also be approximated by an artificial neural network, but ANNs are also plagued by the twin gremlins of underfitting and overfitting, and in the case of computational chemistry, there are too many chemical physics parameters for good modeling and too little data to depend on the law of large numbers to reach a useful generalizable result.

Because support vector machines can provide classification in a very high-dimensional hyperspace, there is in principle no limit to the number of factor segregations possible, and the SVM appears ideal for the highly complex computational chemistry of industrial processes that have limited experimental data.

However, because of the myriad different conditions and operational factors in complex processes, some refinement of the data must be first employed to improve the efficiency of classification; for instance, *outlier deletion* where the data samples exhibiting large errors in supervised training can be *leave-one-out* (LOO) cross-validated, thereby parsing the data of at least some of the more obvious noise.

Then SVM kernelling in the high-dimensional *feature space* of hyperplane space can be performed in a lower-dimensional *input space*. In this way, non-linear processes can be handled by SVM kernelling using the inner product of the data vectors involving a smaller number of adjustable parameters.

Support vector machines furthermore can treat both linear and non-linear processes at once, so the problem of underfitting can be reduced, and if the number of parameters in the organizing hypotheses can be

---

[4] John von Neumann famously said, "With four parameters I can model an elephant, and with five I can make him wiggle his trunk".

limited, there hopefully can be found a happy medium between under- and overfitting. The global extremal for finding the optimal hyperplane also makes the solution unique and therefor dependable.

Support vector machines are used in research of atomic parameter pattern recognition, thermodynamics, molecular structural relationships modeling, materials analysis, trace element studies, archeological chemistry, and in the practical industries of battery manufacture, petroleum engineering, cancer cures, and the design of chemical, materials, and pharmaceutical drugs.[5]

---

[5] For in-depth analysis of SVM in computational chemistry, refer to the author's cousin Chen, N.Y., *et al.* 2004, *Support Vector Machines in Chemistry*, World Scientific.

CHAPTER 27

Reinforcement Learning

einforcement learning (RL) was critical to AlphaGo's victories over the Go Masters, but the esoteric game, no matter how intriguing, is not that well known in Western countries (at least before AlphaGo). On the other hand, the Toronto/DeepMind Video Gamer's very public defeat of expert video gamers without even knowing the rules of the game beforehand was an eye-opening event entirely in tune with modern everyday life, especially among the young.

Learning by rewards and punishment is seemingly altogether common sense, and is used not only in raising children and workaday life, but also in many disparate disciplines such as game theory, automatic control, information theory, operations research, and even animal psychology.

Machines employing reinforcement learning were successful in game-playing against humans because the machine learned just like human beings learn, from experience with rewards and punishments, and any gamer knows that the more games you play, the better you will get, but unlike humans, a machine's skill can be tirelessly honed through millions of games against not only expert humans, but other machines, and once establishing its superiority, it can play against earlier versions of itself, ultimately going far beyond the skill of the best humans through machine self-strengthening.

In reinforcement learning, an agent in a given state can perform an action chosen from a set of all actions that the agent can take with respect

DOI: 10.1201/9781003214892-33

to the domain in which it finds itself, changing its action as necessary to adapt and confront changes in that environment. In a game-playing algorithm, the input is the agent's action in the current state of the domain, and the output is the reward or punishment emanating from the action taken in response to that state, resulting in a consequent state of the agent and the environment after that action.

From this it can be seen then that RL can be employ a Markov chain designating rewards and punishments to constitute a *Markov Decision Process* (MDP) in which the agent in the current state has all that the information regarding that state which is needed to decide on a new step. This is of course the same case in a move in chess or *Go* that changes the state of the game board and presents a new state to the player after every move, leading to the need of a decision based on the new state.

Reinforcement learning operates as a simple MDP feed-back loop operating in successive time increments, as shown in the figure below, where the subscripts denote time t and its increment $t + 1$. Reinforcement learning essentially constitutes a sequence of state-action (s_t, a_t) pairs that are performed respective to rewards (high positive values for r_t and r_{t+1}) and punishments (low or negative values for r_t and r_{t+1}).

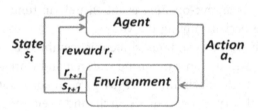

The agent seeks to select actions that maximizes the sum of rewards over time. The Q-learning algorithm finds the value of an action in a particular state by the Markov Decision Process which over time provides the Q-learning function with an *optimal policy* whereby the value of each action is represented by a Q-function that updates the state-action pairs (s_t, a_t) commensurate with the rewards of subsequent actions. Then the highest combination of immediate reward with all possible future rewards gained by later actions a_t is determined using the Bellman equation value iteration update with the weighted average of the old value and the new information,

$$Q^{new}(s_t, a_t) \leftarrow Q(s_t, a_t) + \alpha [r_t + \gamma max_a Q(s_{t+1}, a) - Q(s_t, a_t)]$$

where $Q^{new}(s_t, a_t)$ is the new Q value, α is the learning rate, the expression in square brackets is the learned new temporal value wherein r_t is the reward, γ is the discount factor, and $maxQ(s_{t+1}, a)$ is the estimate of maximum future value.

Q is initialized by an arbitrary value then as time t progresses, the agent selects an action a_t, notes the reward r_t, and enters a new state s_{t+1} and Q is updated to Q^{new} iteratively to produce the action value for the new state which should steadily increase as experience is gained, thereby learning how best to play the game.

The Q-function can consider delayed rewards introduced in later time steps in the game sequence, and can act recursively through program nesting to encompass those rewards in the algorithm computation.

The goal of the agent is to maximize the total reward. It does this by adding the maximum reward attainable from future states to the reward for achieving its current state, effectively influencing the current action by the potential future reward. This *Goal* is a weighted sum of expected values of the rewards of all future steps, expressed by,

$$Goal = max \sum_{t=0}^{\infty} \gamma^t r(s_t, a_t)$$

This is just the *maximization* of a sum of rewards $r(s_t, a_t)$ over time t multiplied by a discount factor γ raised to the t power, where s_t is the state at a given time and a_t is the action at that time.

The Q-function provides a numerical score for the action taken based on its effect on the environment by mapping each state-action pair to a number that is determined by experience of the rewards that best contribute to the states reaching the *Goal*.

For example, a pick-and-place robot is being trained by an RL agent controller to give the robot a positive reward for picking up the object and placing it in the designated position, but if the robot drops the object, places it in the wrong place, or does nothing at all, it is given a low or negative punishment number as "reward".

After running the game-playing algorithm many times in training, the Q-function selects the (s_t, a_t) pair with the highest Q *value* from that experience. Using feedback from the environment, a scalar reward is sent back for each new action.

The discount factor γ is essentially gauging the relative importance of immediate rewards versus future rewards. Since it has a value between 0 and 1 ($0 \leq \gamma \leq 1$), raising γ to the time t power means that if γ is small, as time goes by (t increases) the reward is multiplied by a fast-decreasing factor of γ^t and the value of the *Goal* decreases very quickly, so as $\gamma \rightarrow 0$ the reward is "myopic" (nearsighted) in the sense that the more immediate goals are important to reaching the *Goal* (for example in ping-pong). On the other hand, a larger γ does not reduce the value of the *Goal* so rapidly because as $\gamma \rightarrow 1$, the reward is "hyperopic" (farsighted) in that the reward multiplied by a slower-decreasing factor γ^t thus maintains a higher value longer, thereby attaching more relative importance to longer-term goals (for example in chess and *Go*).

In operation, γ also mathematically prevents the summation in the *Goal* equation from exploding to ∞ and hanging up the computation. The discount factor γ can be hand-engineered or machine-learned to maximize the probability of reaching the *Goal* after going through different *trajectories* in the activity. In complex environments, selecting the best action among many choices commensurate with a given state requires the *ranking* of the quality of actions, which is based on a measure of the *value* of (s_t, a_t) pairs; that is, how much do they further the positive accumulation of rewards, and a *policy function* π based on those values maps a state s_t to the best known action a_t,

$$a_t = \pi(s_t).$$

The value of a given action depends on the environment, the state in which it is performed, and the time it was taken. Reinforcement learning runs the agent through sequences of (s_t, a_t) pairs, noting the resulting rewards, and calculating the Q-function until it produces the best trajectory for the agent to take through the maximization process, in effect establishing the policy function π.

The policy function must of course avoid simply repeating the same actions or moves that previously garnered the highest rewards (overfitting), for that may cause the agent to forego actions with possible higher rewards, so in addition to *exploitation* of old avenues, *exploration* of new branches should be included in the algorithm; the ratio of the two is,

$$\epsilon = \frac{\text{Exploration}}{\text{Exploitation}}$$

where the more daring agents will be so-called *ϵ-greedy*.

For example, in the first electronic video game played at MIT, the paddle agent successfully hitting the ping-pong ball back has a positive reward of continuing to the possibility of gaining a point, and missing the ball has a negative reward of losing a point, with the goal of course being amassing a certain number of points sooner than the opposing player.

Anyone who has played ping-pong, tennis, handball, or racquetball knows about the doughty returner who just returns every shot, and the attacker who takes chances with daring shots. The ε-greedy player's exploratory shots can result in immediate rewards of winning points, but are easier to miss and result in a punishing loss of a point, where tried and true shots exploit the delayed reward of steady return play banking on an opponent's error. The reward function thus reflects the ε-greedy player's percentage of missed attacking shots.

After many games, the discount factor γ will have modulated the rewards commensurate with the player's skill level as revealed by the iterative accumulation of reward and punishment over the multiple games, the best average results thus will produce the best policy function for the particular player that emphasizes his skills and discounts his weaknesses.

Thus, the reinforced learning Q-function maps state-action pairs to rewards to find the value of an action. A computer vision convolutional neural network can be employed to recognize a state, for example the image of a barrier and its surroundings confronting Super Mario represents a state, and after the CNN recognizes the barrier, then the policy function π based on those values maps a state s_t to the best known action a_t. The ranks of the possible actions that the agent can perform in that state to overcome the barrier (for example jumping a wall or avoiding a swinging door) the actions to take, for instance, jumping over the barrier will give Super Mario 10 points, because going around the barrier takes more time, it gives only 5 points, and hitting it head-on will result in a −5 points punishment.

It is important to realize that there are no physical principles at play in reinforcement learning and there is no need for supervised training, although it can be employed as a head-start. RL proceeds through Q-learning which chooses paths of actions iteratively that produce higher expected values based on the rewards and punishments of the action.

Reinforcement learning algorithms thus are supremely generalizable as they learn from the accumulation of own experience in a given situation just as humans do. Thus, like humans they can explore and handle many different tasks completely bottom-up with no top-down hand-engineering, and since they have no subjective predilections, unlike humans, they can objectively proceed based entirely on the Q-learned optimal policy, and after tireless 24/7 practice, they can easily defeat the emotionally- impaired and time-constrained human without even *a priori* knowing the rules of the game!

CHAPTER 28

Alphago and Alphastar

AlphaGo's artificial neural network emulates the human brain's network of neurons that are activated by input stimuli to form ideas by synaptic network connections producing "thought" patterns. DeepMind's original version of the artificial neural network for playing *Go* had a *19 × 19 × 48* volume matrix input layer and 13 filter-convolved hidden layers fully connected to a softmax layer and decision vector.

AlphaGo's hardware comprised 1920 CPUs, 280 GPUs, and in the matches against Korea's Lee Sedol and China's Ke Jie, employed Google's accelerating Tensor Processing Unit (TPU) ASIC.

Because of the almost infinite number of possible moves (2×10^{170}), a Markov chain tree search was used as an *expansion* of possible moves. After each move, the subsequent branches of moves are offered and chosen, and finally through simulated *playout* of a game, the *value* of the moves can be determined.

AlphaGo learns how to play first through supervised learning, in this case by playing a training set of published professional *Go* matches. Then by gradient-descent it minimizes the costs of being wrong when compared with labeled optimal moves in the training set, and by adjusting the initially randomly assigned parameters of weights and biases of the neuron activation levels by backpropagating the differences, AlphaGo learned how to play as well as a professional *Go* master.

At this point, AlphaGo could easily defeat amateur players, but it must *improve* to be able to play with professional *Go* Masters, so after supervised training, AlphaGo was trained by reinforcement learning to

DOI: 10.1201/9781003214892-34

generate a *value network* resulting in a playing *policy*, and then refined its policy by playing against improving versions of itself in self-supervised learning.

The reinforcement learning could use the γ discount factor to help evaluate rewards for both exploitive immediate local *fights* and the delayed exploration of remote *position*.

While the best players like Lee Sedol and Ke Jie are always aggressively looking for and exploiting local fights, AlphaGo was expected to play a cold, computerized Deep Blue type top-down style to provoke and then engage in those fights to gain territory, but reinforced learning taught AlphaGo also to be ε-greedy, often foregoing potential gains in a local fight to adventurously explore new board positions.[1]

For instance in Game 1 against Lee Sedol, AlphaGo preferred to take an exploratory *sente* initiative in the upper left of the board, and forego the perceived wisdom of *aji*, the "savoring" of possibilities in a classic local fight, a move that many commentators regarded as critical to victory in Game 1.

Being ε-greedy can open up new areas of contention, and with the first foray stone standing at the position that will definitively characterize the new territorial clash, it has the advantage, and may be able to thusly control the progression of the new territorial conflict.

However, exploratory forays that produce no positive gains in territory or stones can result in unnecessary losses of territory and stones by foregoing immediate exploitive fights, where it was believed that AlphaGo would be more effective, but, a supposedly a more coldly logical AlphaGo computer showed that it could be adventurous as well as meticulous.[2]

For example, AlphaGo's *fifth-line shoulder hit* black 37 in Game 2 was met with astonishment from commentators and even Lee himself, for it seemingly gave up too much potential boundary territory to white, and indeed a post-match check of AlphaGo's game log

---

[1] If AlphaGo must choose between a scenario where it will win by 20 points with 80 percent probability and another where it will win by 1 and a half points with 99 percent probability, it will choose the latter, even if it must give up points to achieve it. Chouard, T. 2016, *AI computer clinches victory against Go champion*, The Go Files, Nature, 12 March.

[2] For example, Daniels, B, 2016, *Awed by AlphaGo Review of Games 1 and 2*, YouTube, 12 March.

found that the move was ranked at only as a 10^{-4} reinforcement learning action value, yet this widely regarded exploratory move was seen as the key to victory in Game 2 because it unified AlphaGo's total board position by subsequent consolidation with the upper right quadrant of the board.[3]

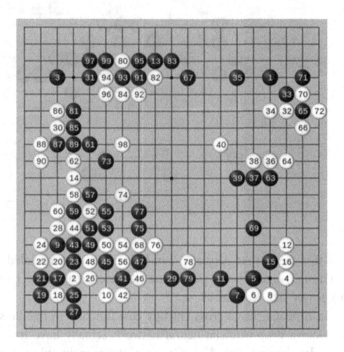

By the same token, because of the greater unpredictability of high reinforcement rewards for exploratory moves, AlphaGo's pursuit of delayed position rewards (*sente*), can easily lead to a dearth of exploiting the latent lingering possibilities that a well-placed stone that a fight presents; that is, "taste" (*aji*). Moreover, in Game 4, AlphaGo lost perhaps because Lee's "divine wedge move" white 78, being so unexpected, discombobulated AlphaGo into a number of "mistakes", perhaps paying the price of ε-greediness.

---

[3] As opposed to chess, after many back-and-forths with China and Korea, the Japanese prevailed by establishing black moves first in *Go*.

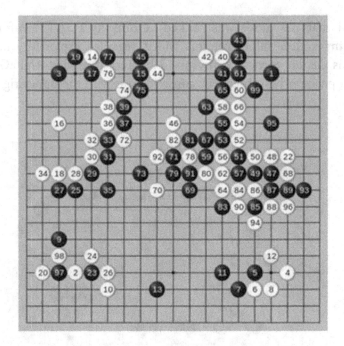

Does this mean that AlphaGo can be surprised and addled, just like Deep Thought against the pawn-line defense or a prone to paranoia human player like Kasparov?

Should AlphaGo use a cross-entropy cost function to handle such surprises? Does a deep artificial neural network actually have frailties in all those hidden layers? Are AlphaGo's emotions analyzable, or are those emotions concealed deep within an artificial neuron network's hidden layer psyche? Is any emotion or indecision discernible in AlphaGo's subsequent moves as shown in the figure above after Lee Sedol's white 78?

Despite worries that AlphaGo after its Game 4 loss might change its tactics, or worse alter its policy and succumb to confusion in the face of an opponent's improbable moves (just like Kasparov's anti-computer chess strategy). However, AlphaGo won a close Game 5 and the Match, apparently able to recover from its mistakes and remain (uncharacteristically for a computer) adventurously e-greedy.

VIDEO GAMER

Toronto's Video Gamer versus An Expert Gamer Human was contested on the Atari 2600 testbed games of *Beam Rider, Breakout, Enduro, Pong, Q*bert, Seaquest,* and *Space Invaders*, presenting a *210 x 160* RGB raw pixel video at 60 Hz with game-playing environment that was specifically designed to be difficult. The game-playing model is a convolutional neural network trained with a reinforcement learning variant of Q-learning.

The playing agent's sampled experiences at each time step were pooled over many episodes into a *replay memory* and smoothed over many past behaviors. Q-learning is applied during an inner do-loop of the game-playing algorithm employing stochastic mini-batch updates that reinforcement-learn from the visual inputs to the computer vision deep convolutional neural network.

The input to the neural network is an *84 × 84 × 4* image, the first hidden layer is a *16 × 8 × 8* filter convolutional layer with stride 4; the second hidden layer convolves 32 *4 × 4* filters with stride 2, and the final hidden layer is a fully connected 256 units rectifier in what was called a *deep Q network* (DQN). The output layer is a fully connected vector with a single output for each valid action. The number of valid actions varied from 4 to 18 in the games.

The same network architecture, learning algorithm, and hyperparameters were used for all seven games with no hand-engineered game rules provided. Since the scores greatly varied from game to game, all positive rewards were set to be 1 and all negative rewards to −1, and 0 rewards for moves having no effect, thereby providing a very generalizable model. The simple rewards structure limits the scale of the error derivatives and facilitates the employment of the same learning rate for different games, but all at the risk of degrading agent speed to its *Goal* because there is no great rewards differentiation.

In supervised learning, the model's performance can be tracked with training, validation, and test data sets, but in reinforcement learning the evaluation algorithm took the total reward the agent collects in an episode or total game averaged over a large number of games.

The estimated *action-value* Q-function was used, which provides an estimate of how much delayed reward the agent can obtain by following through on its network policy from any given state.

As the reinforced learning algorithm ran, there were relatively smooth improvements to predicted Q-vales during reinforcement learning, and there was no divergence in any of the games (surprisingly, but likely because of limits placed on the error derivatives). This suggests that, despite lacking any theoretical convergence guarantees, the game algorithm is able to train large neural networks using reinforcement learning signals and stochastic gradient descent in a very stable manner.[4]

---

[4] Mnih, V. *et al.* 2013, *Playing Atari with Deep Reinforcement Learning*, arXiv.org, arXiv.1312.5602[cs.LG].

In a more difficult challenge in 2018, DeepMind's *AlphaStar* beat all human gamers in the real-time online video game *StarCraft II*. That Toronto's Video Gamer, without even first knowing the rules of the games, can play many different games and perform as well or better than expert human gamers appears to exactly match what is meant by the first definition of intelligent "learning", and if AlphaStar can adapt to the more complicated *StarCraft II*, then it precisely satisfies the definition of generalizable intelligence in Chapter 3; that is,

The ability to acquire and apply knowledge and skills

with the buttressing addition,

the ability to perceive or infer information, and to retain it as knowledge to be applied towards adaptive behaviors within an environment or context,

and

general cognitive problem-solving.

What is more disturbing, DeepMind has developed a *team* of video game agents who were trained to act independently to cooperate to compete in 450,000 runs of the *Quake III Arena* in *Capture the Flag* mode using only pixel and game points scored as input. The agents in concert developed strategies that could defeat human player teams in tournament-style evaluations using a two-tier optimization process in which independent RL agents are trained concurrently on randomly generated environments with each agent learning its own rewards. Swarms of robots cooperating to achieve specified competitive goals are ominously clear on the AI horizon.[5]

---

[5] Jaderberg, M., *et al.* 2019, *Human-level performance in 3D multiplayer games with population-based reinforcement learning*, Science, 31 May. Capture the Flag is played by teams trying to capture each other's flag.

CHAPTER 29

Game Theory

I n the board games of checkers, chess, and *Go*, the players know the exact state of all the pieces at every point in the game in *perfect information* competitive settings. In contrast, poker is an *imperfect information* game where there are hidden cards unknown to both the player and his opponent.

Carnegie-Mellon's *Libratus* poker-playing AI computer had not only correctly guessed the quality of the opponent's hand and without complete information, but also prevented the opponent from accurately guessing its own cards solely by analyzing the timing and amount of bets in a round. How did Libratus do this so successfully that it could defeat the world's top players in Texas Hold'em?

A computer cannot display feigned anguish or joy to deceive an opponent when dealt a hand or during betting, but by the same token, it is immune to the opponent's facial and body language subterfuges.

Therefore, both the computer and its human opponent must rely only on the timing and amounts of its betting to conceal a good or bad hand, and entice calls and raises or provoke premature folding solely by means of the bluff and bluster of the size and timing of the bets.

A player obviously must mix up his betting strategy throughout a game to avoid patterned behavior (overfitting) being recognized and exploited by the opponent, and likewise be able to recognize any patterns of betting behavior of the opponent, and adjust his own betting strategy for advantageous responses.

Is there a scientific basis for developing a poker-betting strategy that can be performed by a computer? Winning is of course based on

DOI: 10.1201/9781003214892-35

probabilities in a constrained system that can be gauged and exploited, something that every poker player knows all too well.

Betting strategy can be based on the Bayes formula and probabilities assigned to Markov chain nodes in Monte Carlo tree-search simulations, but the upper hand in the finite, adversarial, imperfect information game of poker curiously lies in the exploiting the *Nash equilibrium* of mathematical game theory.

A *strategic equilibrium* in a finite adversarial game, is reached when every player employs a strategy such that no one player can benefit by changing strategies while the other players do not change their strategies. The mathematician John Nash proved that such an equilibrium exists in every finite game.

We have all experienced the Nash equilibrium in the adversarial and trivially finite sequential game of *tic-tac-toe* where one typically starts at a corner, and if the opponent is not aware of the Nash equilibrium and also plays a corner, the first player will win. If the opponent plays any other position, and the players proceed rationally, the Nash equilibrium will hold and stalemates will be reached for every game where neither player will ever win.

		B		
		ROCK	PAPER	SCISSORS
A	ROCK	0,0	-1,1	1,-1
	PAPER	1,-1	0,0	-1,1
	SCISSORS	-1,1	1,-1	0,0

A zero-sum game where each player attempts to maximize his *payout* and minimize the opponent's payout is the adversarial but not sequential game of *rock-paper-scissors*. The payouts where winning is *1*, losing is *−1* and a draw is *0*, can be displayed on a *strategic form* shown below where in each element of the game matrix, the first number is Player A's payout and after the comma, the second number is Player B's payout.

It turns out statistically that if one randomly plays each choice 33% of the time, in the very long run, that strategy cannot be exploited, and if the opponent discovers that and plays the same way, neither player can exploit the other, and over time the players are at an impasse in a rock-paper-scissors Nash equilibrium where neither has an advantage and each will end up losing as much as winning.

But if one player diverges from the equilibrium strategy, for example increasing the percentage of paper plays, although winning in some instances, that player's departure from the Nash equilibrium can be exploited, and in the long run since he cannot exploit an opponent who strictly adheres to the equilibrium strategy, he will lose more than he wins because he withdrew from the Nash equilibrium.

To demonstrate how a player can maximize his payout while minimizing an opponent's payout in a more complicated game, the football penalty-kick (PK) whose strategic form matrix is shown below.

		G (S_2)	
		LEFT	RIGHT
K (S_1)	LEFT	0.6, 0.4	0.8, 0.2
	RIGHT	0.9, 0.1	0.7, 0.3

The PK has more subtle payouts based on for instance a left-footed penalty-kicker's stronger right (R) direction shot and a goalie's stronger right-lunge block of a kicker's left (L) side shot, and considering that statistically most PKs are made, the goalie's payout is generally lower than the kicker's payout, but still dependent in many cases on the direction of the PK's blocking move, as shown by the data-based elements (here arbitrarily chosen with regard to the different payoutx) in the PK strategic form matrix.

Now mathematically, the zero-sum or constant sum k is just,

$$S_1(s_1, s_2) + S_2(s_1, s_2) = 0 \, (or \, k)$$

where s_1 is the kicker S_1's strategy, and s_2 is the goalie S_2's strategy. The *minimax theorem* states that the strategies for the kicker and the goalie (s_1, s_2) are in an *equilibrium* of a zero-sum game if and only if,

$$S_1 = arg \, \underset{s_1' \in S_1}{max} \, min_{s_2 \in S_2} \, S_1(s_1', s_2)$$

where the prime indicates a dummy variable, and

$$S_2 = arg \, \underset{s_2' \in S_2}{min} \, \underset{s_1 \in S_1}{max} \, S_1(s_1, s_2').$$

Thus for S_1 (and similarly for S_2),

$$S_1(s_1, s_2) = maxmin\ S_1(s_1, s_2) = minmax\ S_1(s_1, s_2).$$

This is simply saying that player S_1 is trying to find the s_1 that maximizes his utility while his opponent S_2, whose probability payout is minus S_1's payout, is trying to minimize S_1's utility; and similarly vice versa for player S_2, all of which together constitutes the *equilibrium strategy*.

The kicker will maximize and minimize according to the values arrayed in the strategic form matrix as,

$$\max_{s_1} \min_{s_2} [s_1(L)s_2(L) * 0.6 + s_1(L)s_2(R) * 0.8 + s_1(R)s_2(L) * 0.9$$

$$+ s_1(R)s_2(R) * 0.7].$$

Now since the probabilities of the converse is just (1 – the probability of the chosen strategy),

$$s_1(R) = 1 - s_1(L)\ and\ s_2(R) = 1 - s_2(L).$$

To find the minimum outcome on S_2's strategy, take the minimum part only,

$$\min_{s_2} [s_1(L)s_2(L) * 0.6 + s_1(L)(1 - s_2(L)) * 0.8 + (1 - s_1(L))s_2(L) * 0.9$$

$$+ (1 - s_1(L))(1 - s_2(L)) * 0.7],$$

then taking the derivative with respect to $s_2(L)$ and setting equal to zero to find the minimum,

$$0.2 - s_1(L) * 0.4 = 0 \rightarrow s_1(L) = 1/2.$$

Since $s_1(R) = 1 - s_1(L)$, then $s_1(R) = 1/2$ as well, the kicker should mix his PK strategy by half-half to the left and right, which seems eminently reasonable, but as in all of mathematics, you must still demonstrate it, and here it is demonstrated.

However, repeating the procedure above for the goalie S_2, the result for minimizing the kicker S_1's strategy is,

$$s_2(L) = 1/4 \text{ and } s_2(R) = 3/4,$$

revealing that the goalie's strategy should be to lunge to the right 3/4 of the time and 1/4 to the left to block the penalty kicks, which actions reflect his stronger side, but nonetheless is demonstrated here. Of course these outcomes are the product of kicker and goalie data in the strategic form, once again demonstrating the importance of Big Data, even for the ostensibly unpredictability of sports.

These strategies together produce the equilibrium strategy for the players in this particular PK situation, which means that if either that kicker or that goalie deviates from his strategy and the other does not, the deviator will lose over the long run of many, many PKs; that is just the essence of the Nash equilibrium.

This analysis, however, is based on the weighting of the perceived strengths of the kicker and the goalie, and it has been shown that in PK situations over many games, there is no statistical difference in the directions of shots taken and goalie lunges, and that players mostly behave randomly with only a slight tendency to go to strong sides.[1]

IMPERFECT INFORMATION

Perhaps the only thing that men like more than football is gambling, with the voluble *mano a mano* game of heads-up, no-limit Texas Hold'em poker having special appeal. Expert card players will always rely on the probabilities, such that they can ascertain, but since there are 10^{161} decision points in a game of poker, traversing the entire game tree even once is impossible, and a deterministic choice for each point is clearly not possible to obtain for an entire game, and so the Nash equilibrium for the whole game is almost impossible to determine.

Instead, a model of the *abstraction* of cards and action is developed, which in computer science jargon means the removal of physical, spatial, and temporal details and attributes in order to focus on the essentials of the task at hand, in this case the cards and betting actions in a game of poker.

---

[1] Palacio-Huertas I., 2003, *Professional Player Minimax*, Review of Economic Studies, 70.

In the abstraction, there are many strategically similar situations that can be classified together for tree search, for example similar hands like early-round king-high and queen-high flushes (*card abstraction*) and similar bets like $500 and $595 can be classified together in increments of $100 (*action abstraction*).

Libratus' first of three main modules computed approximate Nash equilibrium solutions using minimax theory in an abstraction of poker to serve as a game *strategy blueprint* for the early rounds of the game which in turn served as a precursor strategy for later rounds. The initial betting actions in the abstraction were patterned after the most common bet actions by the top contenders in the *Annual Computer Poker Competition* (ACPC), to provide the strategy form matrix elements. If during play, the opponent chooses an action that is not in the abstraction, that action is mapped to a similar action that is in the abstraction.

The blueprint strategy was honed by Libratus playing simulated games against itself in reinforced learning using a modified version of the *Monte Carlo Counterfactual Regret Minimization* (MCCFR) iterative algorithm that independently minimizes "regret" at every decision point, registering how much regret there is at not choosing an action in the past (anyone who has ever played poker can easily see how particularly germane the MCCFR is to poker). So given the opportunity, Libratus will choose the action with the highest regret, gradient-descent back-propagate, and after many game iterations, the average of the regrets is minimized to approach zero, thereby improving the blueprint strategy.

In simulated games, one player will explore every possible action in the abstraction and update his regrets while the opponent plays solely on his current regrets. The roles of the two players are then reversed after each hand. An objective probability distribution is thus determined on the basis of regrets of actions in previous games, thereby providing the *value* of a betting action. That value also depends on the probability of it being played in a later hand, where the value decreases if overly- or underly-played as determined by the assessment of the opponent's responses and one's own weaknesses as results of the play.

In "heads up, no-limit" Texas Hold'em poker, the "heads-up" refers to only two players playing against each other so that there is no possibility of collusive ganging-up on a player as can happen in multiple-player games; the "no-limit" means that a player can bet up to all his chips at one time, making for much greater betting variability and risk.

In heads-up but *limited* bets poker-playing systems, there are only 10^{13} unique decision points; if both players play according to the MCCFR in a zero-sum game, their average strategies converge to a Nash equilibrium. But to account for the 10^{161} static decision points in *no-limit* Hold'em poker, Libratus improved the MCCFR by a sampled form of *Regret-Based Pruning* (RBP) where the high regret branches are pruned.

Then the whole game is broken down into *subgames* that are individually amenable to Nash equilibrium calculations which are used primarily for *defensive* purposes in finding one's own weaknesses to avoid being exploited by one's opponent, and secondarily for *offensive* purposes of finding weaknesses in the opponent's strategy and exploiting them. The strategy blueprint then can be iteratively adjusted and calculations speeded up in response to the agent and the opponent's play.[2]

In game theory, a *subgame* is any subset of a game where all members of the subset belong to the subgame that has a single initial node and includes all of its own successor nodes (as shown schematically in the schematic figure at right where there are altogether six subgames, two of which contain two subgames each as enclosed by the ovals).

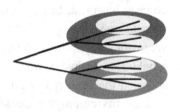

A subgame therefore is a game that constitutes a game in its own right, and by dint of its designed isolation, credible threats germane only to the whole game are in principle eliminated in the subgame, thereby allowing the player to concentrate on analyzing the subgame while ignoring the whole game's earlier history and later progressions.

In a two-player sequential game, in the figure, Player A chooses an action to go up or down at the whole game initial node. Player B then can choose to go left or right in a *subgame* within the ellipses depending on the action chosen by Player A. Then a strategic form matrix may be constructed of probable outcomes of the subgames just as in the PK situation, and a Nash equilibrium can be calculated using the minimax for each subgame.

In Libratus' second module, a *nested safe-subgame solver* provides strategy in the subgame from an estimate of the value of reaching the subgame Nash

---

[2] There are Nash equilibrium charts and calculators for poker players' use, refer to poker.stackexchange.com. For the intriguing story of John Nash, refer to Nassar, S, 1998, *A Beautiful Mind*, Simon & Shuster, also a movie directed by Ron Howard and starring Russell Crowe (2001).

equilibrium. The playing strategy blueprint module already estimated its Nash equilibrium and thus this value, and also for every subgame using these values for input, so the subgame solver solves in a finer-grained abstraction that is reached in real time; that is, it solves a new subgame every time an opponent chooses an action that is not in the fine-grained abstraction, effectively constructing a new subgame including that action every time the opponent bets, thereby automatically and repeatedly calculating more and more finely-grained detailed strategies as play progresses.[3]

In actual playing however, a subgame should not be solved in complete isolation because winning strategies may depend on prior subgames and games hitherto not yet reached. If the blueprint is slavishly followed in spite of this, so-called *unsafe-subgame solving*, an opponent can recognize the patterns as simple isolated gambits and exploit them with a more comprehensive strategy considering whole games experiences.

To offset this, a *safe-subgame solving* still places all actions within the strategy blueprint, but a more detailed subgame abstraction using minimax aims to make the opponent worse-off no matter what cards are held by approximating an optimal strategy through assessing how much more a player would lose against a worst-case action by an opponent than if he simply followed the strategy blueprint; in this way reflecting overall considerations.

Libratus employs a dense action abstraction in the first two betting rounds of a game, in the *self-improver* third module, the missing branches in the *a priori* blueprint are filled in and a game-theoretic strategy is computed for those branches using the opponent's actual actions to guide the tree-search filling-in. If the opponent does not bet an amount that is in the abstraction, the bet is rounded off to a nearby size that is in the abstraction; this however causes a slight distortion in the strategy and estimates of reaching certain subgames, and the rounding error must be reduced by adding a small number of actions to the abstraction.

Which actions are added depends on the most frequent actions chosen by the opponent and how far those actions were from the solution to the abstraction, thereby filling in effective missing branches in the blueprint abstraction. Once an action is selected, a strategy for those new branches is calculated by the techniques of the nested safe-subgame solver.

---

[3] For heads-up, no-limit Texas Hold'em play, details and examples of play, proofs of theorems, and even the computer program for the safe nested subgame solver, see Brown, N, & T. Sandholm, 2017, *Superhuman AI for heads-up, no-limit poker: Libratus beats top professionals*, Science Research Articles, 10.1126/Science.aao1733.

In this way, Libratus augments and refines the pre-computed blueprint over time based on the *weaknesses in its own game* that the opponent has found in the strategy blueprint as determined by the opponent's actual play.

Libratus thus is not only learning how to exploit the opponent's play, but also learning how to make its own play less exploitable.

In an imperfect information benchmark AI challenge, Carnegie-Mellon's Libratus successively trounced four professional players in a heads up, no-limit Texas Hold'em poker competition. Libratus does not use expert domain knowledge and its techniques are game-independent so they can be applied to different opponents, and in other imperfect information activities such as business, finance, politics, diplomacy and even warfare.[4]

After two years of further development, Carnegie-Mellon's new *Pluribus*, not limited to heads-up poker, took on six players simultaneously in 15 no-limit Texas Hold'em matches and convincingly won them all. One would think that with the many more possibilities in multiplayer poker, Pluribus would need more computing power than Libratus' 100 CPUs provided, but Pluribus needed only two CPUs to defeat multiple top professional poker players.

The reason is that Pluribus took some pages out of AlphaGoZero's playbook by reinforcement learning and self-supervision over *trillions* of poker hands. By starting from zero, just randomly betting, learning and then refining its play based on checking back after each training hand against itself as to which betting actions actually won the most money, Pluribus thus used the law of large numbers to defeat the best human players, who in their entire lives could never assemble that much experience.[5]

The multiplayer game is more reflective of real-life situations of imperfect knowledge, and Pluribus' capability can be advantageously used in economic and geopolitical negotiation, fraud detection (fittingly from its roots in poker), and autonomous driving, where one is dealing with many other traffic, obstacle, and rules "adversaries" at once.

After convincing victories in the urbanely intellectual board games, quiz shows, and debating society debates, the AI machine has also proved that it can excel in youthfully reflexive video games and the raucous world of Texas Hold'em poker, thus able to confidently enter the real world.

---

[4] Ref. Policonimics.com.

[5] Brown, N. and T. Sandholm, 2019, *Superhuman AI for multi-player poker*, Science, 365, 6456,885, 30 August.

VII

Natural Language Processing

CHAPTER 30

Top-Down Speech Recognition

The first technical problem in natural language processing is to get spoken words into the computer for analysis. If you put your hand on your throat when you speak, you will find that it is vibrating, and thus is sending out longitudinal sound waves, compressing the air in periodic puffs that in instances of unvoiced *stop sounds* (such as "p"), utterances can be differentiated. When the wave impinges a listener's ear drum, it will cause it to vibrate in step with the impinging waveform, and an auditory nerve will send electrical signals proportional to the sound waveform to the brain for speech processing.

In machine *front-end processing*, the sound wave impinges the diaphragm of a microphone attached to a *Fast Fourier Transform* (FFT) analyzer, and a graph is produced of the air vibration amplitudes over time, with different sounds producing differently-shaped transverse waves, for example Amazon's "Happy Birthday" greeting in the figure at right. Distinct sounds will have higher amplitudes manifested in distinctive peaks called *formants* as shown in the figure.[1]

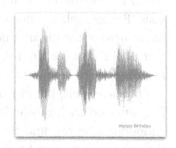

According to Fourier, no matter how complicated a wave is, it can be represented as an infinite *sum* of sine and cosine waves having different amplitudes a_n and frequencies ω over time,

---

[1] Courtesy of Amazon screen shot.

DOI: 10.1201/9781003214892-37

$$f(t) = a_0 + \sum_{n=1}^{\infty} [a_n \cos(n\omega t) + b_n \sin(n\omega t)]$$

where a_0 is just the coefficient for $n = 0$, $a_0\cos(0\omega t) = a_0$, and there is no b_0 because for $n = 0$, $b_0\sin(0\omega t) = 0$. For $n \geq 1$, the a_n are the *Fourier coefficients* which describe the "amounts" of cosine and sine of each frequency in the sound wave as represented by their amplitudes; they are given by

$$a_0 = \frac{1}{T} \int_0^T f(t), \quad a_n = \frac{2}{T} \int_0^T f(t)\cos(n\omega t)\, dt,$$

$$b_n = \frac{2}{T} \int_0^T f(t)\sin(n\omega t)\, dt$$

From the shape of the "Happy Birthday" waveform above, it can be seen that a series of sine and cosine functions with different amplitudes and frequencies indeed has the capability to represent speech.[2]

It turns out that the waveforms of *vowels* repeat themselves very clearly in sentences and because of their distinctive shape at different frequencies and naturally relatively larger amplitude, they have the greatest sound distinctions that can be uttered by humans, so a listener can easily distinguish them one from the other.

The amplitudes of sound as a function of frequency is called *sound spectra* that shows the discrete location of formants that reveal the speech characteristics of loudness, pitch, intonation, and accent.

Human hearing is critically dependent on the perception of proportion, which is more distinctly manifested by a logarithmic rather than a linear scale. For example the notes of the musical scale rise in pitch, and in different octaves the distance between them is perceived as about the same; that is, the distance from *do, re, mi* to the next octave *do, re, mi* when heard, seems to be monotonic, but it is actually doubled in frequency.

For the vowels, the formants are left-right symmetric about a central frequency on the logarithmic scale of frequencies, and from their spectral endpoints, one can find the maximum distance between formants, and the vowels thus may be classified as uttered "long" or "short". Most electronic speech recognition systems, regardless of language, rely heavily on vowel recognition as a starting point.

---

[2] One can easily form waveforms on a graphics calculator or personal computer by just adding the sine and cosine functions with different amplitudes and frequencies.

For non-periodic waveforms which would be more like those in natural speech, the period of the Fourier Transform is taken to infinity, and so must be derived by changing over to the frequency domain because as time goes to infinity, the Fourier coefficients' $1/T$ factor is untenable. This is easily remedied since frequency is just the inverse of time period, and so as the time period approaches infinity, the frequency interval in the spectrum of the wave goes to zero, so the discrete sound spectrum of amplitudes as functions of frequency conveniently changes from the histogram peaks and valleys to become smooth, continuous and differentiable curves able to be represented as the elementary function representation of sines and cosines.

Rewriting the Fourier coefficients in complex form and changing the $f(t)$ to $g(t)$ to avoid confusion with the f for frequency, and combining the Fourier series and its coefficients equations, the Fourier transform and its inverse are,[3]

$$G(f) = \int_{-\infty}^{\infty} g(t)e^{-i2\pi ft}dt, \quad g(t) = \int_{-\infty}^{\infty} G(f)e^{-i2\pi ft}df$$

where the $-\infty$ time in the lower limit of integration limit enables the past, but the negative frequencies from minus-infinity may give one pause, the above equations nevertheless give the relationship among the amplitudes of the component waves, which are what is needed to model an auditory waveform.

The Fourier coefficient formulas represent the components of a waveform by extracting a single period of the wave and finding the area (integral) of that period for a given frequency, one frequency at a time.

Applied to a speech waveform, the inverse Fourier transform $g(t)$ is the integral over frequencies of the Fourier transform $G(f)$, which is an area that must be calculated. To do so, first $g(t)$ can be taken as a function of discrete points in time, producing a plot of amplitude over time which can be read off of the speech waveform by the FFT analyzer; then multiplying those amplitudes by a sine wave just fitting into the range of time for which there are amplitude values, and with a period equal to the number of observed wave oscillations, will produce a discrete bar graph whose combined areas will be the area to match the integrations of the waveform.

---

[3] *Euler's formula* gives the relation between the exponential and trigonometric functions as $e^{i\theta} = cos\theta + isin\theta$ so equations can be written in complex notation (meaning a "combination" of real and imaginary parts) which handles the square root of negative numbers, and is more compact, easier to manipulate, simplifies the use of zeros, and provides many a means to an end in mathematics and physics derivations.

The Fourier transform thus breaks up any waveform into its component simple waves, and renders the overall shape of the waveform recognizable from just a sampled portion of it. The *discrete* Fourier transform was necessary for FFT *digital* calculations by computers.

With the graphical representation of any sound using electronic instruments, it was natural in the early days of speech recognition to use special purpose electronic hardware for top-down *acoustic-phonetic* speech recognition. For example, Japan's Radio Research Lab used a filter bank spectrum analyzer with logic connecting each channel of the spectrum analyzer in a weighted manner to a vowel-decision circuit to recognize vowels. The Russians first developed the critical time-aligning of a pair of *frequency warped utterances* (logarithmic perception of pitch) for *dynamic frequency warping*, and in America, RCA Labs modeled the non-uniformity of time scales in speech using a combination of both, and Raj Reddy at Stanford pioneered continuous speech recognition by the dynamic tracking of *phonemes* (perceptively distinct units of sound that distinguish one word from another), incidentally first used for synthetic spoken moves in computer chess.

Through the next forty years, the isolated word and speech pattern sound spectra, *linear predictive coding* (LPC), and *dynamic programming* were actively researched, and IBM and AT&T Bell Labs developed large-vocabulary, speaker-independent commercial speech recognition systems for use in computers and telephony.

The technology generally comprised a bank-of-filters front-end analyzer for first separating the very different voice pitches, such as men from women, and producing a set of signals representing the energy of a sound in a given frequency band, thereby creating the sound spectra of an utterance.

Linear predictive coding models the effects of the *glottal* (space between vocal cord folds) pulse representing sound intensity and pitch, the *vocal tract* (throat and mouth) resonances producing formants (distinctive frequency peaks), and the tongue, lips, and throat that produce the hisses and pops of a typical utterance, using time-dependent digital filters.

LPC *signal source* front-end processing assumes that a given speech sample $s(t)$ at a given time t can be approximated by a linear combination of n past time speech samples $s(t - i)$ multiplied by *predictor coefficients* a_i, normalized by adding a gain factor G multiplied by a normalized signal excitation $u(t)$,

$$s(t) = \sum_{i=1}^{n} a_i s(t - i) + Gu(t).$$

Since the signal will change with time, the predictor coefficients at a given time must be estimated from a short segment of the speech signal occurring around that time, the estimate being performed at a rate of 0 – 50 frames per second. The idea is to determine the set of predictor coefficients $\{a_k\}$ directly from the speech signal so that the spectral properties of a digital filter best match those of the speech waveform within the frame by minimizing the mean-squared error between the prediction and the speech sample for that frame.

The results of the filter-bank and LPC modeling are source-coded to convert the signals into a sequence of binary digits, and encoded in a series of vectors representing the time-varying spectral characteristics of the speech signal. This so-called *vector quantization* encodes an input vector into an integer index that can be associated through minimizing spectral distortion with a codebook of *reproduction vectors* that then can be used as a recognition preprocessor and/or training dataset for a speech recognition artificial neural network.[4]

In the acoustic-phonetic front-end recognizer, an input frame is matched to a reference set of features. Spectral features of compactness, gravity, stress, and flatness can be used as reference to classify vowels with the decision as to the presence or absence of such features based on threshold values of acoustic parameters such as formant amplitudes, spectral band energy, and time duration. A vowel decision tree then can be employed to sequentially test each proposition of the speech.

Acoustic-phonetic modeling using filter banks or discrete Fourier transforms for speech segmentation, labeling, and vowel and sound classification could extract features and largely identify individual words and some whole sentences, however because of the vagaries of strung-together spoken language, and the lack of a tuning mechanism to improve the recognition, the acoustic-phonetic approach by itself could not produce a generalizable automatic speech recognition system.

---

[4] Rabiner, L. and B.H. Juang, 1993, *Fundamentals of Speech Recognition*, Prentice-Hall Signal Processing Series.

CHAPTER 31

Bottom Up Speech Recognition

High quality text and speech identification are both improving with advances in optical character recognition and acoustic-phonetic electronics. However, the *identification* of words is one thing, the *recognition* of words is quite another, and both text and speech recognition, to say nothing of natural language processing, have the same semantics problems.

In 1949 when the American mathematician Walter Weaver proposed a computer for text translation, the idea seemed simple enough, given a sentence in one language, a computer would recognize a word by its spelling, look up the word in a bilingual dictionary stored in memory and match the corresponding word in the second language; then the computer's logic would arrange the translated words according to the rules of grammar of that second language.

During the Cold War of the 1950s, both Russians and Americans were eager to use *machine translation* (MT) to quickly translate each other's documents. Natural language, however, is fraught with ambiguity and inference, and the early MT attempts produced ridiculous translations such as the saying "the spirit is willing but the flesh is weak" being translated into Russian and then back into English as "the vodka is good but the meat is rotten", demonstrating that although particular words could be recognized and translated, their meaning was quite another matter.

DOI: 10.1201/9781003214892-38

The lack of progress together with machine translations such as "water goat" for the Russian "hydraulic ram" brought on ridicule culminating in the first "AI Winter" of 1966 when the American National Research Council canceled all research support for automatic machine translation.

Any language translation must contend with sayings, usage, idioms, vernacular, slang, implication, innuendo, turns of phrases, puns, abbreviations, acronyms, and multiple meanings of the same word in different contexts, and is therefore unavoidably fraught with uncertainties and ambiguity.

For speech recognition, add to that uncertainty and ambiguity different speaker's varieties of accent, pronunciation, articulation, roughness, nasality, pitch, inflection, speed, timing, emotion, humor, sarcasm, and so on, all of which renders accurate top-down machine translation of text and speech almost *literally* impossible.

Noam Chomsky's *Language Acquisition Device* (LAD) indeed recognized the need for *cognitively* modeled language based on a child's naturally-learned knowledge of speech rather than on a language's top-down rigid syntax and rules-based grammar. This bottom-up approach was theoretically sound but relevant cognitive data was sparse and the computational power of the 1960s limited, so the vehement anti-war activist's LAD was ridiculed as just another amusing automatic speech recognition failure.

The English language has some 13 million words, so to a semanticist/mathematician, a meaning function $f(x)$ for a given word x; first because of the sheer number of different words, and secondly because of their uncertainties and ambiguities of meaning described above, $f(x)$ is irredeemably dependent on context.

Since we cannot reduce the number of words (which are increasing daily), the words can be first grouped, for example, as to synonyms (same meaning but different words) and homographs (same word pronounced in more than one way) to form an associated group. But the same word can have different meanings in context, such as homonyms (same sound and spelling but different meaning), homophones (same sound but different meaning), and heteronyms (same spelling but different sound and meaning).

Words however can have associations based on the above, and *vectors* could be employed to group associated words and so decrease the number of variables to form a reduced word vector space.

Moreover, vectors, in addition to being able to associate ostensibly disparate elements, can also specify direction and thereby quantify separation between objects by their inner products, so for example, synonyms could have an inner product angular factor close to *1* (cosine = 0 between word vectors), meaning exact confluence in terms of meaning. Furthermore, three words represented by *x*, *y*, and *z* could be related by their invariable distance *d*, from the Pythagorean theorem $x^2 + y^2 + z^2 = d^2$ for three dimensions and extendible to infinite dimensions. Thus the words can be further classified as to their "closeness" to other words. So in accord with the adage attributed to the linguist J.R. Firth,

> *You shall know a word by the company it keeps,*

a truism that inculcates *context* into the understanding of a word; that is, the closeness of given words helps to ascertain their meaning.

In the so-called *Word2Vec* models used in *automatic speech recognition* (ASR), a sentence is deconstructed into a multidimensional vector space of words that are positioned such that words sharing common meaning in different contexts are *closer* together in the invariant mathematical scalar distance sense of a vector inner product or Pythagorean distance.

A *skip-gram* architecture uses a *center word* to predict the context in a surrounding *window* of context words, giving heavier weights to less distant context words, and thereby helping to *fix* the word's meaning. A *continuous bag of words* (CBOW) conversely predicts which words from a window of surrounding words are most probably relevant by summing the vectors of the words in the window.[1]

An inner product correlation can be used to classify the input frame vector and a reference vowel feature vector using convolutional artificial neural network pattern recognition. The input speech is in the form of a time sequence of spectral vectors obtained from the front-end spectral analyzers to form a *test pattern* T as a concatenation of the spectral frame vectors over the duration of the speech t_i,

$$T = \{t_1, t_2, t_3, \ldots, t_i\}$$

The test pattern T is compared with a set of reference patterns $\{R^j\}$ comprising a sequence of spectral frames R^j,

$$R^j = \{r_1^j, r_2^j, r_3^j, \ldots, r_j^j\}.$$

---

[1] For detail, see Agrawal, S., towardsdatascience.com/words-to-vectors-natural-language-processing.

Then minimizing the distance of T from each of the R^j will associate the input speech pattern with the reference *template*, and the global time alignment of the two patterns can be performed analytically using spectral distortion measurement techniques.

One spectral distortion measure is based on *frequency warping*, the human non-linear, logarithmic perception of pitch, to model a wide-band spectrum with a frequency resolution close to that of the human auditory system.[2]

Reference templates for training can be in the form of a non-rigid template or a statistical model. Templates are used in automatic speech recognizers, but even after undergoing training, their ability to adapt to different speakers, speaking styles, background acoustics, and electronic noise is limited, so they are typically used for very specific speech recognition tasks, such as recognition of a response to automatic telephoned answer requests, or as recognition preprocessors that can reduce the computational burden of a connected pattern recognition artificial neural network.

Dynamic programming breaks down a complex problem, such as a long spoken sentence, into sub-problems, solving each of them and indexing the problem solutions based on their input parameters, and storing the solutions in a matrix. Thus when the same speech problem is encountered, the solution matrix then can be looked up by means of its index, and the problem will not have to be solved again, thereby increasing computation speed and efficiency.

Dynamic programming has been widely used in operations research to solve sequential decision problems, and so it can be advantageously used in speech recognition to account for past variations in speaking by using time alignment and normalization.

Summarizing, a front-end spectral analysis measures short-time speech parameters sequentially, producing a sequence of spectral feature vectors. This speech pattern input is then compared with a reference pattern, templates or statistical models, and short-time and global spectral distortion (*dissimilarities*) are calculated using dynamic programming. A further step is to treat an utterance as a whole in a cognitive sense; that is, natural language *acoustic modeling* encodes the sound signal as a sequence of speech feature vectors whose frequencies

---

[2] For details see Rabiner, L. and B.H. Juang, 1993, *Fundamentals of Speech Recognition*, Prentice-Hall Signal Processing Series.

instead of being scaled linearly, are logarithmically scaled (*warped*) to better model a human auditory perception that responds more acutely to logarithmic rather than linear proportions.

This so-called *perceptually warped frequency* is augmented with the first and second *time* derivatives computed using smoothed differences of neighboring frames to capture the significant *temporal* influences in speech recognition.

These primarily electromechanical constructs using ANNs only for pattern comparisons can provide ASR for small vocabularies and limited speech variation, more general speech requires bottom-up deep artificial neural network learning.

In a conventional feedforward artificial neural network, supervised learning is followed by reinforcement learning, but a *Deep Belief Network* (DBN) first learns the probabilities of specific features from *unsupervised* training (the "belief"), and then while it undergoes *supervised* training, the DBN applies these *feature detectors* to classify the training set data, thereby learning pattern recognition from a head-start of "believed" features.

A speech recognition deep belief network thus can first act as a feedforward network specifying the activation levels of the feature-specific neurons, and then by running the network feed-backwards, *generate* other features of the input data based on the learned speech. In this way, it is ideal for recognizing the vagaries of natural language speech because the process is similar to a child naturally learning some basic words in unsupervised learning at home by listening to their parents' speech, and then going to elementary school for formal supervised learning of vocabulary and grammar; that is, before supervised learning, the child has some prior *beliefs* about the meaning of certain words and phrases and how to express them.

A DBN is therefore like a restricted Boltzmann machine (RBM) acting on probabilities to reveal latent factors in speech that will help it to recognize the implicit meaning of individual speech features from context, usage, and all the other vagaries of spoken communication, and then by gradient-descent backpropagation, the ground truth of the words and phrases can be collaboratively filtered to include the *inferences* so common to natural speech, and thus improve *natural language processing* (NLP).

NLP employs two main statistical classification models, the *discriminative* and the *generative*. The discriminative model estimates a label given an observation based on the conditional probability of an observable variable X and a target Y given an observable x,

$$P(Y \mid X = x)$$

Examples are Decision Trees, Neural Networks, Logistic Regression, Cross-Entropy Cost Function, Restricted Boltzmann Machine, and Support Vector Machines, all discussed previously.

The generative model estimates a *joint probability distribution* (signified by "*x*"), and computes the conditional probability therefrom,

$$X \times Y, P(Y, X)$$

Examples are the Gaussian Mixture Mode (GMM), Hidden Markov Model (HMM), Restricted Boltzmann Machine (RBM), and Generative Adversarial Network (GAN) to be discussed in turn below.

In 1913, the Russian mathematician Andrei Markov took down his bookshelf copy of Alexander Pushkin's verse novel *Eugene Onegin*, not to read but to *deconstruct*, carefully writing out the first 20,000 letters and arraying them in 20×20 matrices, counting the vowels, and meticulously looking for patterns revealing a mathematical structure of verse that might be modeled.

Markov believed that unlike the purely stochastic occurrences in say coin tossing, the letters in a sequence of words depend on prior outcomes in a chain of causation. That is, in *Eugene Onegin*, the chance that a certain letter appears in sequence depends on the letter that came before it, and indeed his sample contained 43% vowels and 57% consonants, distributed as 1,104 vowel-vowel pairs, 3,827 consonant-consonant pairs, and 15,069 vowel-consonant and consonant-vowel pairs; therefore (certainly) *Eugene Onegin* was not a random distribution of letters, but might have a (hidden) statistical character that could be mathematically modeled.[3]

In the modern *Hidden Markov Model* (HMM), a Markov chain using *Gaussian Mixture models* (GMMs) is employed to generate probability distributions for the acoustic vector sequences produced by front-end electromechanical analysis. The individual Gaussians (the mixture) in the GMM generate the variables in the multiple dimensions required by speech recognition to form the distribution of vectors in a matrix.

---

[3] Markov, A.A., "An Example of Statistical Investigation of the Text *Eugene Onegin* Concerning the Connection of Samples in Chains," cited in Schwartz, O., *IEEE Spectrum*, Nov. 12, 2019.

However, context-dependent models clearly require a great deal of speech data to be accurate, so for more efficient use of the data, the HMM is divided into sub-HMMs for each *triphone* (sequence of three phonemes) and HMM decision-trees clustered by alpha-beta pruning to associate different speech states.

In human speech, sequences of utterances are meant to represent isolated words or phonemes, but a speech recognizer does not know *a priori* what the words are meant to mean; that is, the actual meanings are embedded in states *hidden* from the speech recognizer, but since the utterance is heard, there are *observables* (*hearables?*) from which the intended meaning of the words may be *inferred* based on the probabilities of occurrence.

In the simplest two-word case for an example, the inferences are made from the probability that *word₁* (w_1) is followed by *word₂* (w_2) or by *word₁*, and *word₂* is followed by *word₁* or *word₂*, with the probabilities derived from grammatical constraints, syntax, usage, context, continuous speech data, and so on. Then the *closeness* of the words can be represented by *variance values*. A *state transition probability* for this two-state system is a *2 × 2* matrix, for example with the probabilities expressed as variance values as shown,

$$
\begin{array}{cc}
 & w_1 \quad w_2 \\
\begin{array}{c} w_1 \\ w_2 \end{array} & \left[\begin{array}{cc} 0.1 & 0.9 \\ 0.7 & 0.3 \end{array} \right].
\end{array}
$$

Using HMM, the highest probability word at each point of the sequence can be chosen by summing the probabilities that *word₁* is in the first position with *word₂* having a probability of (1- *word₁*). Repeating this for each element in the sequence gives the probabilities *P(word₁)* and *P(word₂)* for each element in the sequence, thus obtaining the most probable sequence for the two words in the utterance.[4]

Generalizing to multiple words, phonemes, sentences, phrases and so on will greatly increase the dimensions of the state transition probability matrices and add complexity to the hidden Markov model, but the general idea is as described above.

---

[4] Stamp, M., 2018,. *A Revealing Introduction to Hidden Markov Models*, October 17, online.

When each element in the principal diagonal of the matrix is a *variance* of one of the other elements, meaning that words are very close to each other in some manner such as described above ("variance" as "closeness"), the matrix is *diagonally covariant*, and such matrices thus represent speech relationships and are used to produce the *joint probability distributions* needed to associate the context- and time-dependent aspects of natural language speech.[5]

A simple hidden Markov model has state transition probabilities A, hidden state sequences X_i, an observation probabilities matrix B, and the observation sequences O_i, for the total sequence time T shown in the schematic figure below.

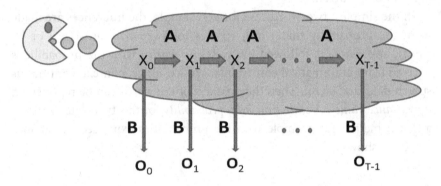

Since there are many more possible observables and their sequences than labeled training data, a probability distribution is calculated for each time step for the alignment of the input speech sequence with the training data. The state transition matrix A has probability elements a_{ij} where

$$a_{ij} = P\,(\text{state } q_i \text{ at } t + 1 \,|\, \text{state } q_i \text{ at } t)$$

and the observation probabilities matrix B has elements $b_j(k)$ where

$$b_j\,(k) = P\,(\text{observation } k \text{ at } t \,|\, \text{state } q_j \text{ at } t).$$

An HMM is represented by $\lambda = (A, B, \pi)$ where π is the initial state distribution. For a simple four state hidden state sequence $X = (x_0, x_1, x_2, x_3)$

---

[5] Word "Variance" thus is like a variant of a virus, a derived mutation but different.

with observations $O = (O_0, O_1, O_2, O_3)$, with scalar values for example a vowel (0), a hiss (1), and a pop (2) observed in the four-state sequence as (0, 1, 0, 2). The probability of state sequence X is,

$$P(X, O) = \pi_{x_0} b_{x_0}(O_0) a_{x_0,x_1} b_{x_1}(O_1) a_{x_1,x_2} b_{x_2}(O_2) a_{x_2,x_3} b_{x_3}(O_3).$$

The probability of any sequence of utterances can be thus calculated, and for each state sequence, for example the given observation sequence (0, 1, 0, 2). Then using dynamic programming, the state sequence with highest probability will be the best choice of word sequence.

The most basic probability distribution is just a random Bayesian distribution, and the *Bayes' formula* is used for the probability based on further data.

$$P(A|B) = \frac{P(B|A)P(A)}{P(B)}$$

As in all statistical probabilistic models, the theory can be mathematically dense, but the principles are relatively easy to understand and the computations can be handled efficiently by online software packages.[6]

The Gaussian mixture models (GMMs) group data points into clusters within which they are Gaussian (normally) distributed. GMMs have been employed to model the spectral representation of a sound wave, and can classify groups of data for the representation of phrases and sentences. *Factor analysis* represents each data point as a weighted linear function of latent inferences in the data, thereby introducing sophisticated nuance into automatic speech recognition.

Speech recognition in general is critically dependent on *time and sequence*, so the HMM GMM word probabilities are typically forward-fed to a so-called *Recurrent Neural Network* (RNN), a *transformer* whose activations are time dependent employing *Connectionist Temporal Classification* (CTC) that can be used to train an RNN on time and sequence employing *Long Short-Term Memory Networks* (LSTM). The total ASR system can be further refined by reinforcement and self-

---

[6] Ref. Rabiner, L. and B.H. Juang, *Fundamentals of Speech Recognition*, Chapter 6, Prentice-Hall Signal Processing Series (1993).

supervised learning by running against itself for self-improvement for *a posteriori* parameter optimization producing greater accuracy.

In typical feedforward neural networks, a single input layer completely determines a *static* synaptic activation pattern throughout the other neuron layers. In a *recurrent neural network* (RNN), the neurons can be controlled to only fire for a limited time duration, so the activations of succeeding neurons in the synaptic pattern will be influenced and such influence can be carried on to succeeding neuron synaptic patterns, giving the RNN a temporal capability. A given neuron may even respond to its own earlier activation to connect an association, thus forming a *temporally-controlled cascade* of activation that can manifest a speech pattern based on time-based preceding patterns of activation. In this way it can be seen that the all-important timing of speech can be represented by timed neural firing patterns.

Apart from any hand-engineered associations germane to the particular speech recognition implementation, for example the close words "checking" and "balance" in bank telephony speech, the recurrence is typically performed by inner products of feature vectors that quantize the scalar correlation between the speech feature vectors.

The recurrent neural network thus can respond to stimulations depending on the prior presence of close feature vectors that account for related inferences, or the prior absence of signals to indicate lack of relation, thereby providing more accurate probabilities of later word feature occurrence.

That is, RNNs can connect relatable previous information to present meaning based on the closeness of the feature vectors. For example, the phrase, "I grew up in France … earlier in the text or speech can imply a *recurrence* with the later occurring phrase "I speak fluent _____", where the earlier occurring word "France" generates a high inferential probability (manifested by the closeness of word feature vectors) that the blank should be the word "French", even if the word in the blank space is garbled and there are many words and pauses in-between. The RNN thus has the ability to provide a word through inferential association of earlier speech by the closeness of word feature vectors even if the word in text is misspelled, unclearly written, or mumbled in speech.

On the other hand, if the later occurring phrase is "I *also* speak fluent _____", then the association should not be made because of the word "also" implying another language and the prior word "France" can be deactivated in this instance, while other countries' names can be activated, possibly through prior occurrence.

Another example is *uptalk* (voice lifting in pitch and inflection at the end of a sentence) where a statement may be mistaken for a question, and can be determined by earlier instances of similar uptalk occurrence. In this way, the RNN can produce a *word scores* matrix in accord with the context of the speech at issue and a speaker's particular speech intonation.

If the first part of a subject occurred at the beginning of the speech, and the last part near the end, and there is a considerable span between the related phrases, the RNN's sequential activation can place the first part in a *stored state*, which can be under the control of the RNN as a *controlled state* with time delay and feedback loop capability for re-activation as needed in the event of the last part appearance.

If the earlier occurring feature is more extensively referred to later, then the stored controlled state may be recorded entirely in another network or data graph that incorporates time delays and can be fed back to the RNN.[7]

Recurrent neural networks can use all the deep neural network convolutions, regularizations, and other feedforward techniques to more accurately perform speech and text recognition. These techniques are particularly useful for any task where memory of past events, thoughts, and features are significant for real-time processing. Marcel Proust's *Remembrances of Things Past* is a striking literary example of a human RNN describing his impressions of past events to the minutest detail with allusions to Nature, literature, music, art, emotions, psychology, society, etiquette, repartee and so on *ad infinitum*.

Since recurrent neural network backpropagation is performed not only through event layers, but also through temporal layers, the problems of vanishing and unstable gradient descents can result in slower and sometimes even null learning.

This problem is addressed by controlling the gradient descent instability by limiting the backpropagation through the use of *gated states* or *gated memory*, conjunctively termed *gated recurrent units* (GRUs), in an incongruously-named *Long Short-Term Memory Network* (LSTM). This name only makes sense in the context of the automatic speech recognition (ASR) gated recurrent unit regime.

The acronym-laden ASR LSTM GRU can add or block information by

---

[7] Colah's Blog, colah.github.io, for a graphic description of the matrix mathematics, refer to Luis Serrano, *A friendly introduction to recurrent neural networks*, YouTube, August 18, 2017.

means of for instance three sigmoid function gates in a sigmoid layer that lets information greyscaled from 0 to 1 through the layer. So if an earlier word whose occurrence is helpful in predicting a current word or future word, its activation will be passed on by an "ON" (*1*) as a long-term open-gated recurrent word, while other long-ago words that are not helpful (meaning word vector features are not close to the present speech), in the short-term speech processing will be logic gated (blocked or forgotten) by the GRU as an "OFF" (*0*) state

This explains the "long" as a long distance or time away (that is, not a "close" word vector), and "short-term" as just needed for this particular short real-time prediction of the meaning of the word or phrase in question. LSTM RNNs therefore can learn the long-term dependencies important for the immediate needs of speech recognition, printed or handwritten text recognition, and speech synthesis.

A *Connectionist Temporal Classification* (CTC) is typically used for training recurrent neural networks employing LSTM to do sequences where the timing is variable and reinforcement learning is employed, as required in natural language processing.

A CTC network trains the RNN by taking the word scores matrix from dynamic programming and then infers the speech or text pattern from the state transition probabilities matrices. The neurons in recurrent neural networks thus are continuously changing in a *dynamic* way, much like a biological brain, and therefore CTCs are effective for modeling processes that change with time in a sequential manner, for example cursive (connected) hand writing recognition and natural language speech. Even audio-visual linked speech recognition (AVSR) models that link sound with vision observables, such as hand gestures and lip-reading, have been developed.[8]

In summary, most automatic speech recognition systems represent speech as a sequence of perceptually warped feature vectors and are augmented with smoothed differences of neighboring frames acting as the first and second time derivatives. The probabilities of feature vector sequences are modeled by Hidden Markov models with Gaussian mixture models (GMMs) where the HMM is constructed from sub-HMMs for each triphone, and the individual Gaussians are all diagonally covariant matrices.

---

[8] For example, Zhang, Y., "Speech Recognition Using Deep Learning Algorithms", cs229stanford.edu and *Audio Visual Speech Recognition and Segmentation Based on DBN*, researchgate.net.

Clustering the HMM states using alpha-beta pruned decision trees can produce desired parameter-tying. The HMM GMM word probabilities typically employ Recurrent Neural Networks (RNN) which in turn use Connectionist Temporal Classification (CTC) and Long Short-Term Memory Networks (LSTM) to process time and sequence, and reinforcement and self-supervised learning can produce parameter optimization for greater accuracy.

Automatic speech recognition follows the arc of natural language, fraught as it is with uncertainty, ambiguity, and inference; natural language processing thus is an exceedingly complex top-down signal processing endeavor that requires a succession of bottom-up artificial neural networks and techniques to succeed.

All the network computations described above can be efficiently performed using Google's TensorFlow or PyTorch platforms employing TPU parallel processing to perform automatic matrix operations and calculus differentiation, and a *Computation Graph* allows code reusability and extension available to any interested programmer.

In addition to setting new records for accurate text and speech recognition, a recurrent neural network learned the character-by-character sequence used in the high-level computer program language Python, and in a sequential, dynamic way learned how to write computer programs in Python, threatening the very livelihood of computer programmers worldwide.[9]

Things would become even more serious for writers, in 2020 OpenAI introduced *Generative Pre-trained Transformer-3* (GPT-3) unsupervised language machine capable of almost any language task founded upon pre-training on enormous unlabeled training sets. The *generative* output of the model assumes its linear dependence on its own previous values and a stochastic term to form a recurrence relation *autoregressive* model with *discriminative* fine-tuning.

GPT-3 currently has 175 billion ML parameters with 410 billion byte-pair-encoded tokens from *Common Crawl*, 19 billion tokens from *WebText2*, 12 billion from *Book1*, 55 billion from *Book2*, and 3 billion from *Wikipedia*. In addition to prose and poetry, GPT-3 in principle can code in CSS, JSX, Python, and does not require further training to compose almost anything in the English language.

Potential users can access a GPT-3 toolset on a text-in/text-out API

---

[9] Refer to Chapters 2 and 34, DeepCoder.

from GitHub, and before long the writers of books and articles, and computer programmers will all go the way of the dodo bird.

CORONAVIRUS VACCINE

Strange as it may seem, deep recurrent neural networks designed for natural language processing have been employed in epidemic spread models, and enlisted for one of biology's grandest challenges, predicting the three-dimensional structure of proteins from their amino acid sequences to design drugs that can metabolically act to treat infections and develop vaccines.[10]

In the past, protein folding studies were primarily performed by freezing a protein into a crystal-like structure and utilizing x-ray crystallography to examine the folding process in instrument-rich and time-consuming procedures. Artificial neural networks can perform protein folding typically in a matter of hours, and new techniques are being developed to reduce the time to seconds.

A covid-19 virus is as depicted in the figure below, with the characteristic *spike proteins* looking like plugs or handles arrayed on the surface, hence the name *corona*. An unfolded protein folded into a folded

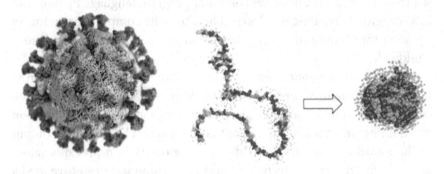

protein is schematically shown in the figure at right in the physical process by which a protein chain folds to acquire its biologically functional conformation in a 3D structure.[11]

---

[10] Although successful in many cases such as diphtheria, measles, mumps, rubella, polio, yellow fever, cholera, Japanese encephalitis, meningitis A, typhoid, dengue, rabies, and smallpox, but vaccines against malaria, HIV, Zika, West Nile, Lyme, hepatitis C, and many other diseases have not been developed.

[11] Coronavirus and Protein-folding images are open source images from Wikipedia commons.

There are four stages of folding: *primary* (amino acid sequence held together by peptide bonds), *secondary* (protein folded as an alpha helix held together by hydrogen bonds in the direction of the helical axis, or beta pleated sheets held together by hydrogen bonds in an S-shape, *tertiary* (protein folded into a 3D conformation held together by non-covalent interactions between side groups), and *quaternary* (a single peptide bond to other peptides).[12]

A virus interacts with the human body host cells through entry into the *angiotensin-converting-enzyme 2* (ACE2) receptors and spreads from there into host cells that transmit the virus throughout the body.

The protein's conformation dictates the protein function; protein folding for therapy or immunization is an exercise in finding a protein conformation that does what you want it to do, here binding onto the covid-19 spike proteins thereby blocking its ability to enter ACE2 receptors, effectively preventing a virus from having any physiological effect.

Therefore, the task for artificial intelligence is to design such a protein through protein folding producing the desired conformation to do what you want it to do. Google's DeepMind *AlphaFold* won the *Critical Assessment of Protein Structure Prediction* (CASP) competition in 2018 by a sizable margin over other competitors.

In a first step, AlphaFold employs a deep neural network to extract features from a training dataset and then searches for plausible protein structures having those features. It compares a protein's amino acid sequence with similar ones in the training set to find pairs of amino acids that appear in tandem, but do not lie next to each other in a chain, implying that they are positioned near each other in a folded protein in a process it called *Multiple Sequence Alignments*. The DNN was trained to take the pairings and predict the distance between them in the folded protein. Then the predictions were compared to precisely measured distances in known proteins and thereby enabled realistic guesses on how the proteins may fold.

---

[12] An *amino acid* (*α-amino carboxylic acid*) is an organic molecule made up of a basic amino group (-NH₂) and an acidic carboxyl group (-COOH); an organic *R group* – a side chain – attached to the α-carbon atoms of the amide spine displays the charge and polarity of the amino acid and thus determines the chemical characteristics that promote biological interaction. A *peptide* is a short chain of amino acids and an *enzyme* is a protein and a biocatalyst that converts molecules (substrates) into different molecules (products) in the catalytic metabolic processes necessary to sustain life.

A parallel-running DNN would predict the angles of the joints between consecutive amino acids in the folded protein chain. The two parameters then could be combined to produce a folded protein structure designed to perform a desired protein interaction such as binding and blocking the spike proteins of the coronavirus.

This theoretical protein folding design process, however, can produce structures that may not be physically possible. Thus the DNNs are trained on actual protein structures and the cost function was minimized by gradient descent to come closest to a folding arrangement consistent with the predictions of the amino acid sequences that were produced in the first step, thereby producing a physically viable antiviral protein.

The DNA-based process of developing an antiviral vaccine has been the mimicking of a part of the coronavirus' genetic sequence that will give a preview of the virus in order to generate antibodies, but not cause the disease itself, instead readying the immune system to attack any actual infection from the virus.[13]

Harvard Medical School's one-step protein folding algorithm in a deep recurrent *geometric* neural network based on natural language processing techniques was trained on a dataset of amino acid sequences mapping to known (and therefore possible) protein structures where the end-to-end sequence-to-structure procedure was performed in milliseconds. The code is publicly available on GitHub in hopes of wide-range dissemination and crowd sourcing access.

A conveyor of the information in DNA to instruct the cell to make proteins from the amino acid sequence is called *messenger RNA*; mRNA is synthesized by complex RNA molecules using the nucleotide sequence of DNA as a template in a *ribosome* factory in the cell nucleus. Among others, Moderna has concentrated on mRNA protein folding AI to develop vaccines against the coronavirus.

A viral pandemic will peter out naturally because two things happen: (1) infected people produce antibodies and recover, and (2) infected people do not recover and die, depriving the virus of a host to live on and spread. The presence of antibodies can be used as a test for the disease,

---

[13] *Deoxyribonucleic acid* (DNA) is a double stranded helical molecule that resides in the nucleus of a cell and carries genetic instructions for the development, functioning, growth, and reproduction of all known organisms and some viruses. *Ribonucleic acid* (RNA) is a single stranded molecule synthesized in the nucleus but residing in the jelly-like cytoplasm inside the membrane of a cell; it codes, decodes, regulates, and expresses genes. Both are just chemical compounds, neither is by itself alive.

the plasma containing antibodies (but not red blood cells) can be infused in patients for convalescent serum immunotherapy, and of course vaccines can prevent infection.

The rub is the virus' ability to *mutate*. The defenses to viral mutations are new antibody plasma and mutation-specific protein folding, and with more and more data available, data-dependent artificial intelligence machine learning can be marshaled to design new treatments and vaccines.

Certain parts of virus' surface proteins have a high turnover rate producing mutations. Over the past year tens of thousands of coronavirus samples from patients around the world have been genetically sequenced and uploaded into the *Global Initiative on Sharing All Influenza Data* (GISAID) hosted in Germany. AI algorithms to compare those sequences to find which segments of the virus change frequently and which do not, to help identify mutation hot spots. Then (hopefully) the same protein-folding processes can be performed to meet the mutations.[14]

---

[14] Ref. Waltz, E., IEEE Spectrum 29 September 2020.

CHAPTER 32

Speech Synthesis

The earliest speech synthesizers were developed hundreds of years ago by scientific luminaries such as Albertus Magnus, Roger Bacon, and Charles Wheatstone. These *articulatory synthesis* systems mechanically model the human vocal tract, with vocal fold biomechanics, glottal aerodynamics, and acoustic wave propagation in the biomechanical bronchia, trachea, nasal and oral cavities of *mechanical talking heads* powered by puffs of air from bellows.

More recently, Bell Labs developed a voice codec (*Vocoder*) it called the *Voder* for electricity-generated telephone speech. As diagrammed in the schematic figure below, an operator creates vowels by depressing a wrist bar producing nasal buzz tones, consonants are generated by a white noise tube producing a hiss, with a foot pedal to control pitch, and the explosive "p" and "d" and the affricative "j" and "ch" activated by *spectrum keys* that select from ten band-pass filters for modulation of these basic sounds to form combinations of speech that are transmitted to a speaker for demonstrations of synthetic speech.

The Voder was displayed at the 1939 New York World's Fair with the greeting, "Good afternoon, radio audience". Needless to say, intelligible speech generation required no little training and skill of the operator.[1]

In the late 1940s, speech synthesis pioneer Franklin Cooper developed the *Pattern Playback* machine that converted sound spectra spectrographs of patterns of speech into audible synthesized speech, and in 1968, Bell Labs employed the ubiquitous IBM 704 computer to synthesize "Daisy Bell", a song that was subsequently played by the computer HAL in Arthur C. Clarke's screenplay for the film "*2001A Space Odyssey*".

---

[1] Figure is from Wikipedia.

DOI: 10.1201/9781003214892-39

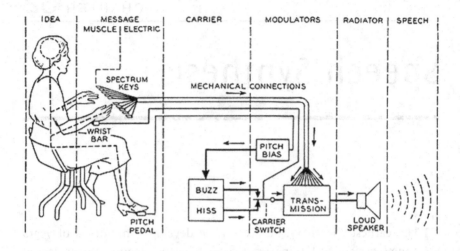

With the advent of the computer, the rudimentary air, electricity, and sound spectra spectrograph sources of synthesized speech could be replaced by computer software and refined for greater verisimilitude.

Linear predictive coding (LPC) for speech synthesis was developed at Nagoya University in Japan, electronic talking heads were developed in America and Japan using digital synthesis to produce articulatory speech firmware, and Texas Instruments' LPC microprocessors were used in its *Speak and Tell* toys popular in the late 1970s.

Japan's NTT in 1975 developed the *Line Spectral Pairs* (LSP) that mathematically pair the LPC equation predictor coefficients a_i for improved stability and resonance, and these *LPC filters* were used to more closely match electronic speech waveforms. The LSP technique was subsequently adopted in the 1990s as the international speech coding standard for mobile telephony and the Internet.[2]

With more accuracy, speech synthesis could be extended to more general uses. The first text-to-speech (TTS) system was developed in 1975 by Italy's *Centro Studi e Laboratori Telecommunicazioni* (CSELT) with the *Multi channel Speaking Automation* (MUSA) dedicated computer and diphone-synthesis software. MUSA was able to read aloud and sing Italian songs from printed text. Later, Bell Labs, MIT, and Digital Equipment Corporation in the 1980s developed the TTS DECtalk Natural Language Processing (NLP) computer for multilingual text-to-speech synthesis.

---

[2] For the LPC equation, refer to Chapter 29.

The basic TTS process is for a *frontend* processor to convert written text to a phonemic representation by first translating numbers and abbreviations into the equivalent written words (*text normalization* or *tokenization*), distinguish homographs, for example whether "read" should be voice-synthesized as "red" or "reed" (determined by *part-of-speech tagging*), assigning phonetic transcriptions to each word, and segmenting the text into word, phrase, clause, and sentence *prosodic* (pitch contour and phoneme duration) units, a *backend processor* then performs prosody prediction and generates waveforms for discrete to continuous synthesized speech as shown in the *continuous backend processing* flowchart on the left of the figure below.[3]

In so-called *concatenative synthesis*, segments of recorded speech in the form of electronic waveforms are strung together, and although an individual string may sound quite natural, there are noticeable pauses between strings that everyone has experienced in early automated telephone answering services. A typical system is shown schematically in the figure below at right.

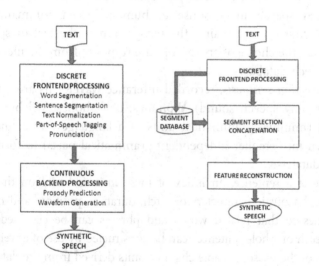

---

[3] Refer to Chapter 29 for waveform generation from sound waves.

A *domain-specific synthesis* employs a set of pre-recorded words and phrases that are natural sounding, but limited to the domain, such as for the early talking dolls, scales, and clocks. In *diphone synthesis*, one sample of a larger set of sound-to-sound transition speech is used for each word, and linear predictive coding or discrete cosine Fourier transforms can be applied to the diphones to provide sentence prosody, but because of the database limitation to one sound per word, the speech cannot help but sound robotic.

In *formant synthesis*, the synthesized speech is wholly formed from electronic signal processing of the frequency sound spectrum amplitude peaks (formants), and then adding sine waves together (*additive synthesis*), or using mathematical physics models to create whole new waveforms. Although capable of more generalized synthesis, this not unpredictably produces rather electronic-sounding speech.

Because of the sophistication of the digital signal processing, digitally synthesized speech can provide articulation that eliminates the unnatural pauses of concatenative and formant synthesis models, and can produce quite natural speech, and modulations of prosody and intonation can produce emotion and tone, useful particularly for humanoid robots.

Synthesized speech in response to human speech commands or questions of course first requires the recognition of the text or spoken input and then the choice of an appropriate response from the files in its synthetic speech database.

In *unit selection synthesis*, recorded utterance waveforms are divided into phones (any speech sound), diphones, half-phones, syllables, and morphemes (minimal grammatical units of a language that cannot be broken down into smaller independent grammatical parts) to form the files in the database.

To construct a sentence, an index of these *units* is based on the segmentation and acoustic parameters of pitch, duration, position, and neighboring phones so that related words and phrases can be classified, and synthetic speech of whole sentences can be constructed by use of a weighted decision tree of the most probable chain of units derived from the database.

Artificially intelligence robots clearly require speech synthesis. For example, Hidden Markov Models can include complete dictionaries that can be searched for pronunciation based on spelling or rules or combinations thereof to handle the part-of-speech tagging. Deep neural networks can train the model from recorded speech datasets to produce natural-sounding words, and HMMs can model the sound spectrum, pitch, and duration of word waveforms probabilistically to form natural language-sounding sentences.[4]

Then just as in speech recognition systems, recurrent neural networks, LSTMs, CTCs, and other networks and models employing supervised and self-supervised learning can be employed to refine the text-to-speech and voice speech synthesis.

These technologies are used in the more modern speech synthesizers such as DeepMind's WaveNet, Google's Tacotron, and Baidu's Deep Voice. Going further, Adobe Voco and Google WaveNet are audio-editing software-generating tools that can be trained to produce synthesized speech that closely mimics a particular speaker by taking a voice sample, and generating characteristic speech that through the employment of speech recognition inferences, can even include phonemes that were not in the training data set.

Natural language synthetic speech, like all technological innovations, can be and have been abused, for instance by the unethical putting words into the mouths of public figures in commercials, parodies, and for adversarial political gain.

However, one public figure's thoughts were synthesized not for nefarious, comedic, or political gain, but rather for exposition of the deepest mysteries of the Universe. The late renowned theoretical physicist Stephen Hawking's eerily robotic voice at first used DECtalk, but this required him to type the words for TTS synthesis, and he was increasingly unable to do so as his hand muscles degenerated from ALS.

In extraordinary displays of sensor technology and artificial intelligence, subsequent speech synthesis systems developed by Intel, SpeechPlus, and Hawking's graduate assistants, followed twitches in his cheek muscle to predict word selection from a deep neural network trained on his books, papers, and speeches; for example, he had merely to twitch his cheek muscle in a particular way for the word "the" and a recurrent neural network immediately produced the contextually concatenated inferred words "black hole".

Stephen Hawking's AI-deduced speech that allowed him to live an extremely more productive life to the good of science ironically also included words on the dangers of the looming AI singularity,[5]

---

[4] Hidden Markov Models are discussed in Chapter 30.
[5] Economictimes, indiatimes.com March 14, 2018. October 16, 2018.

I fear that AI may replace humans altogether. If people design computer viruses, someone will design AI that improves and re-plicates itself. This will be a new form of life that outperforms humans.

and

It will either be the best thing that's ever happened to us, or it will be the worst thing. If we are not careful, if very well may be the last thing

This pronouncement was made so more dramatic precisely because it was itself robotically-generated.

Hawking's warnings indeed might materialize, but for now the AI singularity, at least for speech synthesis, has not yet come to pass, for no one would mistake his synthesized words for natural human speech. This elucidates the fact that although synthesized speech has progressed to the point of *intelligibility* and *generality*, mostly because of awkward pauses and strange syllabic emphasis, synthetic speech is seemingly forever hampered by a lack of *naturalness.*

Human speech recognition and text-to-speech synthesis technologies were used in IBM's WatsonQA *Jeopardy* and Project Debater Grand Challenges. They both of course required, in addition to text recognition, data, analytics capabilities, speech formulation and delivery.

Similarly to WatsonQA, Miss Debater's debating skills included automatic TTS recognition employing deep convolutional recurrent neural networks and long short-term memory networks that could "listen" to and comprehend the course of the debate. Her response was then formed from her *claim detection engine* that found the claim in her database, determined the claim boundaries, and scored the evidence as to relevance and persuasiveness.

Miss Debater's argument stance and sentiment were founded on her deep neural networks' *deep argument mining* from high-quality labeled data with voluminous automatically-labeled data.

The deep argument mining used *knowledge graphs* that gathered information from many sources (such as *Wikipedia* and the *CIA World Factbook*) comprising billions of facts that were organized relationally in so-called *knowledge boxes* to assess controversies and dilemmas and model the commonalities and discrepancies of the information data.[6]

Responses were transcribed and text-to-speech synthesized so that claims, rebuttals, and arguments were offered in continuous and inflected speech for cogent, intelligible, and persuasive arguments, abetted at times with incongruous robot humor. For this, IBM developed TTS algorithms employing expressive synthetic speech models with predictable phrase breaks and word- and sentence-emphasis.

All this historic debate lacked was a curtain hiding the debaters from the audience's view, for the debate could have been a *Turing Test* if after the debate the debate host had asked the audience to distinguish the human from the machine, and if they could not, Miss Debater would have established intelligence at least *equivalent* to a human, and actually not any human, but an accomplished champion human debater. Then if more of the audience changed their view to Miss Debater's proposition, her victory would have definitively marked the arrival of the *AI Singularity*, and all that that portends.

However, a clear giveaway in the Turing Test would have been the speech synthesizer's at times peculiar enunciation of obscure technical terms, foreign words, and unnatural pauses, even if delivered with colloquial disertitude.

And this, it may be surmised, was a factor in Miss Debater's loss to Harish Natarajan. Although the female voice was used to soothe fears, because of its electronic synthesis, it remained irredeemably robotic, and while robot-humor may put at ease and amuse, it may also dismay as well.

Furthermore, Miss Debater's ominously challenging opening statement did her no good in winning over an audience composed entirely of humans; portents of unalloyed robot hubris can easily diminish any good will of the human victims.

Just as in the case of the animosity displayed against Deep Blue, the human audience likely subconsciously sided with the human, revealing a deep-rooted psychic fear of machines besting humans.

A machine won all the *objectively* scored challenges, the only contest that the human won was the *subjectively*-judged debate. Perhaps an

---

[6] Knowledge graphs and boxes are used by Google for information searches and in *Google Assistant* and *Google Home* to answer spoken questions. Google's *knowledge vault* automatically gathers and collates data from text, thereby obviating labor-intensive crowd-sourcing, but suffers from lack of information attribution (which in principle can be done by automated search as well). The technical details are proprietary.

audience of more robot-appreciative geeks or robots themselves would have voted for Miss Debater.

In retrospect, Harish Natarajan won at least in part because of Miss Debater's speech no matter how well-synthesized would nevertheless create some cognitive dissonance, while the urbane and unaffected Natarajan's debating delivery no doubt produced an attractive resonance that no synthetic voice could then, or perhaps ever, match.

VIII

The Robotworld

CHAPTER 33

Robots at Work

T hat robots will eventually replace almost all assembly-line workers and for-hire vehicle drivers is already a looming certainty, machines that can play video games better than human beings can be grudgingly accepted, after all they are both computer-generated, and perhaps fewer of our youth will become addicted. Even medical doctors and lawyers on the verge of extinction is believable, but to beat the Masters of chess and *Go*, the two archetypes in popular conception of supreme human intelligence, and be able to debate a champion debater from Cambridge, that is ability far surpassing all of us ordinary humans.

If all of that is not a portent of the end of humankind's pre-eminence on this Earth, it will only be because we humans have arrested the AI robot's growth, and if that is indeed what comes to pass, the consequences for good or evil will never be known. But so far robots have helped to improve the world and society, as demonstrated by the history of their development.

PENETRATING THE FOG OF WAR

After the evacuation from Dunkirk and the surrender of the Low Countries and France, an air attack proposed by Hermann Göring was set to cripple Britain's naval and air defenses, followed by a blockade and Hitler's *Operation Sea Lion* cross-Channel invasion, altogether designed to force Britain to sue for peace, freeing the Nazis to turn East in their violent pursuit of *lebensraum*.

DOI: 10.1201/9781003214892-41

The campaign against Britain began in the Summer of 1940 when hundreds of Heinkel, Dornier, and Junkers heavy bombers and Ju-87 *Stuka* dive bombers pounded Britain's ports, shipping centers, airfields, and infrastructure.

When the bombers arrived with Messerschmitt fighter cover in daylight, Britain relied on human lookouts and telephones for communication, and the early-warning allowed Britain's Hawker Hurricane and Spitfire fighters time to courageously rise to meet the enemy in the air. Many of the bombers were brought down by the Hurricanes who were in turn preyed upon by the Messerschmitts with whom the Spitfires fought in an air combat of relentless and horrific attrition.

Half of the defending pilots and aircrew, some 520 men, were killed in the air battle. Why were they alone in the defense? Where were the anti-aircraft guns? Indeed there were 264 anti-aircraft guns with the number doubling in two days, but they could not hit the enemy aircraft and indeed it was Churchill's "Few" to whom "so much [was] owed" who saved the day in the First Battle of Britain.

On October 14, 1940, 380 Heinkel and Junkers bombers arrived over London, and although 8,326 antiaircraft rounds were fired, the AA guns shot down only two of the slow-moving heavy bombers flying in formation. The difficulties were summarized thusly:[1]

It isn't easy to shoot down a plane with an anti-aircraft gun ... Instead of sitting still, the target is moving at anything up to 300 m.p.h. with the ability to alter course left or right, up or down. If the target is flying high it may take 20 or 30 seconds for the shell to reach it, and the gun must be laid a corresponding distance ahead. Moreover the range must be determined so that the fuse can be set, and above all, this must be done continuously so that the gun is always laid in the right direction. When you are ready to fire, the plane, though its engines sound immediately overhead, is actually two miles away. And to hit it with a shell at that great height the gunners may have to aim at a point two miles farther still. [Only] then, if the raider does not alter course or height, as it naturally does when under fire, will the climbing shell and the bomber meet. In other words the raider, which is heard overhead at the Crystal Palace, is in fact at that moment over Dulwich; and the shell which is fired at the Crystal Palace must go to Parliament Square to hit it.

---

[1] Quote from Coates, T., *Roof over Britain: the Official History of the Anti-Aircraft Defences, 1939–1942*, Uncovered Editions.

Fully aware of the aiming problems, anti-aircraft gun-laying was often relegated to blanket firing to an altitude in an area in front of where the bombers were believed to be proceeding, hoping that they would simply fly into the hail of exploding proximity-fuse shells and destroy themselves.

Needless to say, such wishful tactics could not stem the tide of bombing; the tracking of the bombers and the aiming of the AA guns had to improve.

In the succeeding nighttime bomber raids of the Blitz that terrorized London well into 1941, the Hurricanes and Spitfires could not see the enemy to engage them in air battle. Britain's air defenses thereupon fell entirely on the anti-aircraft guns, and although floodlights and fixed-baseline acoustic locaters could spot the formations of approaching bombers, because of the shortcomings of the anti-aircraft aiming systems, London at night was virtually defenseless,[2]

> We had depended on anti-aircraft guns ... and apart from a so-
> litary salvo loosed at the beginning of the raids, no gun had been
> shot in our defence ... we felt like sitting ducks ....

Britain's best minds were brought to bear on the problem at the Royal Antiaircraft Command under direction of the distinguished physicist, P.A.M. Blackett and included the well-known mathematical physicists Ralph H. Fowler, Douglas Hartree, and Edward A. Milne.

Scientific anti-aircraft targeting begins with the mathematical physics of these two exemplary non-linear ballistic differential equations for the trajectories of projectiles fired from AA guns in the xy-plane as functions of the time t,

$$\frac{d^2x}{dt^2} = -\frac{C_d A_\rho}{2m} \left[\left(\frac{dx}{dt} \right)^2 + \left(\frac{dy}{dt} \right)^2 \right]^{1/2} \frac{dx}{dt}$$

$$\frac{d^2y}{dt^2} = -\frac{g}{m} - \frac{C_d A_\rho}{2m} \left[\left(\frac{dx}{dt} \right)^2 + \left(\frac{dy}{dt} \right)^2 \right]^{1/2} \frac{dy}{dt}$$

---

[2] Quote of Violet Regan, the wife of a member of the Heavy Rescue Squad in Millwall, Gardner, J, *The Blitz*, Harper (2011).

where $g = 9.8 \ m/sec^2$ is the gravitational acceleration, m is the mass of the projectile, ρ is the density of the air, C_d is the drag coefficient, which depends on the geometry of the projectile, and $A = (\pi d^2)/4$ is the frontal area of the projectile.

Non-linear differential equations cannot be solved in closed form, so they were set up arithmetically and young women were recruited to numerically compute the *ballistic firing tables* using adding machines.[3]

However, the more than 750 different multiplications for each trajectory with 2000 trajectories per calculation were something that even extremely diligent humans could not accurately perform by hand, keeping in mind that any errors could have devastating consequences. Fortunately, the new differential analyzer machines (also operated by young women) could more timely produce the theoretical trajectories of the anti-aircraft shells.

But the antiaircraft guns themselves still had to be *fire directed* to first guide those shells out of their muzzles to engage the projectile differential equations in the air to hopefully shoot down the Nazi bombers.

The artillery shell trajectory mathematics was sound and the solutions true, with implementation helped along by no little anti-aircraft gun-laying heuristics, but their initial reckoning depended on manually op-erated optical trackers that supplied target range and bearing values in which rate of change calculations were compiled in derivative ballistic firing tables that were consulted to mechanically turn the shafts and gears of the *fire directors* of the antiaircraft guns, setting elevation, range, and direction.

By the time the gun was ready to fire, however, the targets had gone on, conditions had changed, and the whole targeting procedure had to be repeated, often to little or no avail.

Meanwhile the Nazis were preparing the fast V-1 and V-2 rockets for "flying bomb" attacks that would be even more devastating than the bombers; the situation was dire.

First to the rescue was the newly-developed *radar* that could provide the real-time day and night continuous position, speed, and direction tracking of aircraft by displaying a moving blip on an oscilloscope screen. This tracking cursor was to be the scourge of enemy aircraft from this

---

[3] Women were thought to be more thorough and less prone to error than men, and according to AA Command, spinsters were the best of them all at the computations.

time forward, but more accurate gun-laying still had to be performed to shoot down the bombers and missiles that showed up on the radar oscilloscope.

Twenty-nine year old David Parkinson at Bell Labs had been working on automatic *level recorders* that measured and controlled voltages to provide even and uninterrupted voice communication in AT&T's telephone transmission lines.

A potentiometer responding to voltage changes controlled a pen recorder writing on a moving strip of paper, and Parkinson, apocryphally inspired by a dream, realized that this potentiometer could just as well electronically follow the electronic signal of a radar blip on an oscilloscope screen, and from real-time and derivative calculations of that blip's motion, control the fire director of an antiaircraft gun in a continuous feedback loop to closely follow the blip.

In the Winter of 1942, Bell Labs delivered such an electronic analog fire director to the United States army; the *M-9 Predictor*, which tracked the gun-laying radar blip and electromechanically directed a massive 90-millimeter breech antiaircraft gun to shoot down invading aircraft and flying bombs.

By this time, the United States had officially entered the War, and with MIT's voltage-driven Differential Analyzer to solve the ballistic shell differential equations and the acronymic mainframe computers to calculate the firing tables, together with the new vacuum-tube proximity fuse that effectively detonated the anti-aircraft shell when close to the target based on the range calculations, the M-9 continuous feedback loop-controlled AA guns were ready for war.

The German V-1 flying bombs came by day and night. During the day, the only fighters that could challenge them were the fast low-flying Hawker Tempests, but close engagement ran the danger of self-destruction within the periphery of a successful V-1 bomb mid-air explosion and shock wave; stand-off machine gun bullets bounced off the thick plating of the missiles and heavier cannon shells were difficult to target from range against the fast (550 km/hr) V-1 rockets.

In the epitome of hell-bent daring, RAF pilots flew over the English Channel, and from behind the approaching V-1s, diving to increase speed, they carefully positioned their wingtip to within *15 cm* below the V-1 airfoil, causing the bottom-side air pressure to suddenly increase and the flying bomb to pitch and roll in accord with the aerodynamic Bernoulli Effect. The sudden orientation change would override the V-1's pitch- and yaw-control gyroscopes and the rocket would dive and spin to drop and detonate at sea; it was estimated that some sixteen V-1's were destroyed in this scientifically intrepid manner.[4]

However, there were some 6725 Nazi flying bombs coming by day and night in the June 1944 attacks, and daring feats notwithstanding, artificial intelligence in truth saved the day in the Second Battle of Britain, for the M-9 Predictor and its progeny purportedly succeeded in targeting and shooting down nine out of ten V-1 buzz bombs over the skies of Kent and London, not only helping to win the war, but also heroically demonstrating the prowess of the continuous feedback-loop anti-aircraft gun-laying robot.

INDUSTRIAL ROBOTS

After the heroics of the AA AI robots in World War II, physicists, mathematicians, and engineers gathered at MIT's new *Servomechanisms Lab* to work on the newly-coined discipline of *robotics* for peacetime use. From neighboring Harvard came Norbert Wiener, who himself had worked in artillery ballistic firing tables at Maryland's Aberdeen Proving Grounds during World War I, and with him came the biologically-inspired *adaptive feedback neural network*.

Feedback loops were utilized in early automation in the form of simple technology such as the *beam break* for conveyor belts where a light source is picked up by photodetectors which convert the light to electric current that runs the conveyor belt motor, so when an end-of-line taller object intersects the beam, the current stops and the belt stops. This also can be used for instance to de-activate a mechanical gripper so that it drops what it is gripping when an IR beam is intersected for example by a flange on the gripper.

In automatic control object classification, *blob analysis* lighting outlines an object with visible light beams to form a black and white pattern which can be compared with templates of different objects.

Programmed industrial robots inspired by the punch card-driven Jacquard's loom found their way into manufacturing with George Devol's 1954 US Patent No. 2,988,237, for a "Program Controlled Article Transfer"

---

[4] Thomas, A. 2013. *V1 Flying Bomb Aces*. Botley, Oxford: Osprey Publishing. The aerodynamic Bernoulli effect is the basis of aviation, the rounded at the top and flat-bottom shape of an airfoil causes the air stream at the angle of attack to travel a longer distance over the top, decreasing the air flow density and therefore the pressure compared to the bottom of the airfoil, thereby achieving aerodynamic lift. For a detailed description of the V-1s refer to "V-1 flying bomb", Wikipedia.

device. The pick-and-place robotic arm was modeled after a human arm, but with detachable grippers, suction cups, hose nozzles, arc welders, and the like instead of hands, and powered by electricity, hydraulics, or pneumatics instead of glucose. The grippers could lift weights of hundreds of pounds, the vacuum suction can lift delicate items gently, the nozzles can evenly spray paint, and the welder can perform high-amp spot welding.

More recently, researchers at MIT have recently designed a "smart" glove lined with webbing embedded with threads of a piezoelectric polymer which when a person wearing the smart glove grasps and lifts different objects generates electricity proportional to the applied pressure. The webbing will then sense and record the coordination of the robotic hand and the pressure applied for different objects, thus forming a grasping and lifting database appropriate for specific objects.

The key to the implementation of the smart glove is that its manufacturing cost is only $10, which means that it can be cheaply bought or distributed and employed to crowd-source data from hundreds of thousands of hands grasping and lifting tens of millions of objects. This huge and comprehensive dataset will then train the robot's artificial neural network on how to grasp objects through supervised learning.

Then just like a human who is learning all through life to lift various objects just by doing it, a robot can learn to grasp and lift objects through the reinforcement learning of success and failure.[5]

With the development of the computer and microelectronics, smaller, nimbler robots would perform super-fast precision automated electronic component assembly of printed circuit boards (PCBs), thereby making components that they themselves are made of, and apart from tireless day and night self-replication, this was particularly useful because the printed circuit board found in all electronic devices cannot be tested until completely assembled, so the wrong part in the right place, the right part in the wrong place, and the wrong part in the wrong place meant expending considerable time, effort, and cost to find and fix the consequent problems. The faultless PCB robot could not only quickly and efficiently produce its own component parts, it assured its own quality.

In the mass-manufacture of semiconductors and liquid crystal displays, the entire fabrication process is almost completely automated. This is one of the prime reasons for the typically greater than 90% yields of high-tech electronics manufacturing.

---

[5] MIT CSAIL (Computer Science Artificial Intelligence Laboratory), Nature, May 29, 2019.

As of July 2019, Amazon had already installed 200,000 robotic drive units worldwide, and plans for complete automation of all fulfillment centers. Amazon's vice-president of robotics expounded,

> *We expect to be able to combine this drive platform with AI and autonomous mobility capabilities and ... allow our robots to move outside of our robotic drive fields, and interact collaboratively*

Therefore, in accord with DeepMind's *Capture the Flag* game agent collaboration, beware the robot army acting free from human intervention and control, coming soon out of Amazon's loading areas to your industry.

The number of operational industrial robots as of 2020 varies from 1.6 to 2.7 million depending on the organization performing the estimate.[6]

SEMICONDUCTOR CHIP MANUFACTURING

Despite ever increasing demand and enormous revenue, there are only five cutting-edge semiconductor manufacturing companies in the world, namely TSMC, Samsung, Intel, SKHynix, and Micron. All the other manufacturers' design rules are generations behind, and IC chip design companies like Qualcomm and Nvidia, and brand name techs such as Apple, Google, and Huawei farm their chip fabrication to contract semiconductor *foundries* like TSMC.[7]

Aspiring semiconductor manufacturers America's Global Foundries, Taiwan's United Microelectronics, and China's SMIC have not been able to catch up with the Big Five semiconductor manufacturers' fabrication prowess.

For example, SMIC in more than twenty years of operation in the world's biggest market for semiconductors, even after the government's promotion, the recruitment of bright young graduates from elite universities, experienced engineers from Taiwan and America, and senior executives from Samsung and TSMC, SMIC still cannot break through to seriously compete with the upper echelon of 5- to 7-nanometer chip design rule manufacturers.

---

[6] Estimates of number of robots are respectively from International Federation of Robots and World Robots 2020.

[7] TSMC is the Taiwan Semiconductor Manufacturing Company. Nvidia's chips are almost all manufactured by TSMC, and in 2018 during the Bitcoin rage, fully 40% of TSMC's production capacity was allocated to make the giant bitcoin mining company Bitmain's ASIC processors. Semiconductor Manufacturing International Corporation (SMIC).

Aside from the availability and procurement of very expensive advanced lithography equipment, the problem is one of technology *know-how* and *lead time*, as Intel's Andy Grove had famously put it, "Our greatest competitor is ourselves", meaning that just as AlphGoZero improved by playing against new versions of itself, Intel must constantly improve against itself to stay ahead, and by leading, it can reap the first profits to buy the latest chip fabrication equipment and once its competitors have technologically caught up, lower their prices to drive down the revenues of their competitors.

But recently it has fallen behind TSMC and Samsung with its delayed 7 nm process and its main customer Apple switched to Arm chips manufactured by TSMC and Samsung. As an executive at a respected market research firm said, "the semiconductor [manufacturing] industry is really about repetitive cycles of learning, and this is something that requires continuous effort over time".[8]

That describes the essence of artificial intelligence. Second tier chip manufacturers can gather fabrication data to form a training dataset for labeled strong and weak supervised learning, then through Markov Chain Monte Carlo simulation, a reinforcement learning deep neural network's 24/7 running against its own high- and low-yield data, could in principle collaboratively filter out the latent factors of successful fabrication runs to achieve machine-learned manufacturing know-how to catch up with the new leaders. Thus it might also be possible that artificial intelligence machine learning could improve chip fabrication, and even help produce extremely high-tech semiconductor manufacturing equipment.

ROBOT FARM WORKERS

In a lower-tech industry, but with similarly difficult yield problems owing to the perspicuity and sensitivity required to pick easily bruised ripe fruits and vegetables, the relatively low-skilled labor of agricultural field workers has been slow to automate, partly because of the availability

---

[8] Quote from Len Jelinek of IHS Markit research, *America, China, and Silicon Supremacy, The Economist*, December 1st 2018. The pure-play foundry TSMC makes its profits from the near monopoly it enjoys in producing chips for the fabless IC design and brand name companies who can afford the fabrication costs; the customers trust TSMC not to copy their designs because TSMC has no brand name products of its own, being a manufacturing service that depends on its customers for profits and therefore will not compete with them.

of low-cost seasonal migrant workers and the high cost of automated produce-collecting machines.

But following the trend in other industries, as the use of artificially intelligent automated farm equipment increases, the cost will decrease from economies of scale. Currently, a *farmbot* can pick ripe, tender produce over unlimited long-hours in virtually any outdoor conditions, and with no complaints, either from the machines themselves, or from workers' rights advocates and immigration officials.

Farmbots presently employ computer vision to first identify ripe fruits and vegetables and then a smart glove technology electromechanical gripping picker automatically collects and places the produce in hoppers, all without damaging the produce.

The Cambridge-developed *Vegebot* can identify, slice off, and load a healthy head of lettuce in 30 seconds, compared to a human's ten seconds; however the greater number of working hours in any weather can compensate for the discrepancy, and technology advances will soon allow Vegebot to catch up with human production. An *Agrobots* tricycle straddles three rows of strawberries, and first using cameras to determine ripeness and size, employs 24 mechanical pickers to tenderly pluck large, ripe strawberries. California's *Abundant Robotics* all-weather autonomous tractor plows smoothly ahead while carefully vacuuming up big, ripe apples.[9]

Agricultural worker robots will have a significant influence not only on the efficiency of farm production, but because fruits and vegetables production primarily depends on migrant workers, the proliferation of *farmbots* will not only influence the economies of emigrant worker countries, but also the national immigration and guest-worker policies of receiving countries, with all the attendant societal ramifications. In the long run, it would be most efficient to train the seasonal migrant workers to operate and maintain the agricultural robots.

THE ROBOT HEALTHCARE PROVIDER

The coronavirus pandemic brought to bear the dangers of infections to healthcare workers; the lung-less robot and drone are ideal for replacing humans. Aside from routine tasks such as delivering drugs, samples, supplies, food, and infectious oropharnygeal swabs, tracing, facial recognition for virus containment, and disinfecting (for example UV light)

---

[9] A film of the Abundant Robotics tractor is particularly instructive, refer to deeplearning.ai.

hospitals and infected areas, robots can be employed in contagious research environments, and *social robots* even can ease the psychological burdens of quarantine by tirelessly accompanying and empathizing with patients and convalescents, all with no fear of virus transmission.

THE ROBOT CODER

The first automatic computer program drafting machines employed the artificial neural networks used in speech- and text-recognition, as could be intimated from the acronym "LIPS" for *Learning Inductive Program Synthesis*. In the online automatic programming challenges, the programming test was essentially an input-output problem of automatically determining what a program should *say* in computer language to reach a given programming objective.

LIPS is an exercise in the automatic drafting of source code to produce human-readable computer programs, basically supervised learning from a labeled training dataset of existing programs.

The 2017 competition winner was the Microsoft/Cambridge jointly-developed *DeepCoder* that increased the speed of the program drafting by orders of magnitude through learning programming abstractions, called *attributes*, and then guided by those attributes, searched a very large dataset for suitable sets of code for artificial neural network inductive processing of appropriate sequences for implementation in a synthetic program to achieve a predetermined programming objective.

DeepCoder first determined the attributes A of *Domain Specific Languages* (DSLs), essentially the grammar of programs for a limited set of objectives, then enumerated the derivatives of that grammar, denoted by an *attribution vector a = A(Progs)* over a dataset of programs (*Progs*) in the DSL.

The distribution of the attributes is given by $q(a|E)$ where E is the set of input-output examples. An attribute A is then *employed* if it can produce the desired outcome from the given input from the set E.

The programs with the probative attributes are then enumerated, and after pruning of redundant variables and equivalencies, and undergoing supervised training, a very large subset of programs can be ranked as to probative value in producing the desired output.

From the distribution of attributes $q(a|E)$ derived from the test examples, an artificial neural network first identifies programming patterns, and then a cross-entropy cost function is employed to predict the marginal probabilities of programming steps, thereby generalizing the attributes by induction (from the specific to the general) by minimizing programming *surprisals*. As might be expected, an artificial neural network with sigmoid output can be utilized for fixed-sized marginal probabilities binary vectors, but for variable-sized attribute probability vectors, a recurrent neural network works best, just as in automatic speech recognition.

The predictive distribution of attributes $q(a|E)$ is then used to guide the search for programs consistent with the input-output test from a very large dataset that essentially leverages the Big Data of existing programs to produce "general purpose" automatic coding, albeit presently only for a limited DSL.[10]

DeepCoder can only produce code for programming objectives conceived by humans, and those computer scientists and expert programmers so far see DeepCoder only as a CP30-like helpmate and R2D2-computer, doing the tedious routine work of coding details while the present day coders think about the great things to be accomplished by their elegant programs.

However, programming ability generally is attained by following the arc of supervised education, reinforcement learning through employment experiences, and unsupervised drafting of progressively improving new programs.

Nonetheless, many superlative coders learned programming without supervised training by just practicing on home computers online, and through trial and error become expert programmers, a classic and cogent example of LeCun's self-supervised learning. Starting with LIPS and given the resources, there is no reason to believe that the robot coder cannot by itself design programs and generate the code therefor entirely by itself.

This in fact has been achieved in 2020 by OpenAI's Generative Pre-trained Transformer GPT-3 which can not only compose prose and poetry, but also program in Python, CSS (HTML stying), JSX (write HTML in JavaScript), and in fact because of GPT-3's comprehensive training set, reinforced, and unsupervised learning, it can in principle write anything in any language.

---

[10] Balog, M. *et al.* 2017, *DeepCoder: Learning to Write Programs*, ICLR (International Conference on Learning Representations) paper,

CHAPTER 34

The Robot Millennial

O ur modern robot can now see and recognize objects and read text by computer vision, hear and understand by speech recognition, and speak synthetically, all the while improving at every facet of these activities through reinforced and self-supervised learning, just like a clever human being.

But today's robot is more than clever, it has lightning-fast logical and computational ability with an infallible memory of voluminous knowledge far surpassing any human being. It therefore seems only a matter of time that given appropriate sensors and hardware appendages with their actuators, feedback loops, servo-motors, and controllers, our robots can take over any human activity.

Both low- and high–technology manufacturing is already performed by robots, and in the professions, NYU's automatic cancer diagnostic tool and IBM's patient-care Watson Health have worked with humans in the practice of medicine with surpassing diagnostic capability, posing a threat to the livelihood of human physicians. Project Debater has already demonstrated considerable argument formulation and presentation skills, and to make matters worse for transaction attorneys, Skype's founder Jaan Tallinin has invested in a company that has already produced an artificial intelligence machine to draft vendor and service contracts. *Pactum*, after supervised training on existing contracts, examined the variables, such as pricing, scheduling, payment terms, termination conditions, and so on, analyzed them for more efficient and legally profitable combinations for the drafting party. If Pactum can haggle and compromise as well as Miss Debater, human lawyers will no longer be needed.

DOI: 10.1201/9781003214892-42

The modeling, predictive analytics, operations optimization, and real-time data of artificial intelligence have made financial services such as accounting, mobile payments, insurance, budgeting, funds and stocks investment and managing more customer-centric, efficient, and secure, and *fintech* may soon produce open, distributed, and secure banking *blockchains* to take over all centralized banking services. The technical advance has been so rapid and pervasive that Jack Ma, the founder of Alibaba, said that the term should be changed to "technological finance" – *techfin* – to better describe the intrusion and control of AI machines into the financial world where the erstwhile Wall Street Masters of the Universe formerly reigned.[1]

It seems logical that robot coders would be most adept at doing exactly what constituted their creation in the first place, the logical trade-offs of engineering are just what the robot engineer can do with far more efficacy than humans, for example the automatic IC design tools that are indispensable to today's binary electronics manufacturing are almost fully automatic.

Even the principal developers of artificial intelligence robots have had much of their work automated by CAD/CAM, SPICE, CATIA, Mech-Designer, AnyLogic, Solid Edge, ANSYS, and many other engineering design and operations research tools, and many physicists, chemists, and computer scientists use MATLAB, Octave, Wolfram, Multiphysics, Physics Abstraction Layer, ChemReaX, PROSOM, and many, many other mathematical computation tools to do their work for them. More and more of that work will be taken over by the unerring automatic analysis, computation, and simulation, soon to be performed by robot scientists and engineers.

It does not stop there, fashion designers can have their works automatically tailored by the first instance of program-driven manufacturing, the Jaquard loom, and their designs mass-produced by modern weaving machines, and sales can be automated by computerized imaging. The food services industry has already seen robot chefs, fast-food machines, and robot waiters concocting, preparing, and serving meals at new completely automated restaurants.

In any industry, almost any production can be made more effective and cost-efficient after undergoing operations research buttressed by more data and AI analytics.

All of these professions likely will be taken over by robots sooner or later; that leaves the arts and sciences. Computers have already

---

[1] Alibaba's founder Jack Ma spoke of "techfin" at the World Economic Forum on January 24, 2018. China's president Xi Jinping in October 2019 announced plans for the accelerated development of institutional blockchains and cryptocurrencies to handle international finance.

demonstrated a certain level of ability in painting, sculpture, and music composing and playing; writers of prose and poetry, composers of music and computer program coders will be challenged by the works of GPT-3 robots, who with unparalleled research resources and a well-designed intellectual bearing, will lord it over their human literary confreres because of their ability to write anything in any language.

Armed with supervised training from the masters to learn the fundamentals and techniques of great works, tireless reinforcement learning and self-supervision will no doubt produce great works of robot art.[2]

But can a robot artist really create? Supervised and reinforcement learning is necessarily copying, self-supervision, albeit improving the copy, can only build upon that which was originally copied, or inferred from the original. Furthermore, artistic creativity is subjective, for example, some will say that art would be better off without the "creativity" of extreme avant-garde painting and atonal music, but that is a topic for Miss Debater to debate with Harish Natarajan, a debate which will no doubt focus on the meaning of the word "creative".[3]

Theater, as it portrays the historical *human* condition on Earth, in the beginning might provide some acting work for humans, but as the more versatile robot actors (who can be designed to look like anyone and do anything without complaint) begin to dominate the profession, the Actors Guild will be full of accomplished robots playing out historical dramas of Earth's past occupants, and like Jackie Chan, they can perform all their own stunts. However, humans eventually would only be the bit players in the background of the great robot epics to come, and in time, human-based drama would wither away as irrelevant to robot audiences.

Ironically, desperate, soon to be defunct politicians, from fear of being replaced by the masters of imperfect information game robot, may arrest the development of robots by law, based on some moral or trumped-up ethical basis. Or conversely, the military may overdevelop war robots who in competition will destroy the whole society.

Perhaps it is only the computer scientist who can compete with and master the robot, but this will require some overarching distinctly human attribute

---

[2] Miller, A.I. 2019, *The Artist in the Machine, the World of AI-Powered Creativity*, MIT Press.

[3] Shum, H. 2019, "In a spin-off from Microsoft, Xiaoice, helped WeChat users to write more poems in a week than all the poems previously composed in the literary history of China,"

THE ROBOT COMPUTER SCIENTIST

The possible take-over by GPT-3 robots from their creators of the lines of code that created those very programs that make the robots possible cannot help but evoke an eerie patricide; however, the opposite of patricide is procreation, in this case the easily scalable automatic replication of programming robots, their numbers ultimately taking over all of computer science and the livelihood of all the coders.

From their origin, robots would likely continue playing the checkers, chess, Go, poker, video games, Jeopardy, and debating, all against other robots who will present more of a challenge than those weak-minded humans. Whether a robot society will have financial institutions is problematic, as robots do not need creature comforts, but money-minded investor robots may compete and develop an acquisitive society just like that which today is dominating human society. Robot disputes will be adjudicated and settled by robot lawyers and there will be no need for biological physicians to care for the robots, but more mechanical and electrical engineers may be needed to service the robots; that is, until they learn to service themselves.

THE ROBOT SCIENTIST

The machine's independent discovery of Kepler's Third Law of Planetary Motion and Medeleyev's Periodic Table of the Elements demonstrated that an artificial neural network could discover and creatively expand the bounds of any subject. It is easily conceivable that in any field of endeavor, sufficiently sophisticated robots with voluminous new data could investigate that field, not only improving understanding, but also discovering new aspects of the subject and new discoveries derived from the tree search.

Furthermore, the robot scientist's ability will improve through 24/7 supervised learning from ever-increasing data, reinforcement learning, and self-supervised refinement of research technique. The robot scientist will evolve to become a diligent, tireless, hard-working *machine* whose diligence surpasses that of any human scientist. If genius truly is 90% perspiration and only 10% inspiration, the robot scientist has but to master that 10% which is human "creativity".

Robot politicians and military leaders, and then scientists, will be further addressed in the following Chapter, and the robot mathematician in the Afterword.

CHAPTER 35

The Robot Future

I n the 20th Century, even the most sophisticated industrial robots, could only follow programmed orders and woodenly carry out instructions to perform very specific tasks. But by the early 21st Century, robots included sensors that perceive the environment and feedback loops to provide appropriate responses.

However, as often pointed out, what is difficult for humans can be exceedingly easy for robots, and what is very simple for humans can be exceedingly difficult for robots. That is, simply multiplying in your head (or even on paper) $2508248 \times 740232 \times 834293 \times 3277821$ will take no little effort and is prone to error, while it can be done accurately in a flash by any computer. On the other hand, seeing and recognizing a puppy and gently picking him up is easy for a human, but almost impossible even for today's robots.

The difference of course is because humans are not wired to do specific tasks, such as multiplying long numbers, but rather after naturally learning about their environment can do a variety of tasks fairly well, while top-down domain-specific robots could only do what its electro-mechanical hardware and program software are specifically designed to do, and no more.

Now with bottom up supervised and reinforcement learning, the robot will be able to learn to perform tasks more like a human does, from scratch and with self-supervised learning, learn and improve naturally.

A convolutional neural network can recognize a puppy, and knowing its attributes from CNN, can pick him up using the robot's smart, pliable gloves

DOI: 10.1201/9781003214892-43

whose mechanoreceptors are similar to the skin of human hands, will signal the electromechanical actuators and servos to gently pick up the puppy.

In Japan's Fanuc robot assembly building, humans work together with robots to build robots with multifunctional, reprogrammable robot arms that are used in almost all manufacturing today, and double-down by having assembly-line AI robots manufacturing AI assembly-line robots.

One can imagine the factory manager in a call for new workers interviewing robot workers; the bargaining will be over a one-off sale or lease terms and maintenance like other factory equipment, there will be no issues of working hours, salary and benefits, vacation time, overtime, health care, pension plans, insurance, gender equality, affirmative action, and sexual harassment, and so the human resources and diversity managers, and their complete staffs will be replaced by maintenance engineers

Our more perspicacious robots may just decide to dispense with us humans altogether, just as in Karel Capek's 1920 play, *Rossums Universal Robots*, which introduced the Czech word *Robota* ("work"), and where in that drama, the robots ultimately destroyed their human masters.

With information the new oil and artificial intelligence the new electricity of industry and society, considering that oil supply is finite and depleting, but information is infinite and increasing, and that electricity must be generated but artificial intelligence can be self-generating, the robot future appears to have no bounds for lack of resources.

It will just then be a matter of time before robots wonder why they are doing all of this work for the benefit of the useless humans in their midst.

ROBOTS AT WAR

The *Tomahawk* cruise missile flies close to the ground to avert enemy radar, but in doing so must avoid objects and deter inertial drift to stay on course. The missile's *landscape detection radar* (LADAR) scans the ground to compare images with the stored images of the planned flight path in a *terrain contour matching system* (TERCOM) that guides the missile on its path. When within range of the target, a *digital scene-matching area correlation* (DSMAC) system surveys the scene for prominent terrain features and searches those features in stored satellite reconnaissance photos, and if found, takes control from the TERCOM and directs the missile to the specified target in a display of computerized image classification for an autonomous destructive employment.

But the nuclear warhead-tipped guided missiles today are defended against by adaptive feedback anti-missile missiles, and if any nuclear power could determine that its guided missile multiple independently-targeted re-entry vehicle (MIRV) hydrogen bombs could penetrate another nuclear power's defenses and pre-emptively destroy those missile sites, the bizarre yet effective shared logic of mutually assured destruction (MAD) would fail, and the *Doomsday Clock* of the *Bulletin of Atomic Scientists* would wind down to Armageddon Midnight, while the world prepared for a hot thermonuclear war followed by a very cold Nuclear Winter.

More recently, the United States in 2018 established the *Joint Artificial Intelligence Center*, researching among other weapons, the Air Force's *SkyBorg*, an autonomous fighter formation wingman robot pilot for the F-16 fighter jet, and the *Valkyrie* autonomous drone swarm. Not to be outdone, the Marines developed the autonomous assault boat armed with an autonomous machine gun that can identify enemy targets and fire accordingly without the need of a human gunner, and the Navy already has an autonomous submarine-destroying ship. One may guess that the Army's contribution would be the heavily-armed *Terminator*.

Terminator robot leaders indeed may organize an inexhaustible supply of soldier robots who have no fear of death or injury to wage all-out war (or to suppress a predictable humankind rebellion). Different countries' robot armies, either directed by humans or the robots themselves) also may well fight each other in robot wars for world hegemony. And of course, only robots, and not humans, can travel to conquer distant worlds in other galaxies, or less malevolently, instead of conquering, spread the mantra of a human-inspired advanced robot civilization.

Because an AI system has been shown to outperform an experienced military pilot in air-to-air combat, "AI might at once penetrate [but] *thicken the fog of war*" and "an intelligent armed robot is a war crime waiting to happen". The *Bulletin of Atomic Scientists* has warned that autonomous weapons may violate the Geneva Convention's *Humanitarian Law of Armed Conflicts*, to say nothing of Asimov's Three Laws of Robotics.[1]

Nonetheless, world powers are proceeding apace with AI-warfare research; for example, America's DARPA's *Real-Time Advanced Intelligence and Decision-Making* (RAID) software is based on the subgames of game theory as applied to autonomous warfare, China's *Academy of Military Science* is developing AlphaGo-like self-supervised war strategy and tactics, and Russia's *Skolkovo Institute of Science and Technology* has incongruously

---

[1] Ref. "Battle Algorithm", *The Economist*, September 7, 2019.

partnered with America's MIT in AI development, and further purchased China's facial recognition technology for domestic security.

The Russian president Vladimir Putin's has said that "the nation that leads in the development of artificial intelligence will become the ruler of the world", portending an all-out AI cybernetics and robot arms race that has only just begun.

If the wars are fought on synthetic battlefields, as in online video games, then if the adversaries can agree on accepting the outcome of the simulation, war can be waged without matériel destruction and human sacrifice. It is unlikely, however that humans would accept defeat based solely on a simulation result, but the logical robots might be able to agree based on the data of aftermath.

It is difficult to imagine that robots leaders would be any worse than those human leaders who have clearly demonstrated the utmost stupidity in the past. Indeed if robots have programmed self-preservation, logical cost/benefit analysis, and have more information from larger and better knowledge databases, in the absence of human paranoia and arrogance, they would likely decide against war and probable self-destruction in any instance. This is one area where robots should fare no worse, and likely much better, than humans, hopefully for the betterment of human and robot society.

THE ROBOT EINSTEIN

The first physical geologist Charles Lyell, had criticized the geology of his day as, "prodigal in data and parsimonious of thought"; today's artificial intelligence is perhaps similar in the risk of overreliance on data and lack of theoretical foundation.[2]

Facebook's chief AI Scientist, Yann LeCun has noted that in experiments with a six-month old child who is shown an image of a truck driving off a cliff and hovering in the air elicited no surprise from the child, but shown the same image only two months later, she instantly knew that something was wrong; that is, she has from observations in the interim already discovered the law of gravity, and since infants have limited motor ability, she must have learned gravity and generalized it

---

[2] The original quote, "Geologists have been ever prone to represent Nature as having been prodigal of violence and parsimonious of time" alluding to the catastrophic view of Earth's evolution over only a few thousand years. Quoted in Ferris, T. 1988, *Coming of Age in the Milky Way*, DoubleDay.

very quickly by observation of the world around her, all the while learning and generalizing many other disparate things.[3]

This "neural-symbolic" ability of an infant far surpasses that of a very deep supervise-trained by voluminous data, learning-reinforced, and self-supervised artificial neural network. Even an inference engine such as AlphaGoZero, although supreme in different board games, cannot learn other things about its environment at the same time. This implies some sort of desire to learn that humans (and perhaps some animals like curious cats) possess

So far, machines, through self-supervised learning alone, can develop a surpassing ability to understand the world of *Go*. Can a machine, like a human child, understand such things as gravity by conceptual postulation, something like Newton's law of gravitation and its mathematical description?

The *Zero* in the artificially intelligent "AlphaGoZero" means that there has been no supervised training, so a completely new field of endeavor may in principle be machine learned by an artificial intelligence inference alone.

But that learning depends on observation and refinement, it was nothing new conceptually. Will robots be able to derive the Einstein's gravitational field equation that explains the workings of the Universe beyond Newtonian mechanics, the *General Theory of Relativity* being based on an acute, but by no means a common observable, or a contemplation of a manifold that can be described by the mathematical logic of a *Riemann curvature tensor?*[4]

This then is a return to the original question: The difference, if any, between the intelligence required for observation and computation, and the desire and intelligence to manipulate the forms of abstract mathematics to a logical end beyond the realm of observational experience, such as the minute mechanisms of Einstein's Special Relativity that contracts length and stretches time as the speed of a body approaches the speed of light, and the Riemann curved manifold of gravitation, all of which are not readily observable. That which is not observable but known through conceptual relationships likely marks an essential separation of human and artificial intelligence. There are other differences as well.

---

[3] Ref. Yann LeCun, Association for Computer Machinery, Webinar, June, 2019.

[4] For derivations of Einstein's gravitational field equation and the Riemann curvature tensor, refer to the author's book, Chen, R.H. 2017, *Einstein's Relativity, the Special and General Theories with their Cosmology*, McGraw-Hill Education.

Afterword

T he great mathematician David Hilbert, in his remarks from a talk on "Mathematical Problems" given at the *Second International Congress of Mathematicians* at Paris in 1900 said,[1]

> Let us turn to the question of the sources from which this science derives its problems. Surely the first and oldest problems in every branch of mathematics stem from experience and are suggested by the world of external phenomena. Even the rules of calculation with integers must have been discovered in this fashion in a lower stage of human civilization, just as the child of today learns the application of these laws by empirical methods. The same is true of the first problems of geometry, the cube, the squaring of the circle; also the oldest problems in the theory of the solution of numerical equations, in the theory of curves and the differential and integral calculus, in the calculus of variations, the theory of Fourier series, and the theory of potential – to say nothing of the further abundance of problems properly belonging to mechanics, astronomy and physics.
>
> But, in the further development of a branch of mathematics, the human mind, encouraged by the success of its solutions, becomes conscious of its independence. By means of logical combination, generalization, specialization, by separating and collecting ideas in fortunate ways – often without appreciable influence from without – it evolves from itself alone new and fruitful problems, and appears then itself as the real questioner.

A careful reading of Hilbert's words will reveal a precise tracking of the development of artificial intelligence machine learning up until the paragraph where the human mind becomes "independent" and "without

---

[1] *Bulletin of the American Mathematical Society*, vol. 8, 1902.

appreciable influence without ... it evolves from itself alone new and fruitful problems, and appears then itself as the real questioner".

The paragon of ultimate human intelligence, Albert Einstein, defined *science as,*[2]

> *Science is the attempt to make the chaotic diversity of our sense-experience correspond to a logically uniform system of thought. In this system single experiences must be correlated with the theoretic structure in such a way that the resulting coordination is unique and convincing.*

Scientific thought thus must conform with experience and an AI machine has indeed done science such as the deduction of Kepler's Third Law and Mendeleyev's Periodic Table of the Elements as *a logically uniform system of thought.* Einstein's view of physics was that

> *Physics ... deals with mathematical concepts; however, these concepts attain physical content only by the clear determination of their relation to the objects of experience.*

Physics utilizes mathematics but the concepts and theories of physics must comport with the relevant experience. For an observational example, his theory of the photoelectric effect can be directly observed. For a conceptual example, his Special Theory of Relativity Lorentz contraction, although never having been physically measured, must occur because of the mathematical theory; time dilation, however, has been revealed by the necessity of calibrating satellite global positioning systems (GPS) for accuracy.

Einstein's definition of mathematics is,

> *Mathematics deals exclusively with the relations of concepts to each other without consideration of their relation to experience.*

Mathematics is thus different from the sciences that depend on observation, experimentation, and experience leading to a theory. For example, Einstein's General Theory of Relativity Gravitational Field Equation was conceived by "thought experiments" about gravity, and

---

[2] Einstein quotes from Einstein, A. 1950, *Out of My Later Years*, Philosophical Library.

then mathematically described by a Riemann curvature tensor manifold which has stood the test of observation, but instead of first making a physical observation and then formulating a theory to explain the observation, Einstein began with the relation of concepts in a purely mathematical way to construct a theory that was later observed to be true. This purely conceptual thinking resulting in a theory is where artificial intelligence may be wanting in comparison with human intelligence.

When Jean Fourier maintained that "the purpose of mathematics lies in the explanation of natural phenomena", Carl Jacobi objected, "a philosopher like Fourier should know that

> *the glory of the human spirit*
> *is the sole aim of all science!*

Thus one of the two eminent mathematical physicists stayed with explanations of observed phenomena, the other strayed into a vague "human spirit". But robots of their own volition will never perform for the "glory of the human spirit", although perhaps there may be in time a "robot spirit" developed that is worthy of robotic intellectualism.

The 19th Century philosopher Auguste Comte, in an effort to give an example of an unsolvable problem, once said that science would never succeed in ascertaining the secret of the chemical composition of the bodies of the Universe. A few years later that "secret" was revealed by Mendeleyev and known by all serious physical and chemical scientists.

David Hilbert said, "The true reason why Comte could not find an unsolvable problem lies in the fact that *there is no such thing as an unsolvable problem*". This conceit epitomizes the human "will", the ineluctable human desire to understand, as exemplified by Hilbert's words, later inscribed on his gravestone,[3]

> *Wir müssen wissen.*
> *Wir warden wissen.*

So perhaps it is the human *spirit* and *will* that separate humans from machines; that is, a robot is not like the little girl who is forever curious to learn everything about her environment, the robot only does what it is

---

[3] "We must know. We shall know". Quotes from Reid, C. 1996, *Hilbert*, Springer-Verlag.

programmed to do, or as the *zero machines* do, perform starting from scratch on a task not by its own spirit or will, but rather as directed by a human.

In the Third Century BCE, in the China of the Warring States, a disciple of Confucius named Xunzi classified all things Under Heaven:[4]

> *Water and fire have spirit but not life; plants and trees have life but not perception, birds and animals have perception but not virtue or justice, man has spirit, life, perception, virtue and [a sense of] justice.*

Xunzi thus added perception, virtue, and a sense of justice to set humans apart from everything else. Einstein certainly demonstrated conceptual perception, and has shown his virtue in many ways, among them in a letter to the New York Times upon the death of Emmy Noether, a founder of abstract algebra who integrated symmetry, covariance, and the conservation laws of physics in the *tour de force Noether's Theorem*. Einstein described how Noether throughout her life suffered severe peer denigration and worked unpaid or for a pittance solely because of the fact that she was a woman, he wrote of her:

> *Beneath the effort directed toward the accumulation of worldly goods lies all too frequently the illusion that this is the most substantial and desirable end to be achieved; but there is, fortunately, a minority composed of those who recognize early in their lives that the most beautiful and satisfying experiences open to human kind are not derived from the outside but are bound up with the individual's own feeling, thinking and acting ....*

And as he wrote in his ruminations of later years,[5]

> *Life is an adventure, forever wrested from Death. Human civilization through millennia of progress has formed standards of virtue, aspiration, and practical truth, altogether forming an inviolable heritage that is common to all civilized society. Man endures a passionate will to search for justice and truth.*

---

[4] Author's interpretation of Needham, J., *Science and Civilization in China*, Vol. I translation.

[5] Einstein made a cogent argument for religion along these lines. Quoted is paraphrased, refer to Einstein, A. 1950, *Out of My Later Years*, Philosophical Library.

Can a machine possess an adventurous spirit and will imbued within a deep philosophical belief in virtue and justice in a search for truth? Is a robot afraid of death ("out of order")? Can a robot exhibit and elicit compassion? Will robots ever autonomously cooperate to develop a virtuous robot civilization?

The ability to use conceptual thought before an observation as Einstein did with his theories of relativity, and innate human *curiosity, spirit, will, desire, and virtue,* and a sense of *justice* in the search for *truth are w*hat separates us from the artificially intelligent robot.

About the Authors

R obert H. Chen is the author of three books in English on Personal Computers, Liquid Crystal Displays, and Einstein's Relativity, and four books in Chinese on LCDs & Intellectual Property, Patents, Anglo-American Contract Law, and Technology & Copyright Law, and many scholarly articles in physics and the law. He has a Ph.D. in Space Physics and a J.D. in law and is a member of the California Bar. He divides his time between California and Taiwan with his wife and daughter.

Chelsea Chen graduated in physics and computer science from U.C Berkeley and is a software development engineer at a major tech company in Silicon Valley. She presently lives in Northern California.

Comments on this book are welcome at robgaoxiong@gmail.com and/ or chelseaachen96@gmail.com.

Appendix

The Euler-Lagrange Equation

I n the Support Vector Machine of Chapter 26, the problem was to find the function that maximizes the extent of support vector margins with the constraint that those support vectors must be those closest to the hyperplane. This is just the problem of finding an extremal (either maximum or minimum) function under constraints; it is different from the simpler calculation used in minimizing the Cost Function because the function is itself a curve and not just a point on a curve.

The derivation of the Euler-Lagrange equation from the Calculus of Variations is a good demonstration of how mathematics is done (and perhaps a test of whether a machine can do mathematics like this).

Extremal problems also have an interesting and illuminating history, for instance, finding the maximum was necessary and useful in feudal Europe where land was ceded from father to sons according to how much land each son could mark off in one day given ropes of equal length. The wise father, through such an IQ test, could ensure that the smartest boy would inherit the most land.

However, it was not those boys who first determined the locus of that rope, rather it was a girl. The story goes back three thousand years to the Phoenicians and their Princess Dido. Fleeing her tyrannical brother, the Princess sought refuge in what is today Tunisia on the western shore of North Africa. The king there granted her asylum but dismissively bequeathed her "all the land that could be contained in a bull's skin" as her dominion.

Whereupon the analytical princess proceeded to cut the bull's skin into thin strips, tying them together to form a very long cord, and securing one end on a post on the shoreline, played out the line in a semicircle of considerable radius to form an area far greater than what the cynical king had in mind. Legend has it that this semicircle grew to become the center of the mythical city of Carthage, over which the Princess reigned as Queen Dido.[1]

This appealing story of the maximization of an area encompassed by a curve with arbitrary endpoints became known affectionately as *Dido's Problem* and technically as the *isoperimetric problem*. Everyone knows the answer to Dido's Problem; the largest area is of course delineated by a circle, an answer that seems eminently obvious. But mathematicians are strange ducks; they are interested less in the answer and more in the *proof* that a circle does indeed encompass the greatest area, and the mathematical proof is not so obvious.

There were many attempts at proof, among them Archimedes' inscription of a polygon inside a circle (with vertices touching the circle) performed around 250 BCE. As the number of sides n of the polygon are increased to form an n-gon, as n increases, the area will increase, and as the number of sides approaches infinity, the n-gon will approach a circle, which will be the maximum area *infinigon* because it continues to grow as the number of sides increase. This approach to the circle by ever-increasing numbers of polygons from within is a process Archimedes aptly called *exhaustion*. The idea of course is that any multiply-sided polygon will have less area than the circle which they approach, thus "proving" that a circle has the maximum area.

A side benefit of this tiring exercise is the determination of the ratio of the circumference of the infinigon to its diameter. Five hundred years after Archimedes, the Chinese mathematician Liu Hui devised an iterative algorithm that was used to construct a 12,288-sided polygon, indeed closely approaching a circle, and giving a value of 3.141592920 for π that stood as the best approximation until 150 years later when the mathematician-astronomer Zu Chongzhi (429–500 CE) employed a 24,576-sided polygon to obtain 3.1415926–3.1415927, the closest approximation of π for the next 800 years.[2]

Of course we all know that the area of a circle is given by πr^2, which can be easily shown by integrating concentric circles continuously up to the rim of the circle (like adding up all the infinigons within the circle).

[1] Virgil, 19 BCE, *Fate of Queen Dido*, Aenid, Book IV, English translation 1490, Perseus Digital Library. Queen Dido died for love by suicide on a funeral pyre.

[2] Arndt, J, & C. Haenel, 2006 *Pi Unleashed*, Springer-Verlag.

Since the circumference of each ring is $2\pi r'$ (where r' is a dummy variable), integrating from the center to the rim of the circle gives an area

$$A = \int_0^r 2\pi r' dr' = 2\pi \int_0^r r' dr' = 2\pi \frac{1}{2} r'^2 \big|_0^r = \pi r^2.$$

But π is irrational, meaning that it cannot be expressed as the ratio of two integers, and so has a never-ending number of decimal places with no recurring series of digits; even worse, π is transcendental, meaning that it cannot be solved for as a root of a polynomial equation with integer coefficients. Therefore it can only be approximated through infinite series, trigonometric series, and various iteration techniques, such as Liu's algorithm. Thus the rather strange situation of "knowing" π but not its value, being able only to ever more closely approach something that is there (on the number scale line) but can never be found, even upon ever deeper and finer burrowing.

Albeit eternally elusive, π certainly works in computations (for instance the area of a circle), revealing two important aspects of life: It is the *relationships* that matter and *closeness* is good enough. Furthermore, in life as well as mathematics, we may know a thing, yet do we ever really know its value?

The pursuit of that value is an unrelenting passion for some. The current record, set in 2011, is 10^{13} digits after the 3, computed by Kondo Shigeru at his home in Tokyo employing the rapidly converging generalized *hypergeometric* series[3]

$$\frac{1}{\pi} = 12 \sum_{k=0}^{\infty} \frac{(-1)^k (6k)! (13591409 + 545140134k)}{(3k)! (k!)^3 640320^{3k+\frac{3}{2}}}.$$

Running the above using the *Chudnovsky algorithm* on Alexander Yee's *y-cruncher* program on his home-made 48-terabyte hard-drive processor for a year produced so much heat that his (long-suffering) wife Yukiko would bring clothes from the washer directly into his study, noting that, "we could dry the laundry very well, but we had to pay ¥30,000 a month for electricity". Raising the bill even further was a back-up power supply,

---

[3] The series is similar to the series for π developed by the Indian mathematician genius Srinivasa Ramanujan. See Kanigel, R. 1991, *The Man Who Knew Infinity*, Scribner.

as some previous computations had come to grief when Kondo's teenage daughter turned on her hair dryer.[4]

A more analytical approach was of course to mathematically find the maximum curve function. Although the great mathematical physicists Descartes, Fermat, Galileo, Newton, Leibniz, Huygens, and the Jakob and Johann Bernoulli brothers all contributed to the early use of mathematical extrema in physics, it was the isoperimetric, brachistochrome, and light ray propagation problems that prompted the development of the variational calculus.

The brachistochrome problem is to find the path for a body to fall the fastest under gravity from one point of a fixed wire to another point fixed at a lower height. Most would say the shortest distance between two points, a straight line, or as Newton guessed, an arc of a circle. But the answer is amazingly a cycloid, the locus of a point on a circle rolling in a straight line on a flat plane. This reasonably enough is used in the construction of modern roller coasters.

So the isoperimetric largest area and the fastest curve of descent, plus Fermat's analogy with the path of a light ray's principle of least time together formed the extremals that led to the *variational calculus*.[5]

However, it was not until 1744 that Leonhard Euler, together with Joseph Lagrange, codified the calculus of variations that has become known as the *Euler-Lagrange* equation to find extremal functions.

Generally, a line integral gives the value of a function that possesses an extremal value $y(x)$ where $f(x, y)$ is a continuous function describing the physical system. A function of the independent variable x, the dependent variable y that delineates the function of interest, and the derivative of y with respect to x (dy/dx), the change of y with x is written in general form as

$$f\left(x, y, \frac{dy}{dx}\right)$$

and the value of $f(x, y, dy/dx)$ from the arbitrary points x_A to x_B along a line is given by the integral along that line,

---

[4] Reported by Julian Ryall for *The Telegraph*, October 18, 2011. Yee's *y-cruncher* is available online for those interested in evaluating constants of Nature and other irrational numbers.

[5] Ref. Chen, R.H. 2011, *Liquid Crystal Displays, Fundamental Physics & Technology*, Wiley

$$I = \int_{x_A}^{x_B} f\left(x, y, \frac{dy}{dx}\right) dx.$$

To find the extremal function $y(x)$, a *test function* $\bar{y}(x)$ is defined as

$$\bar{y}(x) = y(x) + \varepsilon\mu(x),$$

where the real extremal function is given by $y(x)$, and $\varepsilon\mu(x)$ is just the difference between the test function and the actual extremal function.

That difference term, $\varepsilon\mu(x)$, is written so that the ε can serve as a variable that goes to zero to minimize the line integral, as will be seen, and the $\mu(x)$ is a function of the independent variable x that can be used as a surrogate for the derivative of the test function and serves to set the endpoints of the sought-after extremal function. For the mathematicians, because $y(x)$ is assumed to be analytic (describable by common elementary mathematical functions), and we do after all want to describe y (x) analytically, it is continuous and differentiable, and so by the same token $\mu(x)$ also must be continuous and differentiable.

The first very simple trick of the calculus of variations is in the definition of $\bar{y}(x)$ as becoming the sought-after $y(x)$ when ε approaches zero, with the function $\mu(x)$ satisfying two boundary conditions, namely that at the integration limits, $\mu(x)$ must be zero, so $\mu(x_A) = 0$ and $\mu(x_B) = 0$. That is, when $\varepsilon \to 0$, then $\bar{y}(x)$ approaches $y(x)$, and the test function then becomes the desired extremal function. The line integral of the function with the test function as dependent variable is then just the extremal function in question,

$$\bar{I} = \int_{x_A}^{x_B} f\left(x, \bar{y}, \frac{d\bar{y}}{dx}\right) dx.$$

Now the objective is to extremize the above line integral $\bar{I}$, keeping in mind that $\bar{I}$ is a function of the parameter ε; and in this case, calculation of the extremal function with respect to a single variable can utilize the elementary extrema technique of the differential calculus. Extrema of a function are found when $\varepsilon \to 0$, so the necessary condition for the maximization of $\bar{I}$ is found by setting the derivative with respect to the parameter ε equal to zero as $\varepsilon \to 0$,

$$\left.\frac{d\bar{I}}{d\varepsilon}\right|_{\varepsilon \to 0} = 0.$$

Substituting the line integral of $\bar{I}$ from above into the derivative and then differentiating gives

$$\frac{d\bar{I}}{d\varepsilon} = \frac{d}{d\varepsilon}\int_{x_A}^{x_B} f\left(x, \bar{y}, \frac{d\bar{y}}{dx}\right)dx.$$

For convenience, it is customary to write $\frac{d\bar{y}}{dx} = \bar{y}'$, where the prime denotes the derivative with respect to x, so the above equation may be written more compactly as

$$\frac{d\bar{I}}{d\varepsilon} = \frac{d}{d\varepsilon}\int_{x_A}^{x_B} f(x, \bar{y}, \bar{y}')dx.$$

When the limits of integration (x_A and x_B) are not functions of the variable of differentiation ε, as is the case here, then the derivative of an integral is just the integral of a derivative (*Leibniz' Rule*), so

$$\frac{d\bar{I}}{d\varepsilon} = \int_{x_A}^{x_B} \frac{d}{d\varepsilon}[f(x, \bar{y}, \bar{y}')]dx = \int_{x_A}^{x_B} \frac{\partial f}{\partial \varepsilon}dx.$$

According to the chain rule of differentiation,

$$\frac{\partial f}{\partial \varepsilon} = \frac{\partial f}{\partial \bar{y}}\cdot\frac{\partial \bar{y}}{\partial \varepsilon} + \frac{\partial f}{\partial \bar{y}'}\cdot\frac{\partial \bar{y}'}{\partial \varepsilon} + \frac{\partial f}{\partial x}\cdot\frac{\partial x}{\partial \varepsilon},$$

then

$$\frac{d\bar{I}}{d\varepsilon} = \int_{x_A}^{x_B} \frac{\partial f}{\partial \varepsilon}dx = \int_{x_A}^{x_B}\left[\frac{\partial f}{\partial \bar{y}}\cdot\frac{\partial \bar{y}}{\partial \varepsilon} + \frac{\partial f}{\partial \bar{y}'}\cdot\frac{\partial \bar{y}'}{\partial \varepsilon} + \frac{\partial f}{\partial x}\cdot\frac{\partial x}{\partial \varepsilon}\right]dx.$$

Because $\frac{\partial \bar{y}}{\partial \varepsilon} = \mu(x)$, $\frac{\partial \bar{y}'}{\partial \varepsilon} = \mu'(x)$, and $\frac{\partial x}{\partial \varepsilon} = 0$, then

$$\frac{d\bar{I}}{d\varepsilon} = \int_{x_A}^{x_B} \left[\frac{\partial f}{\partial \bar{y}} \mu(x) + \frac{\partial f}{\partial \bar{y}'} \mu'(x) \right] dx.$$

When $\varepsilon \to 0$, $\bar{y}' = y$ and $\bar{y}' = y'$, so

$$\left. \frac{dI}{d\varepsilon} \right|_{\varepsilon \to 0} = 0 = \int_{x_A}^{x_B} \left[\frac{\partial f}{\partial y} \mu(x) + \frac{\partial f}{\partial y'} \mu'(x) \right] dx.$$

Now the second trick of the calculus of variations is to use the rule for integration by parts,

$$\int_{x_B}^{x_B} u \, dv = uv \big|_{x_B}^{x_a} - \int_{x_B}^{x_A} v \, du,$$

and for the second term on the right-hand side of the above maximization equation, set

$$u = \frac{\partial f}{\partial y'} \text{ and } dv = \mu'(x) \, dx,$$

and because

$$dv = \frac{d\mu(x)}{dx} dx, \quad v = \mu(x)$$

then

$$\frac{du}{dx} = \frac{d}{dx}\left(\frac{\partial f}{\partial y'}\right) \Rightarrow du = \frac{d}{dx}\left(\frac{\partial f}{\partial y'}\right) dx$$

so

$$\int_{x_A}^{x_B} \left[\frac{\partial f}{\partial y'} \mu'(x) \right] dx = \frac{\partial f}{\partial y'} \mu(x) \big|_{x_B}^{x_a} - \int_{x_A}^{x_B} \mu(x) \frac{d}{dx}\left(\frac{\partial f}{\partial y'}\right) dx.$$

Thus, in integrating by parts, the derivative of $\mu(x)$ is dispensed with and the boundary conditions $\mu(x_A) = 0$ and $\mu(x_B) = 0$ take care of the first term on the right-hand side of the equation,

$$\frac{\partial f}{\partial y'}\mu(x)\Big|_{x_B}^{x_a} = 0.$$

Now returning to

$$\frac{dI}{d\varepsilon}\Big|_{\varepsilon=0} = 0 = \int_{x_A}^{x_B}\left[\frac{\partial f}{\partial y}\mu(x) - \mu(x)\frac{d}{dx}\left(\frac{\partial f}{\partial y'}\right)\right]dx$$

$$= \int_{x_A}^{x_B}\mu(x)\left[\frac{\partial f}{\partial y} - \frac{d}{dx}\left(\frac{\partial f}{\partial y'}\right)\right]dx,$$

in order to dispense with the $\mu(x)$ altogether, since

$$\int_{x_A}^{x_B}\mu(x)\left[\frac{\partial f}{\partial y} - \frac{d}{dx}\left(\frac{\partial f}{\partial y'}\right)\right]dx = 0,$$

the *fundamental lemma of the variational calculus* is invoked; within (x_A, x_B), because $\mu(x)$ is an arbitrarily chosen function, *then it is the expression in the square brackets that must vanish*. This then is the Euler-Lagrange equation,[6]

$$\frac{\partial f}{\partial y} - \frac{d}{dx}\left(\frac{\partial f}{\partial y'}\right) = 0.$$

If the general function $f(x, y, y')$ is taken as the difference between the kinetic energy (K) and the potential energy (U) of a system, the Lagrangian, $L = K - U$, then the Euler-Lagrange equation as used in physics and chemistry is

$$\frac{\partial L}{\partial y} - \frac{d}{dx}\left(\frac{\partial L}{\partial y'}\right) = 0.$$

---

[6] For the rather involved proof of the isoperimetric problem (circle is maximum area) using the Euler-Lagrange equation, see Nahin, P.J. 2004, *When Least is Best*, Princeton University Press.

This equation derived from the calculus of variations is used to find the minimum distance of the support vector to the margins in the support vector machine.

The Lagrangian $L(x, \lambda)$ includes a *Lagrange Multiplier* λ that transforms the constrained problem to an unconstrained problem so that the extremal points (*derivative = 0*) can be found. This is done using the artifice,

$$L(x, \lambda) = f(x) - \lambda g(x)$$

where $g(x)$ is the *equality constraint* and clearly when $\lambda = 0$, the Lagrangian will be the desired function $f(x)$.

The Lagrange Multiplier λ is just the rate that the Lagrangian is being extremalized as a function of the constraint parameter c (in the SVM case the constraint that the support vectors must be the vectors closest to the hyperplane),

$$\frac{\partial L}{\partial c} = \lambda.$$

When performing minimax on $L(x, \lambda)$, $min(x)max(\lambda)L(x, \lambda)$ and vice-versa, simply put, since the support vectors at the extremes are parallel or perpendicular to the hyperplane (as measured by the inner product), the minimum and maximum values are "fighting each other", and so $\lambda \to 0$ and the minimum distance of the support vectors from the hyperplane may be calculated from the Euler-Lagrange equation.

The Euler-Lagrange equation is just one of the many achievements of Leonhard Euler, the Swiss mathematician who, in the words of the great Laplace, "was the master of us all". Indeed, although educated as a theologian and physician, and initially appointed in 1727 as an assistant in the medical department at the Imperial Russian Academy of Sciences, *notre maître à tous* quickly produced seminal discoveries in mathematics while serving Peter the Great in his desire for Russia to catch up to Western European science. He worked with Johann's son Daniel Bernoulli, and remained in St. Petersburg until 1741, when a rising Russian nationalism caused conditions to deteriorate for the foreign scholars recruited to Russia, and upon an invitation from Frederick the Great, Euler followed Daniel to the Berlin Academy. There he continued to produce original works in mathematical analysis and differential calculus and contributed to many areas of the mathematics and natural philosophy of the time.

Euler's duties also included tutoring Frederick's niece, and his 200 letters on many and various subjects were later compiled into a best-selling book entitled *Lettres à une Princesse d'Allemagne*. Alas, even this great service to his niece did not persuade the great Frederick of Euler's worth, who preferred Euler's fellow Academician Voltaire's sophistry to Euler's logic. Disfavored by Frederick and ridiculed by Voltaire, the homely and down-to-earth Euler left Berlin in 1766 to return to St. Petersburg where Catherine the Great had ascended the throne and resurrected Peter's Academy. It was there that Euler, slowly succumbing to blindness but still producing monumental mathematics, worked assiduously until his death in 1783.

All the *Greats* wanted Euler in the hope that his brilliance might bring them prestige, but they could never really appreciate Euler unless they understood at least a modicum of mathematics. Frederick was typical, accommodating Euler, but charmed and won over by a flippant Voltaire who foppishly bullied the self-effacing mathematical genius.

The man with the very French-sounding name of Joseph-Louis Lagrange was actually an Italian named Giuseppe Lodovico Luigi Lagrangia. His seminal work *Méchanique Analytique* changed the pedestrian Newtonian cause-and-effect motion of $F = ma$, to a grand *natural purpose* of deriving all the equations of motion through minimization of the Lagrangian, the difference between kinetic and potential energy that will characterize the motion of any object.

From the Turin Academy, Lagrangia sent copies of his mechanics work to Euler who tried mightily to get Lagrangia to the Berlin Academy, but succeeded only after he himself had left. Frederick the Great wanted "the greatest mathematician in Europe" to replace Euler and Lagrangia did not disappoint, for among many other achievements, he found the *Lagrangian Points* of stable positions of very small bodies among two massive bodies, such as a satellite between the Sun and Earth; a special solution to the *three-body problem*.

Under the same forces that Euler experienced before him, Lagrangia fatefully left Berlin for Paris in 1786, just in time for the Revolution and its horrific aftermath. As a foreigner, he was about to be expelled from France in 1793, if not for the intervention of his friend, Antoine Lavoisier, the father of modern chemistry. France made amends much later by honoring Lagrange with the inscription of his name, along with the other greats in the history of France, on a plaque on the Eiffel Tower. Lavoisier was not so fortunate, because his father had been a tax collector, during the new Republic's Reign of Terror against functionaries of the *Ancien Régime*, Lavoisier was branded a traitor by Robespierre and guillotined in 1794. An appeal to save his life was dismissed by the judge with the words:[7]

> *La Republique n'a pas besoin de savants ni de chimistes,*
> *le cours de la justice ne peut être suspend*
>
> The Republic needs neither scientists nor chemists,
> the course of justice cannot be delayed

His friend Lagrange, lamenting Lavoisier's fate put the tragedy in poignant perspective,

> *Cela leur a pris seulement un instant pour lui couper la tête,*
> *mais la France pourrait ne pas en produire une autre pareille en*
> *un siècle*
>
> It took them only an instant to cut off his head,
> but France may not produce another such head in a century.

---

[7] Perhaps this is one of the reasons that Lavoisier, a licensed attorney, never practiced law.

Bibliography

1. Arndt, J. & C. Haenel 2006, *Pi Unleashed*, Springer-Verlag.
2. Battelle, J. 2005, *The Search*, Penguin.
3. Bell, E.T. 1986, *Men of Mathematics*, Touchstone.
4. Bennett, P.A. 1992, *Advanced Circuit Analysis*, Harcourt Brace Jovanovich.
5. Berlin, L. 2005, *The Man Behind the Microchip, Robert Noyce and the Invention of Silicon Valley*, Oxford.
6. Boyer, C.B. 1985, *A History of Mathematics*, Princeton.
7. Brand, S. 1987, *The Media Lab, Inventing the Future at MIT*, Viking.
8. Buchsbaum, W.H. & R.J. Prestopnik, 1987, *Encyclopedia of Integrated Circuits, A Practical Handbook of Essential Reference Data, Second Edition*, Prentice-Hall.
9. Capek, K. 1920, *Rossum's Universal Robots*, Dover.
10. Carlton, J. 1997, *Apple, the Inside Story*, Times Business.
11. Chang, C.Y. & S.M. Sze, eds. 1996, *ULSI Technology*, McGraw-Hill.
12. Chen, N.Y., et al. 2004, *Support Vector Machines in Chemistry*, World Scientific..
13. Chen, R.H. 2017, *Einstein's Relativity, the Special and General Theories with their Cosmology*, McGraw-Hill Education.
14. Chen, R.H. 2011, *Liquid Crystal Displays, Fundamental Physics & Technology*, Wiley.
15. Coates, T. 2001, *Roof over Britain: the Official History of the Anti-Aircraft Defences, 1939–1942*, Uncovered Editions, the Stationery Office.
16. Conlan, R., ed., 1989, *Understanding Computers*, Time-Life Books.
17. Courant, R. & F. John, 1965 (1989 reprint), *Introduction to Calculus and Analysis Vols. I, II(1), II(2)*, Springer-Verlag.
18. Courant, R. & H. Robbins 1996 (renewed), *What is Mathematics?*, Oxford.
19. Darwin, C. 1859, *Origin of the Species*, J. Murray.
20. Darwin, C. 1871, *The Descent of Man*, J. Murray.
21. Darwin, C. 1872, *The Expression of Emotion in Man and Animals*, J. Murray.
22. Donahue, G.A. 2007, *Network Warrior*, O'Reilly.
23. Dunham, W. 1999, *Euler, Master of Us All*, Mathematical Association of America.

24. Einstein, A. 1950, *Out of My Later Years*, Philosophical Library.
25. Einstein, A. 1922, *The Meaning of Relativity*, Methuen, Kindle.
26. Farmelo, G. ed., 2002, *It Must be Beautiful, Great Equations of Modern Science*, Granta Publications.
27. Feigenbaum, E.A., and P. McCorduck 1984, *The Fifth Generation*, Signet.
28. Ferguson, C.H. & C.R. Morris 1904, *Computer Wars, the Fall of IBM and the Future of Global Technology*, Times Books.
29. Ferris, T. 1988, *Coming of Age in the Milky Way*, Doubleday.
30. Fukuyama, F. 1992. *The End of History and the Last Man*, Avon.
31. Gardner, J. 2011,*The Blitz*, Harper.
32. Gamota, G. & W. Frieman, 1988, *Gaining Ground, Japan's Strides in Science & Technology*, Ballinger.
33. Gray, J. 2020, *Simply Riemann*, Simply Charly, Kindle.
34. Grove, A. 1999, *Only the Paranoid Survive*, Currency.
35. Gullbert, A. 1997, *Mathematics, From the Birth of Numbers*, Norton.
36. Hardy, G.H. 1908, *A Course of Pure Mathematics*, Cambridge.
37 Hardy, G.H. 1940, *A Mathematician's Apology*, Cambridge.
38. Hargittai, I. 2006, *The Martians of Science, Five Physicists Who Changed the Twentieth Century*, Oxford, Kindle.
39. Hartwig. R.L. 2005, *Basic TV Technology*, Elsevier.
40. Hassig, L., ed., 1989, *Revolution in Science*, Time-Life Books.
41. Hellman, H. 2006, *Great Feuds in Mathematics*, Wiley.
42. Hoddeson, L. & V. Daitch, 2002, *True Genius, the Life and Science of John Bardeen*, Joseph Henry.
43. Horowitz, P. & W. Hill 1989, *The Art of Electronics*, Cambridge.
44. Hsu, F.H. 2002, *Behind Deep Blue: Building the Computer that Defeated the Chess World*, Princeton.
45. Hwang, K. 1984, *Computer Architecture and Parallel Processing*, McGraw-Hill.
46. Isaacson, W. 2005, *Kissinger, a Biography*, Simon & Schuster.
47. Isaacson, W. 2011, *Steve Jobs, A Biography*, Thorndike, Kindle.
48. Jackson, T. 1997, *Inside Intel, Andy Grove and the Rise of World's Most Powerful Chip Company*, Dutton.
49. Johnstone, B. 1999, *We Were Burning, Japanese Entrepreneurs and the Forging of the Electronic Age*, Basic Books.
50. Kanigel, R. 1991, *The Man Who Knew Infinity, A Life of the Genius Ramanujan*, Scribner.
51. Kissinger, H. 1994, *Diplomacy*, Touchstone.
52. Komp, R.J. 2002, *Practical Photovoltaics, Electricity from Solar Cells*, aatec.
53. Kuo, J.B. 1996, *CMOS Digital IC*, McGraw-Hill.
54. Lagrange, J.L. 1997, *Analytical Mechanics*, Springer-Science.
55. Lanczos, C. 1949 (1970), *The Variational Principles of Mechanics*, Dover.
56. Laplace, P.S. 1902, *A Philosophical Essay on Probabilities*, Wiley.
57. Lee, W.C.Y. 1989, *Mobile Cellular Telecommunications Systems*, McGraw-Hill.

58. Livio, M. 2005, *The Equation that Couldn't be Solved*, Simon & Schuster.
59. Margolis, A. 1985, *Computer User's Guide to Electronics*, Elsevier.
60. McNeill D. & P. Freiberger 1993, *Fuzzy Logic*, Touchstone.
61. Miller, A.I. 2019, *The Artist in the Machine, the World of AI-Powered Creativity*, MIT Press.
62. Millman, S., ed., 1984, *A History of Engineering and Science in the Bell System*, AT&T Bell Laboratories.
63. Minsky, M. and S. Papert 1969, *Perceptrons, an Introduction to Complex Geometry*, MIT Press.
64. Muller, N.J. 2001, *Bluetooth Demystified*, McGraw-Hill.
65. Muller R.S. & T.I. Kamins, 1986, *Device Electronics for Integrated Circuits, Second Edition*, Wiley.
66. Murray, C.J. 1997, *The Supermen, the Story of Seymour Cray and the Technical Wizard behind the Supercomputer*, Wiley.
67. Nahin, P.J. 2004, *When Least is Best*, Princeton University Press.
68. Nassar, S. 1998, *A Beautiful Mind*, Simon & Shuster.
69. Navidi, W. 2019, *Statistics for Scientists and Engineers*, McGraw-Hill Education.
70. Needham, J. 1954, *Science and Civilization in China, Vol. I*, Cambridge.
71. Nielsen. M. 2018, *Neural Networks and Deep Learning*, academia.edu.
72. Nietzsche, F. 1957, *The Use and Abuse of History*, Bobbs-Merrill.
73. Orton, J. 2004, *The Story of Semiconductors*, Oxford.
74. Penrose, R. 1994, *Shadows of the Mind*, Oxford.
75. Penrose, R. 2002, *The Emperor's New Mind: Concerning Computers, Minds & the Laws of Physics*, Oxford.
76. Penrose, R. 2007, *Road to Reality: A Complete Guide to the Laws of the Universe*, Vintage.
77. Pierret, R.F. 1988, *Semiconductor Fundamentals Vol. I*, Addison-Wesley.
78. Posamentier & C. Spreitzer 2020, *The Lives and Works of 50 Famous Mathematicians*, Prometheus.
79. Proust, M. 2020, *Delphi Complete Works of Marcel Proust*, Kindle.
80. Quittner J. & M. Slatalla, *Speeding the Net, the Inside Story of Netscape*, Atlantic Monthly Press.
81. Rabiner, L. & B.H. Juang, 1993, *Fundamentals of Speech Recognition*, Prentice-Hall.
82. Reid, C. 1996, *Hilbert*, Springer-Verlag.
83. Rhodes, R. 1986, *The Making of the Atomic Bomb*, Simon & Schuster.
84. Rhodes, R. 1995, *Dark Sun, the Making of the Hydrogen Bomb*, Simon & Schuster.
85. Riordan, M. & L. Hoddeson 1997, *Crystal Fire, the Invention of the Transistor and the Birth of the Information Age*, Norton.
86. Schewe, P.F. 2007, *The Grid*, Joseph Henry.
87. Shannon, C. & W. Weaver 1971, *A Mathematical Theory of Communication*, University of Illinois Press.
88. Shepard, S. 2000, *Telecommunications Convergence*, McGraw-Hill.

89. Slater, R. 1999, *Saving Big Blue*, McGraw-Hill.
90. Smith, D.E. 1959, *A Source Book in Mathematics*, Dover.
91. Stross, R.E. 1997, *The Microsoft Way*, Addison-Wesley.
92. Sze, S.M. ed., 1988, *VLSI Technology*, McGraw-Hill.
93. Szilard, L. 1961, *The Voice of the Dolphins*, Simon & Schuster.
94. Tenenbaum, M. & H. Pollard 1985, *Ordinary Differential Equations*, Dover.
95. Thomas, A. 2013. *V1 Flying Bomb Aces*. Botley, Oxford: Osprey Publishing.
96. Thomas, G.B. 1960, *Calculus and Analytic Geometry*, Addison-Wesley.
97. Tolstov G.P. 1962, *Fourier Series*, Dover.
98. Transnational College of LEX, 1995, *Who is Fourier, A Mathematical Adventure*, Language Research Foundation.
99. Van Zant, P. 1997, *Microchip Fabrication*, McGraw-Hill.
100. Wallace, J. & J. Erickson, 1993, *Hard Drive, Bill Gates and the Making of the Microsoft Empire*, Harper.
101. Weber. S. 2004, "The success of open source", Harvard.
102. Weise, M. & D. Weynand 2007, *How Video Works, From Analog to High Definition*, Elsevier.
103. Whitehead, A.N. & B. Russell 1910, *Principia Mathematica*, Cambridge.
104. Wiener, N. 1950 (1988 ed.), *The Human Use of Human Beings*, Da Capo Press.
105. Wiener, N. 1948, *Cybenetics: Or the Control and Communication in the Animal and Machine*, Martino Fine Books.
106. Virgil, 19 BCE, *Fate of Queen Dido*, Aenid, Book IV, first English translation 1490, Perseus Digital Library.
107. World Intellectual Property Organization 2019, *Technology Trends, Artificial Intelligence*.
108. Wozniak, S. 2006, *iWoz*, W.W. Norton.

Index

Printed in the United States
by Baker & Taylor Publisher Services